The Best of Times, The Worst of Times

Andrew Greeley and American Catholicism 1950–1975

John N. Kotre

Nelson-Hall Company nh *Chicago*

Library of Congress Cataloging in Publication Data

Kotre, John N
    The best of times, the worst of times.

    "Books by Andrew M. Greeley": p.
    Bibliography: p.
    Includes index.
    1. Greeley, Andrew M., 1928-   2. Catholic Church—Clergy—Biography.   3. Clergy—United States—Biography.   4. Catholic Church in the United States—History.   I. Title.
BX4705.G6185K67   282'.092'4 [B]   78-14224
ISBN 0-88229-380-X (cloth)
ISBN 0-88229-597-7 (paper)

To: John F. Kotre, Elizabeth
C. Dyker, and the corner of
Bell and Chase

Acknowledgments

For help extended along the way I wish to thank the staff of the Rebecca Crown Library of Rosary College, Philip Scharper, Sue Ann Holden, and my wife, Ann Marie. To Robert Coles I owe special thanks: for gracing this book with a foreword, but especially for passing on in his own work a certain spirit that spoke, long before I ever conceived of this project, to some of the things I hoped to become. I am also grateful to one Charles Dickens for providing the title to a volume that is very much a tale of two cities—and of a man caught between them.

Contents

Foreword

There are many ways to come to know a particular society. The subject of this biographical effort has done more than his share to tell us about ourselves—through a strenuous outpouring of articles, essays, published data, newspaper columns, and not least, books containing a wide range of inquiry and comment. Moreover, Father Greeley has recently been moving toward additional genres—stories, poems. He is a remarkably conscientious, determined, steadfast observer and writer—only one citizen, but an important asset for a nation that badly needs to understand what it is about. He is also a man of considerable courage, who has not felt the need to fall in line —to yield to the intellectual "powers and principalities" which have their own special ways of demanding compliance, conformity.

For years now Father Greeley has walked a number of tightropes with dignity, persistence, and a smile that has indicated a certain rebellious amusement at his own fate. An intellectual of broad and deep sensibility, he has refused to distance himself (in spirit or in the nature of his work, his concerns) from the working people of this country. A man of obvious social compassion, he has kept a keen eye on the hypocrisies and pretenses, and worse, the smug arrogance that can more than occasionally bedevil those who want to "reform" society. A social scientist, adept at various quantitative "instruments" of research, he writes strong, clear, often quite touching prose—a much needed example to his colleagues. A Catholic priest, he has dared show his love for the Church by pointing out exactly where he thinks it stands, where it is headed—and at what cost to its flock.

In a sense, Father Greeley combines in a striking and gifted manner the pastoral and prophetic elements of the priesthood—and of the secular priesthood which we call "social science." He has made dozens of important interpretations, clarifications, analyses, and predictions—thereby telling us what is happening to a large, rich, powerful, but sometimes rather torn and confused nation. He has also kept close to his own roots and to those of many other Americans— their memories, hopes, worries, dreams. And always, he has shunned the faddish, the clever postures that upper-middle-class intellectuals no less than others are susceptible to. He offers us not only opinion and shrewd observation, but mounds of carefully sifted and evaluated evidence—some of it, over these past few decades, a wonderful reminder that all too much of the received wisdom of the day is, in fact, a porridge of self-serving distortions or rationalizations.

Father Greeley's working man—Irish or Italian or Slavic, or yes, black—is not always the liberal or radical intellectual's version of the same. He knows and has tried to do justice to the ironies, ambiguities, contradictions, inconsistencies, and paradoxes of our social, economic, political life. He comprehends and does not fear acknowledging the conflicts in men and women all to readily written off as "prejudiced" or "narrow-minded" or "provincial"—by those who have their own wordy, self-important ways of exhibiting meanness, a limited intelligence, and thorough insularity. And as his recent, exceptionally instructive and movine book *Neighborhood* reveals, he knows what people crave, and still have, if lucky, despite the easy and clever dismissals of various critics: a sense of place, a sense of tradition, a sense of affiliation, all concretely realized in streets, houses, stores, schools, and playgrounds, where relatives and friends are to be found—neighbors in much more than the spatial or incidental meaning of the word.

This is the book of a young colleague who has found a decent, imaginative, independent-minded mentor and has chosen to celebrate that discovery—not to mention the considerable body of work that has a life of its own, once put into print. John Kotre's writing is lucid and forceful, a fitting tribute to the man whose complicated, unusual, vigorous life is evoked in these pages. A lot of people who know and love Andy Greeley will be grateful for this book; but one hopes his critics will find their way to it and will have the courage to face its thrust with an open-minded, inquiring spirit. Andrew Greeley has never issued heavy-handed, dour fiats—is himself a man of wit, liveliness, and wide-ranging concerns. He has never been anyone's (in the secular world) piece of property, and he deserves an attentive, reflective audience, willing to learn from him, and one hopes, to appreciate his singular, rewarding presence on the American religious, scholarly, and journalistic scene.

—Robert Coles
April, 1978

Preface

Andrew M. Greeley is an Irish Catholic priest of the Archdiocese of Chicago and a sociologist whose Center for the Study of American Pluralism is located at the University of Chicago. But as I write, neither the archdiocese nor the university wants anything to do with him. In 1950 Greeley was hidden in a seminary, four years from ordination, thinking of anything but a career in writing. In 1975, he was beginning his third decade in the priesthood and contemplating his sixtieth book. In the twenty-five intervening years, American Catholicism, and the country itself, had undergone enormous change. This is a record of one very expressive man, living through those times of change, loving them, hating them, taking hope from them, despairing of them, and always—*always*, in the case of Andrew Greeley—doing battle with them. It was the best of times; it was the worst of times; and somehow for this Irish Catholic priest— and for American Catholicism along with him—they came in that order.

Greeley *is* expressive; his books are coming out more rapidly than ever before. They bear such diverse titles as *The Education of Catholic Americans, Come Blow Your Mind with Me, The Jesus Myth, Sexual Intimacy, Building Coalitions.* He has published hundreds of articles—in *Commonweal, America,* and the *Critic*; in the *New Republic, Redbook,* the *Village Voice,* and the *New York Times Magazine*; in the *American Journal of Sociology,* the *American Sociological Review,* and the *Public Opinion Quarterly*; in the *Scientific American,* the *Bulletin of the Atomic Scientists,* and dozens of other journals. Add to that a weekly column syndicated to fifty Catholic diocesan newspapers, biweekly columns in fifty city newspapers, meditations mailed out twice a month to subscribers of the Thomas More Association, another continuous assignment that is published anonymously, and whatever else he writes but fails to mention in an interview because his work comes forth almost unconsciously. He was asked to write his first book, and 80 to 90 percent of what he has produced since then has been initiated at the request of a publisher or an editor. A volume he described to me as his *magnum opus* (a misnomer—he has written no *magna opera*), which was reviewed as "generous, intelligent, and often courageous theology," was dictated from notes in a single week—more than three hundred pages of typewritten copy. Better, he has said, to write an incomplete book at the right time than a complete book at the wrong time. Is he repetitious? Absolutely. Predictable? Even his loudest critics say no. Clear? For his own good, probably too clear.

Within a period of a few years, one and the same man, Andrew Greeley, wrote all of the following:

> It is also interesting to note that there is relatively little short-circuiting going on in the model. Most variables exercise their influence "further down the line," indirectly rather than directly. There are only three short-circuit linkages, the -.20 already mentioned between age and a desire to marry, the -.21 between age and loneliness, and the -.50 between age and modern values. Age, then, is the only variable in the model that is likely to cause short circuits.[1]

> And the woman will be semiconsciously dwelling on similar questions. When will he start? Will it begin even before supper or will he wait? Where will his hands and his mouth go first? Will he be in one of those moods when he wants to strip me leisurely? Shall I turn the tables on him tonight and strip him first, or will I surprise him with my plan to trap him at his work in the library when I approach him wearing only panties and a martini pitcher—or maybe only the martini pitcher? Will I kneel on top of him, forcing my body down on his?[2]

> I know what you're going to say. You were indeed quite explicit about the need to become like little children. And what you meant was that we should have the faith and the trust and the enthusiasm of little children. But you were just speaking figuratively, weren't you, Lord? You really don't expect me to become like that small creature? It would be absurd. Wouldn't it?
> *Amen.*[3]

> As I sat on an eroding Lake Michigan dune watching the Democratic party destroy itself in July of 1972, I kept asking myself what

picture these people had of the American public. Do they really know what it does to the American voter to be told that Bella Abzug, Shirley MacLaine, Jesse Jackson, Bill Singer, Walter Fauntleroy, Robert Drinan, Abbie Hoffman, Jerry Rubin, and the Minnesota and New York representatives of gay liberation belonged on the floor of the Democratic convention while Richard Daley did not?[4]

Q. *(Triumph)* Most Holy Father—
A. I'm not Holy, and I'm certainly not Most Holy, and I'm also certainly not your father or anybody else's, so call me Pope, or Mr. Pope, or Bishop, and drop the rest of that nonsense.[5]

Critics accuse him of spreading himself too thin. Only a dilettante, they say, could possibly cover the ground that he does, and, if he has a wide readership, it is because he is a "popularizer" and not a "serious scholar." There is suspicion of the man settling, like the medieval Jew, on the fringe of our intellectual domains, who has connections with other lands and other ways of thinking, who wants to be part of us yet not assimilate our premises, who has the gall, the *chutzpah* (may Greeley's patron saints forgive me) to tell us—his hosts—that our assumptions are only culturally relative. Much as we mouth the value of "cross-fertilization," we are likely to view the outsider as one who brings germs, not seeds, and our impulse is to treat him like the first astronaut back from the moon: two weeks in an isolation chamber to make sure we are not "fertilized" by his parasites.

When one adds to the role of migrant intellectual the personality of Andrew Greeley, who crosses borders to plant mines as often as he does to sow seeds, who is in such a blur of motion that one can project anything onto his person (he has been called a "sunny optimist" and a "gloomy pessimist," a "stereotypical New Leftist" as well as an "apologist for Daley"), who loves to get his readers flowing one way and then to cut back against the grain, one has conflict of the highest—and, I might add, the most instructive— order.

I first met Andrew Greeley when I walked into his office with an idea for dissertation research on young adults from Catholic backgrounds: Why did some of them wish to retain their identity as Catholics and why did others wish to sever themselves from the Church? I was, of course, studying myself. Father Greeley was receptive to the idea and proved to be an ideal dissertation director: he left me alone except for suggestions at critical moments and was on the phone to me with immediate feedback whenever I dropped several chapters off at his office. At the same time I sat through his course in the Sociology of Religion—now the books *Unsecular Man* and *The Denominational Society*—attending perhaps half the sessions, watching the attendance dwindle from a crowd in the beginning to a handful at the end. The course left no great impression on me, simply memories of a Roman collar, of percentages on the blackboard, of Freudian slips, of quips about illiterate bishops, of springtime growing outside a dirty window.

I saw little of Father Greeley after I left the University of Chicago in 1969. I remember reading his condemnation of sensitivity training and recall columns in which he psychoanalyzed those who were leaving the priesthood (and, it seemed, anyone else who disagreed with him). A *Commonweal* column, entitled "Andrew Greeley, Divine Sociologist," accused him of "sneers, name-calling, and distortion . . . a cavalier attitude toward the truth."[6] I saw a brief appearance on the national news in which he expressed the growing anger of lower-middle-class whites at being "left out," and I did not miss his scathing attack on the Catholic hierarchy; "morally, intellectually, and religiously bankrupt" was the delicate way he spoke of the nation's bishops. It seemed that a new book was being advertised or reviewed every few months, but I paid little attention because "it was just Greeley sounding off again."

At the time I was involved in the impersonal mathematics of survey research at the University of Michigan. Something in me had to counter that excess of rationality and logic; it led to a book on fantasy and the search for a genre that would enable me, as a social psychologist, to touch the lives of people more directly. People had so much more to offer than variables. They were concrete, reactive, emotional—and they unified and focused issues in a way that abstracts of research did not. I read Robert Coles's book on Erik Erikson and said, yes, that is something I would like to do, and it was not long thereafter that I decided to try it with Andrew Greeley.

I chose Andrew Greeley because there was always a stir about him, because he was saying things at that time that were not being said in my environs, because at the core of his polemic there often appeared a kernel of truth that could not be shucked. Here was a man who had lived and breathed, encouraged and fought American

Catholicism during some of its most tempestuous years, who knew its people from the inside, who researched their social, political, economic, and religious behavior, who wrote about the spiritual underpinnings of their existence. Through him, through what he had studied and what he had lived, one could tell the story (true, *his* story) of the American Catholic people over the past quarter of a century.

And so I wrote Father Greeley with a proposal to get all that he had written into one volume. He told me he was astonished and flattered at the idea, offered to cooperate in any way he could, and sent me an up-to-date bibliography (which wasn't up-to-date at all). I began, then, not as an intimate of Andrew Greeley, but as a former student. Over a period of four years I got to know him well, reading nearly everything he had written, interviewing him extensively, consulting the archive of his materials available at Rosary College in River Forest, Illinois. Through it all, my goal was not to systematize his thought (that would have been impossible) nor to tear it apart (that was being attended to quite nicely) but simply to return it to its source—the ebbs and flows of a single human life.

I like to think that this book is about the *eyes* of Andrew Greeley. When Father Greeley speaks to you, his eyes are in constant motion, working hard, dancing nervously about the room, seeking not so much the variety there as that which exists in his own mind. The eyes are on the trail of ironies and paradoxes—primal unities in diversity—that surprise, perplex, confuse, yet capture truth. They pounce on one-liners that offend one person and make another laugh (of a Pentecostal meeting: "The Holy Spirit had bad breath"). Greeley has argued, in his public life, that the metropolis is not an even mass but a patchwork of ethnic color. He has championed the unstable pluralism from which the American political system emerged and shouted out for those parts of the system not being heard. Of schools, of the organizational Catholic Church, of the priesthood he has said that without experimentation in alternative structures they will decay. He believes the unfaithful spouse is one who is monotonous, who fails to explore and surprise, in the marriage bed. He believes that life itself is a preparation for the surprise of death and that God was drunk when He created the universe, so great and colorful is the variegation that exists within it.

1 A Recurring Dream

In the early 1930s a number of Chicago's newly affluent Irish Catholics spent their summers at a Knights of Columbus camp in Twin Lakes, Wisconsin. Among them was the family of Andrew T. Greeley. Each Fourth of July, they boarded a train for a trip through Illinois chain-o'-lakes country, through Lake Zurich, Crystal Lake, McHenry, and Genoa City, to a tiny station just across the state line. Then, the children's excitement growing, they climbed aboard a truck for a bumpy ride to an old castlelike building atop a great green lawn that ran between outlying wooden cabins and sloped down to the shimmering water.

They had returned! For two months it was all little Andy and his sisters could ask for: charging madly down the hill to the beach, shooting down the metal slide to the lake, devouring roast beef with potatoes and gravy in the screened-in porch of the clubhouse, staying up in the stone-and-concrete "pergola" to watch the moon dancing on the water's surface. One night at the end of summer all the wooden crates that had been stored in the kitchen would be set ablaze, and the flames, it seemed, would light the entire sky.

Twin Lakes meant a great deal to the Greeleys. It was there that Andrew Greeley, Sr., just starting his own stocks and bonds business, had met his wife Grace McNichols, a clerk at Sears. To the children who came along—Andy, Grace, and Mary Jule—it became the promise of joy as regular as the return of summer. The Depression was raging elsewhere, but it kept its distance from Twin Lakes.

At least for a time it did.

On one of those glorious vacation days Greeley, Sr., arrived from Chicago and spoke quietly, alone, and very seriously with his wife. After that everything seemed to change. Greeley still worked as hard as ever, he still went to church faithfully, he still avoided "the creature" (unlike others in the clan), he still read voraciously. He kept the respect of family, friends, and neighbors. But a leprechaun, a lover of play, had flitted off and left behind a somber, silent, distant man. The joy had left Twin Lakes, and the Greeleys rarely returned.

The Depression had hit, not hard enough to leave the family penniless, but hard enough to destroy years and years of their father's effort and hope. Greeley never mentioned the Great Crash to his children, but its lesson did not escape his only son: a lifetime of work can be washed away in a single moment; even the promise of summer can be broken. No one—no matter how honest, how fair, or how generous—is exempt. He is in a summer house on a lake watching great waves wash up at the foot of the house. They are beautiful, awesome waves. They begin to lap into the house and fill up the porch and front room. But they go no father and the home is left intact.

The dreamer, Andrew Moran Greeley, was born on February 5, 1928, in the Chicago suburb of Oak Park, just across Austin Boulevard from the city itself. Both his parents were the children of immigrants from County Mayo on the west of Ireland, but beyond that, little is known of their roots. Andrew's father grew up in what is now Old Town in Chicago, and his father's mother taught school. Perhaps it was she who instilled in her son an insatiable passion for ideas.

Though Andrew T. Greeley had only a high-school education, he was a bright, energetic man and an omnivorous reader—far and away the best read man among his peers. He loved to argue, says his son, "but he never held an argument against you." He was a writer, too, for newspapers and magazines of the Knights of Columbus (an organization of Catholic laymen to which he was deeply committed) and for another of his loves, the *Indoor Baseball Guidebook*. He was not an "intellectual" and probably knew no intellectuals, but, in the words of his son, "knowledge was respected," and to judge from the picture of his father reading everything in sight, it was not only respected but devoured. That was unusual for Austin Boulevard in the 1930s.

Andrew's mother, Grace McNichols, had been born fifth in a

family of seven children and grew up on Western Avenue in the Holy Family–St. Ignatius district of Chicago. Both her parents died when she was in her early teens, her father, from years of working in the sewers, her mother, of the plague, so she and the rest of the family were raised by an older sister. Grace went to St. Mary's High School for two years, thought about becoming a nun but decided against it, and went to work at Sears for five dollars a week. She continued at Sears for a decade and a half until she married in her early thirties. While the crash was borne by his father in silence, Greeley recollects, it rocked his mother visibly. She spoke of it to her son, of what it had done to them, of what it had done to his father. The family was not poor after the crash (they were able to purchase a brick bungalow in 1937), but they were "hurting," especially in view of what might have been theirs—indeed, if hard work gets its just desserts, in view of what *should* have been theirs.

The family atmosphere, Greeley recalls, was "even." "There were not highs, and there were not lows." There were few shows of affection, little demonstration of feeling, absolutely *no* conflict that ever came to the surface. The children succeeded, and their success was noted without any further comment. Were failures criticized? "We didn't fail," Greeley says matter-of-factly. Young Andrew was obedient; he lived by the rules. But he was curious, extraordinarily so, inquisitive in a pushy way, constantly asking questions, delighting to tell others (even, for a while, the nuns who taught him) that they had gotten something backward.

It was assumed in grammar school that all the children, the girls included, would go to college. It was unusual for any of the Irish of that time and place to think of college for their children, and singularly remarkable that plans for higher education should include daughters as well as sons. But Greeley, Sr., was incapable of imagining anything else. "Politically, my father was a New Deal Democrat. In mainstream, nonideological liberalism, you don't discriminate against people because of sex; I mean, you just don't." No crisis, no conflict, no heated arguments about the matter—it was just one of the assumptions of that silent, even atmosphere, and only in retrospect does it seem in any way out of the ordinary.

Not that the children *had* to go to college. They were not manipulated, never held in check or forced to conform by that middle-class Irish respectability that Greeley would criticize in years to come, not cut down to size by "What will people say?" and "Who do you think you are?" There was nothing of "Irish ridicule" in his family, save from his sister Grace. The children, all of them, were free to do what they wanted. A decision would be greeted with "Fine"—no more, no less, in the same tone, and seemingly with the same involvement, with which one commented on the weather.

The Greeleys were not extraordinarily pious. "Being a Catholic was as natural as breathing," says Greeley. The family attended Mass each Sunday at St. Angela's (his father rarely went to communion), and when the children were old enough, they went to the parish school. The family was not active in parish organizations. They did have great respect for the nuns who taught their children and for the priests who said Mass and administered the sacraments (one of the elder Greeley's closest friends, in fact, was a priest on the same softball team as he). But God and religion, like so many things, were rarely mentioned in the home; rather, *they were absorbed*. With this absorbed religion came a belief (hardly formulated as such) in what Greeley calls the "ultimate graciousness of reality." Their God gave the Greeleys hope, not joyous expectation, surely, but the resilience to bounce back from the effects of a devastating financial loss. Their religion kept them going, enabled them to survive. "They were Irish," Father Greeley says—three words and a thousand years of history.

St. Angela's was truly a center of young Andrew's boyhood years. It was a depression parish, the streets lined with tidy bungalows and two-flats, the atmosphere as stable and gray as that in the Greeley home. The parishioners were almost entirely Irish, with a handful of Germans and Italians (when the latter moved in, residents feared that the neighborhood would soon "go Italian"). The people got around on foot and on streetcars and buses. The children played baseball in empty lots (called "prairies"), touch football on the asphalt streets, and basketball on the backs of garages. In winter they had snowball fights with the "publics." People didn't say they were from Austin or Mayfield Avenue; they said they were from St. Angela's. It was a world so entirely Irish and Catholic that one was not self-conscious about it; one could not imagine anything else. Indeed, its people simply felt they were "Americans."

The church itself was a frame building, later replaced by a gymnasium that served as a "temporary" church for almost two decades. The monsignor was a kindly man in failing health; the curates were friendly, affable, wisecracking. Young Father Hayes (an early hero of Greeley's) was teaching the doctrine of the Mystical Body, organizing Catholic action groups, and even saying a dialogue Mass as early as the mid-thirties. Some of the nuns in the parish schools were "crabs" and some were "nice," but they did their job. The children were orderly and always looked up the Legion of Decency rating for a movie before trotting off to see it at the Manor or the Iris. The parish had carnivals and raffles, novenas and missions, and repeated appeals to build the new church. Without bothering to think about it, you knew it was where you belonged.

One incident stands out in Greeley's memories of his early years of grammar school, something that happened when he was in the second grade. "This nun said one day, 'How many of you are going to be priests when you grow up?' About half of us raised up our hands, and she said, 'Well, maybe one of you will be one,' and I thought to myself, OK, that'll be me. And I've never really had any second thoughts about that. I made up my mind then and never really changed it."

In the early years of elementary school Andrew was insatiably curious. He loved history and geography, thought the religion books dull. He was outspoken, too, realizing now that he must have "threatened the hell out of the nuns" but having no idea of it then. But after the fourth grade, he became quieter. The criticism of teachers began to take its toll; classmates were nastier; there was no longer the hope of Twin Lakes; his father was more somber than ever. At home, there was no reinforcement of any kind, positive or negative. There emerged "a certain silence, a certain feeling of being different." He was still inquisitive, still read a good deal, still had friends, but he was "the odd one." And if he was a gifted child, he would have been astonished to know it. Friends who knew him in the later years of grammar school can hardly believe that the same person is today so brazenly articulate.

When Andrew told his parents that he wished to be a priest, they said, "Fine." His mother made it clear that it was *his* vocation, not hers, that he was free to change his mind at any time. In September, 1942, then, Andy Greeley and five of his friends from St. Angela's began their daily excursion to Quigley Preparatory Seminary. He caught the Central Avenue bus, met the others at the corner of Chicago Avenue (you had to be there by 8:10 A.M. or miss them), and rode the "red rocket" down Chicago Avenue, through Polish and Italian neighborhoods, to the gray Gothic building with the beautiful stained glass windows on Chicago's Near North Side. The trip lasted an hour; along the way, the city's diversity got on the streetcar, paid its fare, and rode along beside you.

Students came to Quigley from all over Chicago. "Looking back on it, I, probably more than most people of my generation, was aware of the ethnic complexity of the city because Quigley was probably the most ethnically heterogeneous high school that there was. One became aware of Poles and Czechs and Lithuanians and Slovaks and Slovenes and Italians." The diversity was tolerated but played down. St. Patrick's Day was celebrated but only as "First Rector's Day," the birthday of the school's first principal. The faculty, like the clergy in Chicago at large, was predominantly Irish, but national languages were taught because students would be returning to their communities after ordination—and they had to hear confessions. "In retrospect," says Greeley, "Quigley's attitude toward ethnicity was a pure assimilationist perspective, but it was a tolerant assimilation. They were going to let people assimilate in their own time."

The regimen at Quigley was demanding, but neither strict nor stern. No smoking was allowed (but the smoke pouring out of the washrooms was ignored by passing faculty) and students could not date (though there was no way of checking whether students dated or not). Each student was expected to attend Mass every day before coming to school. School was in session on Saturday, but Thursday was free. Once a week all the students were herded into chapel for a spiritual conference, and twice a year each one spent twenty minutes in a counseling session with his spiritual director. Homework was not excessive—Andy usually had it done by the time he got off the Chicago Avenue streetcar. Quigley was a good place—Father Greeley has fond memories of it. There were spiritual directors like Father Mohan, teachers like Father Grady. He wanted to be like *these men.* He kept the rules. "I was very happy there, actually. The

people who attended it were nice people. I mean there was just a lot
less negative reaction to me there than there was in grammar school.
Now there was some, surely, but a lot less, both from the faculty and
from the students. I didn't threaten the faculty and the students
nearly as much as I did in grammar school. I was very happy at
Quigley. Extremely happy. They were five good years."

Quigley is where Andrew Greeley came alive intellectually. He
discovered John Henry Newman, Joseph Conrad, Charles Dickens,
William Shakespeare. He followed politics in *Time* (which his
father brought home every week) and read the *front* half of the newspaper. He lived the saga of World War II. "I was old enough to be
fascinated by it and young enough not to be able to understand all
the suffering," he says. At the end of his first year at Quigley he was
given as a prize Theodore Maynard's *The Story of American Catholicism*, and he devoured it. It awakened him to history, "not history
as something one read about in textbooks, but history as a drama,
history as something on which one stood." He happened to pick up
a Father Brown mystery story from a paperback rack and learned of
G. K. Chesterton. *The Everlasting Man. Orthodoxy. The Ballad of
the White Horse.* Chesterton was romantic and hopeful, and he had
a way of saying things. "Life is too serious to be taken seriously."
"Hope is a virtue only when the situation is hopeless." "It's not that
Christianity has been tried and found wanting; it's that Christianity
has been found hard and not tried." The paradoxes would appear
time and again in years to come.

Greeley graduated from Quigley in 1947 and began major
seminary at St. Mary of the Lake in Mundelein, Illinois, in September of that year. Ten days after he arrived he received news of his
father's death. The elder Greeley had been ill, but everyone thought
he was getting better, so the death came as a shock, an overwhelming
one. "Characteristically," says Greeley, "I don't think any of us
could really express grief at it. Even today, probably, some of that
grief is still locked up inside." There was never a thought that
Andrew would have to leave the seminary to support his mother.
She did not complain, even adjusted with "some ease and elegance." The crash, it seemed, was harder for her because of what it
did to *him*. After his death, Mrs. Greeley bounced back and went to
work. She was Irish. She had her religion.

The years at St. Mary of the Lake were pleasant and leisurely. There was no tuition. Greeley calls the seminary a "comfortable, well-appointed ivory tower. There was no chance to mature there. All the decisions were made for you—when you got up, when you went to bed, what you ate, how you spent your time." The teaching was from textbooks. No attempt was made to return to sources or to encounter the major trends of contemporary American thought. Philosophy courses relived the hoary controversies of the Middle Ages. Spirituality was just as up-to-date. Theology was better, but that was because Greeley was reading so much on his own. The best that could be said of the atmosphere at the major seminary is that it provided the opportunity for self-education.

During his years at Quigley, Andrew held a variety of summer jobs. He was a conductor on Chicago's "el," a clerk for the Pullman Company, a stockboy at Carson Pirie Scott. There was always a week or two for a trip north, and on one of them he returned to Twin Lakes. During major seminary he worked in the summers in the warehouse of the Catholic school board. And in his last three summers at St. Mary of the Lake, there was a six-week "villa" at the diocese campground near Eagle River, Wisconsin. "A glorious, glorious place," he remembers, "six weeks—every, every second of it, every day of it, a joy. It was supposed to remove us from the cares and the worries and the temptations of the world. It didn't, but it was an awfully nice place—the lake, golf, tennis, movies every night. Splendid."

In the summer of 1950 Greeley was introduced by John Crean, a friend who had recently left the seminary, to a group of Catholics in graduate school at the University of Chicago. Most of them were there because of the GI Bill and many would be gone in a few years. They were in economics, sociology, social psychology, physics—a broad range of fields. For a brief interlude these people were a vigorous, creative Catholic presence on campus. They founded communes like the Greenwood Community; read *Concord*, a Young Christian Student (YCS) publication from Notre Dame; and traveled to Notre Dame in the summer to hear the French theologian Jean Daniélou. Says Greeley, "They encountered the secular university world with a combination of zeal and inferiority. They were going to drag the rest of the Church along with them, and they had things they thought they wanted to say to the secular university world. They were, in a way, militant Catholics and militant intellectuals.

"I remember standing on an elevated platform after a conversation with some of these people, saying to myself, in 1950, these are the first Catholics to be in this. I don't know where in the world, at that stage of the game, I was capable of having that insight—but they were. It dawned on me that, well, these are our first intellectuals."

Greeley visited the Catholic community at the University of Chicago every summer until after his ordination. By that time its fervor was declining (the Korean War had something to do with that, and so did the encyclical *Humani Generis*), and he was too busy with parish work. He felt great respect for the university at those times—he found it open, tolerant, dispassionate, a "font of knowledge." He understood something of the friction between an emerging Catholic intelligentsia and the established Church. But he had no intention of becoming a student at the university. He still wished to be a parish priest like Father Hayes, Father Mohan, Father Grady, and the upperclassmen who were by now ordained and in parish work.

It was through these contacts at Chicago (ironically, hardly at all through faculty at St. Mary of the Lake) that Greeley learned of the new thinking of the French theologians. He could read French, and so, during the years of his theological training, he would send away for the latest work of Jean Daniélou, Henri de Lubac, or Yves Congar and study it. One or two friends discussed the "new theology" with him; and Father Edward Brueggeman, a teacher of French and sacramental theology who had been to school with some of the theologians, kept him abreast of the latest titles. In the main, however, it was a journey he made alone. He returned from it absorbed in a vision of a Church as people, not hierarchy, of religious ideas as open-ended, not immutably fixed.

Near the end of his stay at St. Mary's, Greeley culminated his study of French thought with a paper, "On the Nature of the Act of Faith." Daniélou, de Lubac, and Congar, he discovered, had their roots in the French phenomenological theologians of the early twentieth century—in Pierre Rousselot, Ambrose Gardeil, Maurice

Blondell—and these in turn were influenced by (an old friend now) John Henry Newman. The earlier French theologians opened for Greeley "a whole new style of theologizing." He saw them as the source of the "new theology" of the late forties and early fifties, as forerunners of Pierre Teilhard de Chardin. In retrospect, these were seeds, planted even before World War I, of the growth that would culminate in the Second Vatican Council. Faith, Greeley concluded in his paper, was more than intellectual assent; it was the commitment of the entire personality. The position was one that enabled Greeley to find company, a decade later, with Mircea Eliade, Clifford Geertz, and Langdon Gilkey, a position evident in his later reflections on religious myths and symbols.

But scholars of religion could not have been more remote from the mind of the young man who was ordained a priest on May 5, 1954. Nor could he possibly have foreseen himself as a writer, particularly as one criticized for being too prolific. Father Greeley's mind was filled instead with a vision as grand as the waves of his dream. He saw a vibrant new parish of the people, modeled on the blueprint of French theology.

Yet the grandeur of his vision, like that of his dream, triggered a fear. What if I fail? What if the crash comes back? What if the waves destroy me? A parish priest had to deal with people, not just think about them, and Andy Greeley, isolated for years in the seminary, was sure he could not. "I was particularly afraid, literally afraid, of dealing with kids."

2

The Young of Beverly Hills - and a New Breed

In June of 1954, a few weeks after his first Mass at St. Angela's, a letter reached the brick bungalow where Andy Greeley had spent his childhood years. Its content was straightforward: You have been assigned to Christ the King parish in the Beverly Hills district of Chicago. Greeley phoned the pastor and asked when he should report The answer: I'll schedule you for Mass next Sunday.

Years later Greeley reflected on his first moments at Christ the King:

> The first day I drove down the broad tree-lined streets of the parish, with its wide expanses of neatly manicured lawns surrounding large and gracious suburban homes, I knew I was in a different world from St. Angela. My first view of the almost finished parish church, the first modern church in our diocese, confirmed my hunch that I was involved in a whole new ball game. I had been trained for a place like St. Angela but I had been sent to a parish whose existence had completely escaped our seminary faculty.[1]

Never before had American Catholicism seen the likes of Christ the King. In the beautiful homes of Beverly Hills lived the American Irish who had "arrived"—successful, well-educated business and professional men, their handsome, well-groomed wives, and their baffling and talented children. "Spoiled rich kids," the older priests and nuns told the new curate. "Their parents have given them everything. They respect nothing and nobody."

Greeley's first months at his new assignment, coming after seven years of prolonged adolescence, left him reeling. "I lost twenty-five pounds," he remembers. "I couldn't eat." He was swept up in bake sales, bridge clubs, plays, concerts, picnics, basketball games, discussion groups, dances, teen clubs—and hundreds of "spoiled rich kids." The surprise was that he loved his work and was good at it. And Christ the King, it seemed, was ready to become his new parish. "Loyalty to the parish, enthusiasm over the church—at least as it was perceived—generosity with time and money, commitment to every new project that the parish sponsored (be it the Christian Family Movement or bridge marathons) in Christ the King made St. Angela's look stodgy by comparison."[2] The enthusiasm of the parishioners was a strange mixture of the old and the new: Sorrowful Mother novenas next to Cana conferences, October and May rosaries side by side with Gelineau psalms, *Our Sunday Visitor* and *Commonweal* on the same pamphlet rack. Some people read *Extension*, others the *New Republic*. Some were obsessed with the fear of Negro "immigration"; others were organizing to bring about racial integration. But there was enthusiasm. The people were active, intelligent, intensely loyal, religiously committed (at least insofar as they understood religious commitment). They were coming into money, power, positions of social and political leadership. It was probably the most favorable environment in the diocese for an energetic priest, fresh from the seminary and bristling with ideas from the new French theology.

Still, there were problems. When one's priestly training had been aimed at "cap-and-sweater" people, what did he make of country clubs and Cadillacs? How did Christian asceticism relate to these? And how was the new theology to be applied? Seven years ago at St. Angela's, nobody thought of college for their children; here, everybody did. There, aspirations to move up were few indeed; here, "making it" was an obsession. In the quiet of seven ivory-tower years a remarkable transformation had taken place in the Catholic Church of Andrew Greeley's experience.

There were more questions. European clergy writing in the Catholic press were predicting that the Americanization of the children and grandchildren of Catholic immigrants would bring about a *decline* in religious observance—to the level, say, of that in France. But there was none of that at Christ the King—just the opposite, in fact. On the other hand, *Commonweal* was insisting on greater lay participation in the Church. It was the laity's Church, too; *they* should be in positions of power. But no one was beating down the rectory door at Christ the King and demanding an expanded role in the Church. In what, then, did the religiousness of these people consist? What did their loyalty, their enthusiasm, mean?

That Greeley began to puzzle over these questions on paper he regards as ironic, one of the "tricks of the Spirit." From his seminary days on he knew he could write—he completed assignments rapidly and got good grades—but no one told him he had talent; no one encouraged him to develop his writing skills. (On the other hand no one discouraged him—the environment was as silent as the one at home.) Besides, diocesan priests, expecially young ones, were not supposed to write. If they did, their pastors and bishops said, who was going to hear confessions?

The Spirit's first trick, apparently, was to put Greeley's name in the ears of editors of two Catholic magazines for teen-agers. One of them, based in Milwaukee, was called *High Time*, and the other, situated in Chicago and edited by John Cogley, was known as *Today*. Asked to write articles of a catechetical nature, Greeley demurred and then responded with a trick of his own, submitting several under the pseudonym "Lawrence Moran."

His principal response to the challenge of suburbia's "spoiled, rich kids," however, was both more open and more ambitious. Organizing them into study groups, he exposed them to the American Church's finest thinkers, people such as Godfrey Diekman, Gustave Weigel, Sydney Callahan, and Daniel Berrigan. Greeley's confederation of student groups, drawn from parishes throughout Chicago, was known as the Student Lay Apostolate Conference (SLAC). SLAC's first study week took place in the summer of 1956 at St. Procopius College (now Illinois Benedictine College) in Lisle, Illinois, just outside Chicago. *Ave Maria* editor Donald Thorman happened to arrive early for a speaking engagement at the conference and dropped in on a talk being given by Father Greeley. Like many Catholic editors at the time, Thorman was on the lookout for new authors. He approached Greeley and asked him to write up his talk for *Ave Maria*. Greeley agreed, and Philip Scharper, a new editor at Sheed and Ward, happened to read the results. Shortly thereafter he spent an afternoon at Christ the King planning the first book of Andrew Greeley's prolific career.

Greeley's decision to write that first book was not made easily.

Writers were still suspect in the archdiocese, and he had dropped his pseudonym for the *Ave Maria* piece. But older friends in the priesthood—men such as George Higgins, Jack Egan, and Bill Quinn—not only encouraged him to go ahead but also secured the approval of Cardinal Samuel Stritch and even convinced the chancellor of the archdiocese to write an introduction.

The book that Greeley produced for Scharper was entitled *The Church and the Suburbs* (1959). In it, he reflected on his experience at Christ the King, analyzed its suburban soul, and inquired about its spiritual possibilities. "I am fully aware that suburban Catholicism is impressive, that the material affluence of the suburbs represents a remarkable triumph over poverty and misery," he said. But "the purpose of the book is not to pay compliments or describe happy living, but rather to ask questions and pose problems."[3]

What is suburbia? he asked. It is first of all a place to live, complete with climate—simple, inexpensive, crowded housing for the newlyweds just getting started; a brick home with basement and three or four bedrooms for families moving up; curving, tree-shaded streets, well-manicured lawns, a choice of house styles for middle-rung executives, engineers, insurance brokers, businessmen, and union business agents who, at the age of forty, are successful but not yet rich; and finally, the fashionable homes of the old families and top-bracket executives for the few who had the fortune or had made the extra effort to afford them. Suburbia is color TV, freezers, big hi-fis, barbecue pits, two cars in the garage—the good life. At a deeper level, it is an escape from the city, "a new humanism, an attempt to build as perfect an earthly paradise as is possible."[4]

Suburbia is affluence, Greeley said, but there's a catch; its economic security is not now but just around the corner, at the next stop, in the next development. And so suburbia is also bleeding ulcers, nervous breakdowns, heart attacks, and tranquilizers in every medicine cabinet.

The suburbanite participates fully, frantically, in social affairs—in Cub Scouts, PTA, Little League, and the country club, in T-Groups, S-Groups, and C-Groups. In his quest for community is a longing for the primary group ties that industrialization in the city has weakened, and yet, tragically, community in the Promised Land appears to mean little more than conformism. If the Protestant ethic is hard at work in suburbia, so, too, is the social ethic, soliciting the residents to be well rounded, well adjusted, and well balanced. The suburbanite is buying it all—groupism, team spirit, other-directed-ness, togetherness. It has even become fashionable to be a noncon-formist—just like everybody else.

There are three or four children in every house. If there were not, Greeley said, mothers would not feel needed and fathers would not have a refuge from the rat race of making a living. Indeed, fathers have become more and more domesticated. They are dish-washers, repairmen, recreational supervisors (in part to expiate the guilt of devoting so much time to their careers). Families are doing more and more together. The intimacy of the family is very impor-tant, even critical, yet husbands and wives, parents and children, of-ten feel as though they are sharing a roof with strangers.

Suburbia, Greeley continued, means crowded churches (and if the church has yet to be built, it means folding chairs in an audi-torium), long lines at communion rails, meetings of the Christian Family Movement, and two thousand children per parish wanting Catholic education but having no place to be educated. The move to suburbia has brought with it a religious revival, a nationwide in-crease in church membership that began in the late forties, the soci-ological evidence for which is unquestioned. What the return to re-ligion *means*, however, is not so certain. Highbrow journals ridicule it; others speak of it as an opportunity for spiritual growth. The suburban religious revival is paradoxical and complex—St. Chris-topher medals in Cadillacs, the penitential ashes of Lent beside a Florida swimming pool.

For his analysis of the safe, button-down mentality of suburbia Greeley drew upon social scientists of the day—David Riesman, William Whyte, Margaret Mead, Peter Berger, Robert Lynd, John Kenneth Galbraith—and upon greats of the past—Max Weber, Emile Durkheim, Charles Horton Cooley. The influence of Will Herberg was decisive. In *Protestant, Catholic, Jew*, Herberg had written that religions in America served the function of superethnic groups, giving people a sense of location in a context of fantastic re-ligious and cultural pluralism. *That* was it, said Greeley. *That* ex-plained the high levels of religious observance in Beverly Hills. People sought not only meaning from their religion but also a sense

of belonging. As the residents became more American they were becoming more, not less, Catholic. Social observers like Herberg were
frequently cited in *The Church and the Suburbs*, much more so than
spiritual or theological writers. They were never questioned or
criticized, merely used as experts to open one's eyes or to drive home
a point the author was bent on making. Occasionally they had to be
legitimized to an audience new to them, and so Greeley pointed out
that what they said had been said before by great spiritual writers.

If Greeley's diagnoses of suburbia came from a fusion of personal experience and popular social science, his prescriptions for
Christian living (and prescriptions were obligatory in a book
written by a Catholic priest for a Catholic audience) were drawn
from traditional Catholic theology. Mortification, he advised, one of
the oldest ascetical principles, could never have been more necessary than in the affluence of suburbia. The suburbanite had to become the master of his gadgets, not their slave, and the only way to
do that was to deny himself some of them. Generosity was necessary, too—not merely financial generosity, but the giving of one's
whole person in works of active charity or active social justice. To
the dilemma of conformity versus community Greeley offered the
Church's view of itself as the Mystical Body of Christ. "The Catholic Church is sympathetic to modern man's quest for community;
but its idea of community is considerably different from the narrow
self-contained little world of the modern conformist." The Church
was not to be a place of escape but a source of strength to go forth
and "transform the institutions in which men must live and work
and try to save their souls." Greeley's prescriptions ranged far and
wide—good taste, for example (you get closer to God on FM than
AM), and intellectual curiosity ("the biggest single need of the
American Church is more lay people who read").[5]

As for the young—it was the era of rock and roll, Ivy League
clothes, movies like *Hot Rod Rumble* and *Juvenile Jungle*—they
needed to become engaged, committed. If they did not, they would
become victims of Erich Fromm's "guilt" or David Riesman's
"suburban sadness." It was a point at which Greeley hammered
away. Chapters of *The Church and the Suburbs* were entitled "The
Young People of Suburbia—Not Exactly 'Shook Up,' " "The
Waning of Enthusiasm," "Beat, Cool—and Lonely." In December

of 1959 Greeley asked the readers of *America* why hero worship had become a thing of the past. Why did not Tom Dooley stir up the enthusiasm that Charles Lindbergh had in 1927? Because "we want to be left alone," he answered, "so we can enjoy our Good Life free from social responsibilities."[6] Three months later he was back in the pages of *America* (a magazine fighting contraception and communism at the time) with "No More Radicals?" Wrote Greeley, "The young people of the 1960's may drink too much and may be much more relaxed about sexual morality, but at heart they are dyed-in-the-wool conservatives."[7] They are selfish, he said, incapable of commitment to anything save beer, marriage, and having a family. Where are the poets to come from, Greeley complained, the planners, the artists, the prophets, the philosophers, the saints?

"Oh, they loved to be told they were apathetic," says Greeley of that era's youth. "Of course, the apathetic people were the ones who weren't as·excited as I was."

Assured early in his ministry that he could communicate with teen-agers, Greeley was now torn between conflicting feelings. "There was a good deal of ambivalence because these were people I liked and found attractive—and yet also maddening. They were so reluctant to move, so mired in their own parochialism. I can remember walking over to the church one Holy Thursday evening and thinking about them when suddenly I saw a book. I came back after services and wrote an outline. By Pentecost the book was off to the publishers."

He called the slim volume *Strangers in the House* (1961). In it he revealed in the souls of his docile, unimaginative teen-agers not sins but neuroses. Do they drink? The reason, he said, is to kill the pain of a bleak, ready-made future, one with no alternatives, with nothing to capture imagination, vigor, and commitment. Do they go steady (and going steady was "morally dangerous" and "socially and psychologically harmful")? They do that to prove their·success in the social marketplace and thus to establish their value as persons. Do they cheat? If so, it is because their parents think nothing of cheating, because policemen think nothing of taking bribes, because TV quiz contestants who take answers in advance (one of the scandals of the day) say that everybody's doing it—and so do Korean War prisoners who make propaganda broadcasts for the enemy.

Teen-agers are immature because their parents neurotically maneuver and manipulate them into making exactly the decisions the parents want. Despite their superficial poise and self-control, the young are not in sufficient possession of themselves. "Their emotional state is such that many of them use the confusion of their society as a means of punishing themselves for the vague but powerful guilt which torments them." Entrapped by the need to be liked, to adjust to any group in which they find themselves, they lack the personal force to exclude unwanted elements from their personality and build an identity out of the elements they truly desire. This, then, is the ultimate cause of the age of apathy: "Young Americans are apathetic because they feel that they are no one, and they are right."[8]

Like *The Church and the Suburbs, Strangers in the House* contained prescription, advice, suggestion, what to do and how to do it—less of the practical, perhaps, than much of the Catholic "spiritual writing" of the time but still, in retrospect, a great deal. Young people, for example, had to be taught the proper use of alcohol. Alcohol was a creature of God and therefore good, but its use had to be limited and restrained by periodic abstinence. For parents of steady daters Greeley advised not adamant opposition but "killing it with kindness." As for cheating, the Rx was simple: let the parents stop first. And, in general, let parents love their children for their own inherent worth as human beings and not for what they might produce. Let them guide (and even punish) their children, but let their guidance not be manipulative nor their punishment excessive.

For the young themselves Greeley asked, "Can an organization man be a saint?" It was like other questions he posed, all of them asking whether the separate worlds of his experience could be brought together. "Of course he can," was the answer—if, that is, he engaged in regular contemplation, if he made a yearly retreat and a monthly day of recollection, if he developed a *spirit* of poverty (the Cris-Craft didn't *have* to go), if he practiced personal charity. The advice came from Greeley's seminary days and its details, really, are unimportant. What matters is the hope behind them, the hope that suburbia could move in the direction of its best impulses, that it could become Christian, and (even more) that this new event in

American Catholicism—the upper-middle-class parish—could become the salt of the earth.

The promise of the Christ the Kings appearing throughout America was in its young, in its "saving remnant" (so Greeley separated the sheep from the goats). In 1960 the saving remnant were the graduates of ordinarily stupefying Catholic colleges "who have caught a glimpse of something beyond the ordinary, the mediocre, the banal. Each year a few of these search for something more and find it. They are ordinary people with ordinary talents and ordinary problems. The extraordinary thing about them is that they have refused to believe that there are no more opportunities for greatness." Curious, generous, courageous, the saving remnant has had first-hand experience of involvement in challenging and satisfying action; it has known the meaning of group spirit and enthusiasm; it has felt the power of attractive individuals who radiate the Christian vision. The saving remnant is John Martin, Mary Jo Shultz, Kevin McCarthy, Mike O'Donnell—fictitious names for real people involved in racial and poverty work, leading sections of CCD, YCS, CFM, and other Catholic action organizations. They are not yet saints, "but at least they are living proof that the twenty thousand graduates each year will never be able to plead lack of opportunity or lack of challenge as an excuse for mediocrity."[9]

Strangers in the House won accolades: a favorable judgment in the *Saturday Review* ("the first big review I ever got," Greeley says), a Thomas Alva Edison award when Greeley broadcast excerpts from it on the "Catholic Hour" radio series. The *New York Post* called it a "sensitive and compassionate work of sociology," and most of the Catholic press agreed. The Divine Word Press in Techny, Illinois, asked Greeley for some pamphlets on teen-agers, and he quickly delivered. Apparently people were interested in what he had to say. It was a time to be inspired.

Hope begets new attitudes toward progeny, gentler attitudes, more fatherly ones, the sense that one does, after all, have something of value to pass on. Greeley's burgeoning hope, his sense of fatherliness, came to express itself in the form of letters to his young parishioners. The letters—in another time they might have been called epistles—were first published as pamphlets (to date, they have sold over a million copies) and later expanded into books. *And Young Men Shall See Visions* (1964) was addressed to "John"—and to all the male members of the saving remnant. *Letters to Nancy* (1964) was addressed to a young woman of Christ the King—and to her counterparts everywhere.

And Young Men Shall See Visions found John alone in Paris for his junior year of college. It was very important that he was away from home, away from the influence of suburbia:

Dear John,

The more I think about it the more I become convinced that your journey abroad this year may be one of the most important things that has happened to you during your life. I remember when we talked about it last fall in Worcester I thought I might be in Europe at the same time and that we would drive from Paris to Rome together. But it was good for you things didn't turn out that way. The best part of your year in Europe is not meeting new people and getting to know an ancient civilization and a style of life different from your own. What is really important is that you have gotten away from the neighborhood, from your family, your crowd, your various romances, your parish . . .

What the good Lord has done for you in the last couple of years, John, is to give you your life. He gave it to you physically, of course, long before, but now He has given it to you for your very own. It is no longer—at least on the level of ideas—under the direction of your parents or your teachers or your clergy, at least in any way near the fashion it used to be. It is yours to do with as you will. It is only the beginnings of life, only the first tiny, very hesitant movings of thought and love. It will take long and diligent practice, John, before you have mastered the skills and the discipline necessary for mature thought. You will have to be wrong many times before you are so close to being right that you will be able to admit your mistakes. You will have to make many missteps and undergo considerable sacrifice and suffering before you begin to know the meaning of love. But the Lord has opened to you during these few years the possibility of growth. He has said to you, "You are a man, you can think and love if you wish; be yourself and you will grow. What is still very small and frail in you can become great and strong, so great and so strong that it will sweep the world before you. If you wish, turn away from this possibility of growth; be content with mediocrity, but do not blame Me if you are unhappy."

All of these marvelous possibilities begin to materialize at precisely your age because now you can think for yourself, form your
own ideas, and be free. This is the great decision you must take before you return from Paris. Are you going to give the weak spark of
freedom within you a chance to turn into a steely flame or are you
going to blow it out?

God bless,[10]

In ensuing letters Greeley repeated recent Church teaching on
the role of the laity. "The Church is not just the bishops and the
priests and the religious; it is every follower of Christ sharing in the
work of Christ. As Pope Pius XII pointed out—*you* are the Church,
you are Christ working in the world, *you* are Christ bringing life to
men and order and truth and light to the confusion which death has
caused in the world." The liturgy of the Eucharist is to be the core of
one's life. Without it, "social action can readily become frantic activity without depth or purpose." As for one's career—and "career" is
such a concern of John's contemporaries—let it be a way of achiev-
ing excellence and so reflecting the goodness of the One who brings
life. "One bears witness to Christ, as Cardinal Suhard has put it, not
by engaging in propaganda but by living one's life in such a way
that one would be fooled if Christ were not the Son of God."[11]

In his very first letter to John, Greeley had stressed the intellect:

Do you remember the first idea that you ever had that was really
yours and not someone else's . . . At that point, when you discovered that you had the basic human faculty—the intellect—you
began to emerge as a human being. I am sure you remember the
thrill of discovery that followed that experience, a thrill which is
still going on as the joy of intellectual discovery increases. For suddenly there was the WORLD, no longer a *given*, no longer a closed
system, no longer to be summed up in a few adolescent cliches.
Now it was a place of fascination and mystery, a splendid and confusing place which demanded an explanation and which was
going to be compelled to stand before you so that you might pass
judgment on it.[12]

Half a year later came advice on education and intellectual
growth, complete with "some prejudiced suggestions" for reading.
The lay apostle, Greeley wrote, has to be up-to-date theologically.
He should read Karl Rahner, Hans Küng, Daniélou, de Lubac, John

Courtney Murray, John McKenzie, Roland Murphy, Bruce Vawter, Clifford Howell, Joseph Jungmann. Sociological works are a must—books such as *The Organization Man; The Lonely Crowd; Street Corner Society; Protestant, Catholic, Jew; The Exploding Metropolis; The Politics of Urban Renewal.* "Nor can you pass up volumes on the race question, particularly *The American Dilemma, Black Metropolis, Negro Politics,* or *The Nature of Prejudice."* The *New York Times* is essential, said Greeley. Periodicals like the *New Republic, Atlantic, Harper's,* the *Saturday Review,* and the *Reporter* all got his recommendation. The liberal Catholic point of view is presented in *Commonweal, America,* and the *Catholic Reporter.* And for strictly spiritual reading, there are the works of Hubert Van Zeller, Gerald Vann, and Thomas Merton, though "I am somewhat prejudiced in favor of the books of my friend Daniel Berrigan."[13]

Throughout his young friend's year in Europe, Father Greeley urged him to faith, to patience, to anger, to the intellectual life, to risk-taking, to independence, to the "harsh reality of choice." He called him away from the stagnation of the lonely but powerful crowd of Beverly Hills and to—perhaps the best summation—*freedom.* For John, freedom meant not a moratorium on the Christianity of his upbringing—a time, say, to experience other world views, other religions—but a call to greater Christian enthusiasm:

> These are great days to be alive. The lay vocation has always existed in the Church but only in our time has its full meaning become clear. It is perhaps more exciting to be a Catholic today than for any time in the last thousand years. With the II Vatican Council the Popes have thrown open the window and the strong winds of change are blowing. You are riding the wave of the future. For millennia to come, people will look back on our time and say, "how wonderful it must have been to be alive in those days."
>
> God bless,[14]

In *Letters to Nancy,* Greeley passed on new looks in old theological concepts. Grace he defined as not so much the "absence of mortal sin" or even a "supernatural gift of God" but "God calling on us to be as thoroughly human as we can possibly be." Sin was refusing to become one's best self, because "when you turn away from yourself, you are turning away from God." Regarding the Cross, he wrote, "it is the work of the Christian to keep human suffering at an absolute minimum," but suffering for the purpose of perfecting human love, suffering leading to triumph—that is what is symbolized by the Cross. Poverty was "not being satisfied with superficial goals in life," devoting a bare minimum of one's time to material things because one realizes they are unimportant. Chastity was power, not weakness, disciplined power like that of the artist, "the harnessing and focusing of sex so that it will operate in the proper fashion."[15]

Greeley's strongest caveats to Nancy regarded the "marriage mania." Betty Friedan's *The Feminine Mystique* had just been published, and he recommended it to his young correspondent:

> I would like to submit that the notion that motherhood is *the* feminine role is nonsense and is in fact dangerously close to heresy. . . . You can be fully a woman before you are married (indeed, you better be or you won't be much of a wife) and fully a woman if you should lose your husband. You can be happy before you have children, or after your children are dead, or even if you cannot have children. You can survive and you can survive very happily without husband and children and you can survive as a happy *woman*. You need not be afraid that you will feel useless or unfulfilled or unloved or unlovely.[16]

He was not opposed to matrimony or parenthood, Greeley explained, merely to the way these are approached in our society. He was especially embittered by the fact that the marriage mania had called so many promising young women from the vision.

Greeley had other names for the same sin: the family heresy, the housewife heresy, the good parent heresy. Girls in particular, he said, are prone to it. It would not be easy, he said, for Nancy to resist the temptations that would increase over the next few years. Great love *would* come to her life, said Greeley, but, he advised, "do not push, do not hunt it down relentlessly, do not compulsively look for it with every boy you meet. . . . Look not for weakness you can mother nor for force which will overpower your identity. Look rather for strength which will match your strength, for maturity which will supplement your maturity, for vision which corresponds to your vision." Sex is not something to be exploited (much less something to be ashamed of); it is a resource to strengthen and deepen the personality, giving a girl in particular the vigor to make

sustained sacrifices for the one she loves. "Our Vision demands that
we give; sex teaches us how to give."[17] Because sex is so powerful,
however, it needs control, the discipline of a poet, a ballet dancer, or
a great painter. That is why the traditional Judeo-Christian standards of premarital chastity are so important.

"Intelligence in a woman—what a fascinating subject." Girls
get better marks in school than boys, said Greeley, but they try to
cover their intelligence so they will not threaten fathers, brothers,
suitors, husbands, teachers. They take copious notes in the lecture
hall and study hard for tests but do not ask tough, critical questions.
Greeley urged Nancy to be intellectually alive, though he wrote, "I
do not really think I need urge this on one whose mind is as keen as
yours." Our spiritual life *is* our intellectual life. "The intellect is the
spark of the divine in us and when it seeks its object—Truth—it is
also seeking Him who is Truth. . . . God can be in contact, through
special grace, with a non-intellectual, but it is difficult, indeed, for
Him to be in contact with an anti-intellectual, with one who denies
the importance of that very faculty which distinguishes man from
the beast." Because, in our culture, the intelligence of women seems
to concentrate on the practical and the concrete and that of men on
the theoretical and abstract, "I would think that the purpose of educating a girl is in part to add a masculine element to her thought
processes, just as the purpose of educating a boy is, in part, to add a
feminine element to his thought processes."[18]

At the end of the school year Greeley closed his correspondence
with Nancy as he did with John. It was a great era in the Church, the
best in nineteen hundred years.

> Enough. There is just so much your friends can do for you or say to
> you. Your decisions or series of decisions in the next few months
> are going to have to be made alone—in the chill loneliness that
> each soul must endure when it is locked with its God in the awful
> moments when its destiny is determined. Your own restless tem-
> perament which makes your longings for the Absolute more
> powerful will both drive you to a decision and make the decision
> more agonizing. During these moments there is very little we can
> do; watch, wait, if need be, listen, pray. What will happen? None of
> us knows for sure, but, appearances to the contrary, I am an incur-
> able optimist.
>
>   God bless,[19]

Never again would such fatherliness flow from the pen of Andrew Greeley, but then never again would he exude such hope. *Letters to Nancy*, a book that was stimulated by Greeley's friendship with feminist Alice Rossi, won the Catholic Press Award in 1965 as the best book of the year for young people.

In these early works Greeley's intellect was in the service of his pastorate. He thought of himself as a parish priest, not a writer, an academic, or a scholar. He wished to explain to his people (it turned out that his readers were mainly priests and nuns) the stuff of sociology and theology, to make it clear to them, to tell them what difference it ought to make in their lives, to tell them—since they always asked—what to do. Greeley called *And Young Men Shall See Visions* "middle-range spirituality," existing somewhere between the general principles of ascetic theology and the grassroots experience of people living in parishes, parts of the book "little more than a watered-down version of my dimly remembered ascetics course in the seminary."[20]

An expression can be found in these books, an aphorism of the times, one that did not look to the past as much as it opened up a future. "Grace builds on nature and nature prepares the way for grace," it read.[21] Though not of recent coinage, the words resonated with new theological overtones that had reached Greeley in his later seminary years. It meant the Spirit was no longer at war with the flesh, the church-in-here at odds with the world-out-there. The world and the flesh were "nature," not evils to be dominated, infidels to be converted, but the soil into which God poured His grace. One's task, therefore, was to prepare nature for the action of God— to see, for example, to the basic economic security of people before one spoke to them of salvation. Another expression, cited by Greeley in an article that antedated *The Church and the Suburbs*, revealed the same spirit: "The majors of our syllogisms might come from a papal encyclical, but the minors have to be supplied by realistic economics and sociology."[22]

One needed experts, then, in the "natural" or the "temporal" order. Experts were the Catholic laity in general but also professionals, Catholic and non-Catholic, in sciences like sociology. "To describe what sociology does in terms which are relevant to theology we could say that sociology studies the natural social base on

which grace and supernature must build"—that was for a symposium on "New Horizons in Catholic Thought" in the summer of
1962.[23] What was exciting in this new outlook was the belief (which
was really more of a hope) that, if each were fully understood, grace
did not contradict nature; the two were in harmony. Thus what sociology discovered as true about man could not conflict with Catholic
doctrine. As Greeley wrote in 1964, "We know that grace does not
destroy nature and so if a seemingly Christian insight is contrary to
a valid natural insight—then it is not really Christian."[24] What's
more, Catholic doctrine could speak to many òf the temporal order
dilemmas of which sociologists spoke (such as that of conformism
versus community) and bring to it a solution (such as the concept of
the Mystical Body). Sociological in tone, Greeley's first books nevertheless carried the *nihil obstat* and *imprimatur*, ecclesiastical guar-
antees that they were free of moral or doctrinal error.

All his expectations in these, the best of times, reached a peak in
an article that appeared in *America* on May 23, 1964. The piece,
called "A New Breed," was one of those rare instances of perfect
timing. "I doubt," he wrote two years later, "if anything I have ever
written has created quite this volume of reaction."[25] No data were
used in the article, but none were needed, for the description itself,
naked as it was, had the power of persuasion. A month after its appearance *America* devoted the cover and substance of an issue to the
comments of readers. Ninety-five percent were favorable; 100 percent agreed with the portrait drawn. People felt understood for the
first time. A few thought Greeley had created a monster. Soon thereafter the article became a pamphlet and its title a catchword, a
slogan, a cliche. Readers took hope, a result that bears testimony to
the power of a name.

> There has risen up a New Breed that was all but invisible five years
> ago. There are not very many of them; they might not show up in
> any sample; the majority of their classmates in the colleges, the
> seminaries, the juniorates of the country continue to be listless and
> indifferent. But the New Breed is making so much noise that one
> hardly has time to notice the majority. Almost any college presi-
> dent or seminary rector will admit their existence and will confess
> puzzlement about what they want.[26]

The major impression Greeley had of the New Breed was their concern for honesty, integrity, and authenticity. Those in the seminaries—and particularly the young Jesuits—suddenly wanted to sit down and discuss the reasons for an order before they obeyed. Their honesty, however, was a two-edged sword; it also brought a total lack of tact, patience, and diplomacy. "Truth must be spoken even if speaking it does no good and may even cause harm. To do less would be to debase one's authenticity. . . . They seem to feel that the mere repetition of what they take to be true will eventually carry the day."[27]

The New Breed is intensely worried about personal fulfillment, Greeley went on. "They feel that they can help others only if they can relate as persons and that they cannot relate unless there is a possibility of 'fulfillment' in the relationship." They are uncertain about their ability to love. "They have no doubt that they can be sexually stimulated, but they are not sure that they can be 'friends,' that they can 'encounter' a sexual partner or anyone else."[28]

Because they want to be liked, because they are wedded to no ideology, they are not radicals, not the Catholic equivalent of the New Left. They work for civil rights, enter the Peace Corps, the Papal Volunteers for Latin America, and the Extension home missions and even, on occasion, throw up picket lines, but they are not active in militant civil rights groups or the peace movement. They are interested in politics, but their approach is pragmatic rather then ideological. Above all, "The New Breed wants to help people and wants to be loved by them." They say, "We're getting more out of it than the people we are supposed to be helping."[29]

They are not, for all that, naive do-gooders. Once they have decided on a course of action they proceed with a cool competence that is anything but amateurish. They know how to handle committees, write brochures, give speeches, raise money, and issue press releases. Indeed, CALM (Chicago Area Lay Movement) "managed to get stories into the newspapers about its work *before it had begun to work*—which is surely the height of something or other . . . . Grace Ann Carroll, the cofounder of CALM, spoke for most of the New Breed when she said, 'Before we're finished, we're going to think up a lot more things to do, so that everyone who wants, no matter what their age or responsibilities, can get involved.' " The New Breed proceeds with the supreme confidence "that they will live to bury those who stand in their way."[30]

Since everything is a matter of principle to them, changes cannot be put off until tomorrow. They may mellow in this regard, especially if they see progress, said Greeley, but don't count on it. Whatever the case, do not expect them to leave the Church; they have been told they are the Church so often that they actually believe it, and, if they are restless with the organization, it is the restlessness one has toward the fair bride he loves.

The prophet of the New Breed is Teilhard de Chardin, its patron saint John Kennedy. The latter's "youthfulness, his pragmatism, his restlessness, his desire for challenge and service, his vision of a new freedom, reflected in so many ways what the New Breed wants to be."[31]

The New Breed is a puzzling lot, Greeley concluded, self-confident yet anxious, organizationally efficient but ignorant of diplomacy, eager to engage in dialogue but often inarticulate, generous with the poor and suffering yet terribly harsh in their judgments of elders and superiors:

> It should be clear that I am ambivalent about the New Breed. I am fascinated by them and I admire their courage; yet they frighten me. In another quarter of a century they will be taking over the American Church. . . . I don't know quite what their Church will look like and I wonder how much room there will be in it for someone like me. The New Breed has reason to be confident. Everything is on their side—their youth, time, the wave of history, and, one suspects, the Holy Spirit.[32]

Yes, the Spirit was alive in those days. From a listless generation sprouted new bearers of the vision. The life of this young curate knew frustration, anger, and depression, but it was all *for something*, it was *going somewhere*; and if there were thorny problems, he had the drive to seize them by their roots and dispose of them. During his years of youth work Father Greeley began and completed a doctoral program at the University of Chicago and published his first effort in empirical sociology. And the marvelous thing was that they all seemed to fit—work with youth and intellectual curiosity, theology and sociology, Christ the King and the University of Chicago, the spiritual and the temporal, grace and nature.

The country and the Church, too, were brightened by a spring-time. Freedom rides and lunchroom sit-ins bore witness to the conscience of a nation quickening to centuries of racial injustice. Russian satellites scored their trails in the darkness about the earth, and in response *we* were going to put a man on the moon. Money was pouring into the sciences, and a good deal found its way into the sciences of man. There were new leaders, new theology, a new Council, new grassroots organizations. In the Church, seminaries were full and growing but still could not meet the demand for priests; schools were bursting at the seams; publishing houses were booming. Whatever its meaning, there *was* a suburban religious revival and the promise of a new spirituality.

And a solitary priest commuted from a local parish to a neighboring school, living the rapprochement between church and university, between religion and science. His God told him to go forth, to send others forth, into a land that was no longer hostile but open and receptive. He was to bring out the best in that world and (the same thing, really) to restore it in Christ. His journey was a seed; all of these events were seeds. They brought the promise of life, yet carried, as a secret all their own, the unrelenting mechanism of future death.

3   Where Are the Catholic Intellectuals?

In the mid-fifties, when American intellectuals were bemoaning their image as eggheads, John Tracy Ellis, a Church historian at Catholic University, caught the spirit of the times and decried the pitiful contribution of the Catholic Church to American intellectual life. In an article for the Fordham University Quarterly *Thought* (Autumn 1955), he marshalled data to support an observation made over a decade earlier by Denis Brogan, a professor of political science at Cambridge University, that "in no Western society is the intellectual prestige of Catholicism lower than in the country where, in such respects as wealth, numbers, and strength of organization, it is so powerful."[1] Though part of the explanation for the failure of the American Church to produce went back as far as the original English settlers and their virulent anti-Catholicism, the chief blame, Monsignor Ellis contended, lay with Catholics themselves and "their frequently self-imposed ghetto mentality."[2]

His sober essay released a torrent of commentary in the Catholic media, some of it adopting his self-critical stance and arguing it more forcibly, some of it denying the problem altogether. Those in Ellis's camp maintained that the authoritarianism of American Catholicism inhibited the development of scientific curiosity, that the clergy dominated American Catholic life and steered the "smart boys" into the priesthood instead of scholarly careers, that Catholic emphasis on the other world led to a neglect of this-worldly scientific research, that, indeed, Catholics *feared* scientific knowledge and the whole "liberal" aura of the intellectual life. In Catholic thinking, Thomas O'Dea argued, the intellect was subordinated to a "more holistic orientation of man towards God"[3] or simply to "obedience." Catholics suffered from "formalism," "moralism," "indoctrination," "control." Some of the self-critics took note of the immigrant status of Catholic groups and asked in a sympathetic vein how one could think of the intellectual life when he was trying to survive in a strange country. But the principal target of the in-house Catholic critics, and it was hit time and again, was the "defensive mentality of the ghetto," brought on perhaps (but only perhaps) by the experience of immigration. It dictated loyalty above all and smothered the voices of criticism as so many threats to existence. How could the intellectual life flourish in such a restrictive environment? Hard questions were asked and harsh judgments pronounced, and it was all done with a vengeance.

The works of Ellis and O'Dea, along with an essay by Gustave Weigel, had been commissioned by William Rooney, a Chicago priest on the faculty of Catholic University, in his role as secretary of the Catholic Commission on Intellectual and Cultural Affairs. Father Greeley had been at Christ the King for little more than a year when Ellis's critique (which was the first) made its appearance, and it had an immediate impact on him—upon his work with youth (SLAC was geared to the intellectual life of its participants), upon his books about suburbia, upon his letters of inspiration to John and Nancy. But it never occurred to Greeley that he himself might fill the void at which the critics were so appalled. The Church needed trained scholars and Greeley *was* thinking of graduate school, but only at the urging of Fathers Quinn and Egan, who wanted someone to acquire the practical skills that would make Cana, CFM, and other action programs more effective.

Quinn and Egan urged Cardinal Stritch to send Greeley to graduate school, but their efforts were in vain. The archdiocese believed there was a shortage of priests; ideas, scholarship, and graduate training were fine ideas, but they were luxuries to be indulged in only in an era when personnel were abundant.

When Stritch died in 1958, Albert Meyer came to Chicago as archbishop. Meyer shocked Greeley by calling him in and saying he liked what he had written. In the future, Meyer said, keep me informed of what you are writing, not because I want to censor it, but because I want to be prepared for repercussions. Of that simple meeting, of that simple, unsolicited show of support, Greeley says emphatically, "It was *decisive* in my life."

When Greeley returned to the archbishop's office with the galleys of *Strangers in the House,* Meyer looked them over and said he would be sure to read the book. Then he added, "Is there anything I can do to help you?" Greeley saw his opportunity and broached the question of graduate training.

"Oh," the archbishop said, "that's a good idea. You're probably going to do more of this and you should get the professional skills. But we're just so short of priests here—could you continue with Christ the King too?"

"If you clear it with the pastor," Greeley replied.

"Well, you could go to Loyola, then."

"Or Chicago."

"Yes, that's closer to you, isn't it?"

That's closer to you. Greeley remembers that phrase with astonishment. For thirty years no priest of the archdiocese had been permitted even to think of attending classes at the University of Chicago. It was an evil, pagan place—"Moscow Tech." And now a long period of estrangement would end because an archbishop with a deep respect for knowledge made the very practical observation that Chicago was closer.

So Andrew Greeley began the double life of curate and graduate student while he set about to obtain a master's degree in sociology. He still thought he was learning skills that would make him a more effective parish priest. He began his program in September 1960 and found the first few months "absolutely befuddling." He had not seen a mathematics text in seventeen years and, although he seemed to follow his professors, he could not fathom his fellow students. "These kids seemed so bright—I didn't understand what they were talking about." An *A* on a midterm exam turned things around for him. "I felt great that day. I said, 'I've got this place cased.' " One of his professors, James Davis ("the best teacher I ever had"), offered him a job at the National Opinion Research Center, but Greeley turned him down because he was in a hurry to finish. In June 1961 his M.A. was completed, his thesis an examination of golf partnerships at "Westwood" (in actuality it was Beverly Hills) Country Club. Though Protestants and Catholics were "integrated" at the club, he wrote, Catholics from "St. Praxides" (Christ the King) chose fellow parishioners as golf partners seven times

more frequently than they would have had there been no seg-
regation on the fairways (and everyone insisted there was none).
Friendship ties were clearly cut along religious-ethnic lines. Will
Herberg's model was alive and well in the community of
"Westwood."

Half a year into his program Greeley discovered that Meyer
would give him the green light—and the tuition—for a Ph.D. In the
back of the archbishop's mind was a diocesan office for planning
and research, and he was grooming Greeley to run it. The prospect
of sociological research for the archdiocese, combined with parish
work, could not have pleased Greeley more.

So his thoughts turned to doctoral research, and he recalled the
study that Davis was undertaking at NORC—a study of the career
plans of the June 1961 college graduates. This was an excellent opportunity, thought Greeley, to obtain data on the very things of
which Ellis and O'Dea had written. He approached Davis and
NORC director Peter Rossi and asked whether they needed someone to analyze the impact of religion on career choice. Specifically,
were Catholics failing to choose academic careers as the self-critics
had charged? Davis and Rossi offered to hire Greeley, but he replied, "Don't pay me. Just let me analyze the data."

When Greeley joined the project, the completed questionnaires
were just beginning to trickle in. As the bulk of them arrived over
the ensuing months, Greeley reviewed the available literature on
Catholics and anti-intellectual values.

There was not *that* much evidence, he found—at least since
World War II—to substantiate the claims of the self-critics. The best
was a two-volume study of the origins of scientists and scholars co-
authored by Robert H. Knapp.[4] In it he reported that Catholic colleges were far below average in the proportion of future scientists
they graduated, even though science was the field of their strongest
contribution. The overall pattern discovered by Knapp, and it was
known to Ellis, was that Catholic colleges were "exceptionally un-
productive in all areas of scholarship."[5]

In 1958, three years after the Ellis article, a study of the Detroit
area by Gerhard Lenski revealed that its Catholics were more "anti-
scientific" than its Protestants. In addition, they scored lower than
Protestants on questionnaire items indicative of "economic ration-

ality." To the surprise of many sociologists, the Protestant ethic was alive and well in the Motor City, and the Catholic ethic—which, according to Lenski, valued obedience above intellectual autonomy and put the family and kin group above other relations—was continuing to work at conscious and subconscious levels to inhibit the development of scientific careers.[6]

While Knapp's data referred to graduates before 1950 and Lenski's concerned itself with the Detroit area alone, they carried a great deal of weight, for there were simply no other data in existence that contradicted them.

It was with the expectation that more of the same would turn up that Greeley drew up a set of hypotheses about the 1961 graduates of the nation's colleges. If the intellectual life of American Catholics was at the low point its critics insisted it was, then a number of predictions could be made, principally (1) that fewer Catholics than non-Catholics would *be* in college and graduating in 1961, (2) that fewer Catholic graduates would be planning to attend graduate school, (3) that those Catholics planning to attend graduate school would steer away from the arts and sciences, and especially from the physical sciences, and (4) that those Catholics who, in spite of everything, headed for the arts and sciences, would be "less Catholic" than other Catholic graduates and on the verge of abandoning their faith.

In May and June 1961 over 33,000 seniors from 135 colleges across the country spent half an hour responding to NORC Survey 431. One has to remember that this was *not* a study of intellectuals or scholars and so could not address itself to some of the contentions of the self-critics. It did, however, sample the graduating seniors at 135 representative schools. It is hard to imagine more forward-looking (and therefore more tenuous) data. The data were about twenty-one-year-olds, about their hopes, their dreams, their aspirations, what they *planned* to do rather than what they actually had accomplished. But then a good deal of what the Catholic self-critics had to say was about precisely that—the hopes, dreams, and aspirations the Church instilled in its young.

One morning in the fall of 1961 Greeley drove over to NORC to pick up the first tables that had been compiled from the completed data. When he arrived he found that Davis had written something across the top of the first page: "It looks like Notre Dame beats Southern Methodist this year." It did not take Greeley long to flip through the printout pages and discover what Davis had meant.

Were Catholics underrepresented in the nation's colleges? Apparently not. The 1957 census put Catholics in the country at 25.7 percent of the population, and Catholics constituted 25 percent of the June 1961 graduates. Were Catholics less likely to plan to attend graduate school? Thirty-four percent—compared with 28 percent of the Protestants and 47 percent of the Jews (who were 8 percent of the graduates)—were to begin graduate training in the fall. Were the Catholics who planned to attend graduate school avoiding the arts and sciences? Clearly not. Forty-six percent of them—compared with 43 percent of the prospective Protestant and 39 percent of the prospective Jewish graduate students—were choosing these fields of specialization. And what, in particular, of the physical sciences? The answer was the same. Looking at enrollees in arts and sciences, only a statistical hairsbreadth separated the proportions of the two religious groups entering the physical sciences. Finally, were there signs that potential Catholic scholars in the arts and sciences were "less Catholic" than other Catholic graduates? If there were hints of future apostasy, they were only the vaguest. While potential Catholic scholars did attend church somewhat less regularly than other Catholic graduates, and while 2 percent more of them were already apostates, the future Catholic scholars were astonishingly loyal to their faith.

Page after page, ream after ream of printout filled in the details of the same story. Catholic graduates, looking to the future, saw themselves in scientific, intellectual roles and at the same time saw themselves as Catholics. Nor did the story break down or show even the slightest crack when a host of controls was brought to bear on the findings. The results could not be explained away when sex, hometown size, socioeconomic status, income, parents' education, and a variety of other background variables were taken into account, nor when Protestant graduates were examined denomination by denomination. It did not matter whether the Catholics came from Catholic or secular campuses—in fact, the Catholics from Catholic schools were more "intellectual" and "Protestant" than Catholics from non-Catholic schools. If one looked at measures

other than future career plans, Catholic graduates were still as intellectually oriented as the rest of the sample. They expressed as much
interest in the science and math courses they had taken as under-
graduates, and they were as Protestant as the Protestants in their
reasons for choosing an occupation. The findings regarding the
anti-intellectual and anti-scientific hypotheses were entirely negative. Catholic seniors were indistinguishable from the great American mean, "no more anti-intellectual than anyone else."[7]

It was a rude but pleasant surprise. To a man concerned about
the development of a Catholic intelligentsia, here was hope that the
intelligentsia was on its way. Either things had happened in the past
decade that the critics were not attuned to, or indeed the critics had
been remarkably effective in the span of five years. Whatever the
case, this was good news, welcome positive reinforcement during a
time of collective self-punishment.

Greeley reflects on the discovery as "an immense experience. At
that moment you and you alone know something that no one else in
the world knows." It taught him the importance of *data*—those
simple statistics said more about social change than anything he had
witnessed in his move from St. Angela's to Christ the King. Says he,
"I sensed changes in the Church at Christ the King, but I didn't
know they were happening that rapidly or that dramatically."

With time, the data were analyzed more carefully, and a theory
of what had happened emerged. An apparently minor detail provided a clue: It was the brightest students at Catholic colleges who
reported the most faculty influence on career plans, whereas at secular colleges the situation was reversed—the least gifted had reported
the most faculty influence. Davis provided an interpretation of that
fact: Schools wanting to improve their status concentrate on their
best students, trying to steer them into prestigious graduate schools,
while schools secure in their status focus on less gifted students on
the premise that these are the ones most in need of assistance.
Alumni with Ph.D.'s are status symbols to be collected by schools on
the upgrade, and it was apparent that the Catholic colleges wanted
to corner a goodly share of the symbols. There were strong suggestions in the data that the cries of the self-critics had not been
wasted on Catholic schools and that those schools were recruiting
their most gifted students for academic careers.

On a larger scale the class of 1961 may have represented a milestone in the Catholic acculturation process, indicating that the immigrant trauma was over at last. Catholic immigrants apparently had taken care of first things first, establishing a secure financial and political base and leaving it to their progeny to "prove themselves" in intellectual matters. Perhaps it was World War II and the GI Bill that turned the tide. Certainly the efforts of the self-critics and the resultant recruiting by teachers and counselors at Catholic colleges hastened the process of turning Catholics to scholarly careers.

Yes, the data represented good news, and their interpretation was fascinating, but it was all too good to be true—or, rather, too good *to be perceived* as being true.

Greeley wrote up his results quickly. In June 1962, twenty months after he began his graduate program, his dissertation was completed and his Ph.D. in hand. When Peter Rossi extended to him an offer to stay on at NORC, Greeley had to check first with his archbishop. Meyer said it was a fine idea; Greeley would get more training and it would reflect favorably on the Church. Greeley's pastor at Christ the King thought otherwise—what good was it to him to have someone who was an assistant in name only? But Meyer prevailed and Greeley accepted the offer, specifying that his salary would be for a half-time position.

Greeley asked Philip Scharper if Sheed and Ward would be interested in publishing his dissertation. (Greeley was, at this time, beginning work on *And Young Men Shall See Visions* and *Letters to Nancy.*) Scharper said they would—they wouldn't make any money on the book, but it was important that it be published. Greeley's findings on the anti-intellectualism hypothesis appeared in 1963 under the title *Religion and Career.*

When the book came out sociologists began to pick at it. Gerhard Lenski, who had argued the opposite side in *The Religious Factor,* had doubts about the adequacy of the sample, saying it was unwittingly stacked with students from the better Catholic schools. Controls were inadequate, he said, other research on Catholic anti-intellectualism was ignored—and, besides, if this was a study of potential intellectual leaders, why did it not focus on the portion of the class from which those leaders were most likely to come—that is, "the brightest and best trained males"? Catholic graduates received National Science Foundation, Woodrow Wilson, and other national awards at only *half* the national rate. Did this portend the preeminence that Greeley saw on the horizon? Another reviewer asked whether Catholic graduates were being accepted at *quality* graduate schools. After all, the data did not distinguish between seniors hoping to complete ten graduate hours in education at a local Catholic university and those envisaging a Ph.D. in nuclear physics from Harvard. Other lines of questioning should have been pursued in the survey. More data were needed. They had to be analyzed more carefully. *Relevant* comparisons had to be made if the charges of Catholic anti-intellectualism were to be dismissed definitively.

But the real hostility was to come from Catholic audiences. Greeley wrote about one meeting of Catholic educators in which he and several NORC colleagues presented the survey results:

> The reaction from the floor of the meeting was violent. It was perfectly clear to our listeners that their colleges had to be inferior; the very thought they were average was quite intolerable. Finally, one questioner exploded, "You people just don't know all the anti-intellectual deans that we have to put up with." My colleague, Peter Rossi, leaned over and whispered in my ear, "What the hell makes him think he has a monopoly on anti-intellectual deans?"[8]

A decade later Greeley told me that people just would not *believe* the data. Greeley was an optimist, critics said: he wanted to be a bishop. They simply would not acknowledge the promise spelled out in his statistics. "The very hostile reaction to that book in the national Catholic liberal community was a real surprise, and a blow, and a disillusionment to me," says Greeley. "I think John Ellis has never forgiven me for our findings."

A principal contention of those who resisted the data was that the results were only the self-projections of graduating seniors. As George Shuster said in *Commonweal*, "not every rosy-fingered dawn blossoms out into a bright day."[9] John Donovan observed in the same journal that Greeley could talk only about the intellectuals Catholics *might* have some day in the distant future, not about intellectuals they had *now*. And besides, "Father Greeley's

40   *The Best of Times, The Worst of Times*

empiricist concern with the hard facts of computer sociology barely conceals its own modest anti-intellectualism"[10]

Donovan's charge of anti-intellectualism aside, there was a point here. Would the aspirations of these intelligent-but-not-yet-intellectual graduates stand the test of time? Fortunately, there was enough government and private foundation interest in the class of 1961 at large for the answer to come forth. In June 1962, a year after graduation, a second questionnaire was sent to the original respondents. Of those who said they were going to graduate school the autumn after graduation, 80 percent of the Catholics, 81 percent of the Protestants, and 87 percent of the Jews had actually done so. Catholics were in arts and sciences programs at the *top twelve* graduate schools in the same proportion as Protestants (though both groups trailed Jews). Of all the 1961 graduates, 21 percent of the Catholics, compared with 22 percent of the Protestants and 24 percent of the Jews, affirmed their intention of getting a Ph.D. Apparently Catholics in graduate school were not just getting ten hours of education credits at the local Catholic college. Nor were they finding their religion incompatible with graduate school life. At the end of a year there was only a meager drop in the percentage of those identifying themselves as Catholic and attending church weekly, and the situation at the top twelve schools was no different from that at graduate schools in general.

In 1963 and again in 1964 the class of 1961 was surveyed with no modification in the basic findings. Protestants and Catholics were very much alike in their graduate school experience, though both were still less oriented toward Ph.D.'s than were Jews. Catholics were just as successful in graduate school, including the very best schools, as were Jews and Protestants. And Catholics *from Catholic schools* (alleged bastions of anti-intellectualism) were closer to receiving their Ph.D.'s than Catholics from secular schools. Their allegiance to Catholicism, in the meantime, had changed very little. At the top twelve universities 98 percent of the graduates of Catholic colleges professed the same religion they did in 1961 (this compared with 54 percent of the Catholic graduates of non-Catholic institutions). In addition, an *independent* NORC sampling of June 1964 graduates found nothing that failed to confirm the conclusion of *Religion and Career*. Lenski's doubts about sampling variation could now be laid to rest.

Data from an altogether different source—a survey of scientists in 1960—confirmed both the picture drawn by the self-critics (respondents from parochial schools *were* underrepresented among scientists) and the change predicted by Greeley (parochial school graduates were underrepresented because they *took longer* to secure their highest degree; among the *youngest* scientists, parochial school attendance showed no inhibiting effect). And in 1968, when the 1961 graduates were tapped for a fifth time, their story had not changed: 4.3 percent of the Catholic college alumni (and 5.8 percent of those whose education through college was exclusively Catholic)—in contrast to the national average of 3.9 percent—had received the doctoral degree. Pages of the *American Journal of Sociology*, the *American Sociological Review*, the *Journal for the Scientific Study of Religion*, the *Journal of Higher Education*, the *American Catholic Sociological Review*, and its offspring *Sociological Analysis* were peppered with notes, communications, letters, and articles to this effect.

In reporting his data in the Catholic press Greeley came to refer to the "breast-beating," the "self-flagellation," the "mass masochism" of the critics who would not accept the implications of his findings. They were reveling in an "orgy of self-criticism," those Manhattan Catholics standing in awe of the prestigious Eastern universities, dazzled by European Catholicism. He would never budge from that perception. In a 1967 volume and again in 1969 he spoke of a massive "inferiority complex, . . . one of the grave weaknesses of East Coast Catholicism . . . so very powerful in the American Church."[11] And while he did what he could to beat down the masochism of the self-critics, they proceeded on, describing their efforts as "a process of intellectual fermentation," "a valuable service," "a spur to reform."[12]

Greeley also applied his findings to secular sociology, picking this time on the prima donna of sociological theories—the Protestant ethic hypothesis. Created by Max Weber at the turn of the century to interpret the rise of capitalism several centuries earlier, this theory was still revered enough to be called upon to explain economic achievement in mid-twentieth-century America. The hypothesis had many variants, but its basic tenet was that Protestants were more economically ambitious than Catholics because of their different theological and political orientation. As summarized by R. W.

Mack, R. J. Murphy, and S. Yellin in the *American Sociological Review*:

> The Catholic ethic propounded a culturally established emphasis
> on otherworldliness; the rationale for the performance of earthly
> tasks was otherworldly: reparation for sins and purification
> through humility. Luther and Calvin sanctified work; they made
> virtues of industry, thrift and self-denial. Wesley preached that the
> fruits of labor were the signs of salvation. The culmination of the
> Protestant Reformation, then, was to give divine sanction to the
> drive to excel."[13]

In a paper presented at a meeting of Catholic sociologists—and
later published in an issue of *Sociological Analysis* honoring Max
Weber—Greeley asked that the hypothesis be given a decent burial.[14]
Why should it be allowed to live—more than that, to inseminate research—when eight separate studies in the past decade had failed to
confirm it? Take the work of Mack, Murphy, and Yellin. Using a
nonrandom sample of 2,205 white males in three white-collar pro-
fessions, the authors found no differences in the social mobility patterns or aspiration levels of Protestant and Catholic respondents. Or
take the work of Joseph Veroff, Sheila Feld, and Gerald Gurin. They
employed TAT tests with a representative national sample and
found that Protestants lagged behind Jews *and* Catholics in mani-
festing a need to achieve. The least Protestant of the respondents,
it turned out, were the Protestants themselves.[15]

If the facts indicate that the hypothesis is over the hill, why do
sociologists disagree? Ignorance of the pluralistic nature of Catholicism is one reason. Wrote Greeley, "David McClelland states, as
though he had just discovered it, that Catholicism is a congeries of
subcultures; but, of course, one feels like saying, this ought to have
been obvious to everyone . . . Sociologists still think that if they
find one manual that says, for example, that Catholics ought not to
be interested in worldly gain, they have uncovered the official
Catholic position as well as the practical orientation of most 'good'
Catholics. When someone tells them this is not so, they feel that the
rules of the game have been violated." In particular there is an in-
carnational, humanistic, "Christ in culture" orientation, long a part
of Catholicism—springing in fact from the same humanistic ration-

alism that produced the Calvinistic ethic—that supports worldly striving. "Indeed the rationalization of human striving attributed to the Calvinists can with equal justice be attributed to the Jesuits. Ignatius of Loyola was the last of the Calvinists (or the first of the Methodists)." Sociologists, however, are quite unaware of it all. "The blunt fact is that most sociologists are uninformed about Catholicism and hence when they try to summarize what they take to be Catholic theology or practice end up with distorted cliches and caricatures which become truth if they are repeated often enough."[16]

The Protestant ethic mythology lingers on, too, because of a misunderstanding of Max Weber. Just before he died, Weber wrote another introduction to *The Protestant Ethic and the Spirit of Capitalism*, and in it he bent over backward to insist that he did not claim that Protestantism "caused" capitalism. In fact, having spent a number of years in the study of Eastern religions, he now felt that it was the rationalizing tendency of the West, a tendency antedating the Protestant Reformation by several millennia, that, as much as anything else, explained the rise of capitalism. Protestantism and capitalism were related, to be sure, not because one led to the other, but because both sprang from a common source. And, Greeley added, there is a strong rationalist tradition in Catholicism that is as much a manifestation of the occidental spirit as are Protestantism and capitalism.

If the data were used to lay to rest at one and the same time the Protestant ethic and the Catholic anti-intellectualism hypotheses (and few people were reading the obituary in those days) they were also a harbinger of future development. A constant complaint of Greeley was that no one, especially Lenski, bothered to look at obvious ethnic differences within the Catholic population. And these differences were telling. Immigrant groups, such as Italians and Eastern Europeans, that came in later waves no doubt experienced slower acculturation than those—like the Irish, Germans, and British—who came earlier. Hence they would be less inclined to plan college attendance and academic careers or to be oriented toward economic achievement.

But no one seemed to be interested in ethnicity. In the first NORC wave of questionnaires to the 1961 seniors, not one ethnic question was asked. Sociologists went right on accepting the melting pot theory—along with the Protestant ethic and Catholic anti-intellectualism theories—and it was their loss. Wrote Greeley:

> If sociologists do not soon put aside the outmoded melting pot assumption and return to the study of what is *happening* to the ethnic groups, then what may well be the most significant sociological experience that has gone on in America—or indeed anywhere anytime—will be forever beyond our comprehension.[17]

By intent or not, Greeley had now assumed the role of the empiricist in possession of the fact that could be used to burst the bubbles of contemporary wisdom. "This is . . . perhaps the most delightful thing that sociology can do—debunk myths," he said in the summer of 1962. "Make fun of statistics if you will, but there is no surer way of cutting through the accumulated nonsense of the conventional wisdom than a modest statistical table."[18] Was he an antitheoretical empiricist, because of his "concern with the hard facts of computer sociology?" In the closing lines of his paper calling for a moratorium on the Protestant ethic hypothesis, Greeley lamented that:

> . . . instead of plunging into research that will enable us to fashion new theory, we turn to the past and obtain antecedent theory from the few people who seem to have fashioned it for the sociology of religion—which is to say Max Weber, Emile Durkheim, and Ernst Troeltsch. Even when the categories which these men devised have ceased to be fruitful in research projects, we continue to use them because they are "theory" and "theory" we must have.[19]

Real theory, not Parsonian intellectual exercise, generates testable hypotheses, predicts or fails to predict variance. It can be confronted with reality, quantified reality. "The only numbers in Peter Berger's work," he once complained of a fellow sociologist, "are the page numbers."

If the early NORC years drew Greeley into the role of an empiricist attacking the conventional wisdom, they also indicated something about the Catholic people of whom he was one—and, more specifically, about the ones who were the "intellectuals." That something he discovered empirically, not with the highly quantified empiricism of computerized research but with the unmistakably direct empiricism of a fighter being pummeled by, and pummeling in return, a friend who had become a foe. What he thought was good news preached to the Catholic self-critics turned out to be an unwelcome intrusion. To understand why, one must crawl inside that now infamous ghetto mentality of apologetic Catholicism—a mentality whose existence was acknowledged by Greeley *and* his critics—and capture it just as it was opening up to the world outside the walls.

For there were essentially two explanations for the absence of Catholics from the intellectual life of this country. The first was that the problem was theological, somehow inherent in Catholicism itself, and the second was that it was historical, lying in circumstances attendant upon Catholicism's arrival in America. The first explanation—really, the first way of *blaming*—struck deeper, hit harder, hurt more, while the second deflected blame onto nonessentials. And the irony of the situation is that those outside the Church who argued the merits of the first, the more strongly indicting, explanation were outdone in their zeal by Catholics who felt a need to punish the Church of their upbringing. For to them the demon was no longer *out there* but *in here*, inside the very walls of the garrison.

The mechanism of what, in retrospect, was such a rapid transposition need not concern us. It does seem that by 1960 Catholicism, with a secure political and economic base, was ready for America and that America, with John Kennedy about to enter the White House, was ready for Catholicism. Outside the United States, the Church was taking a new look at the modern world. Teilhard de Chardin had experienced that world as a divine milieu and Pope John had blessed it and legitimized entrance into it with the convening of Vatican II. The world was a place where young men with vision were to be sent to find Christ even more than to bring Christ. God was with Freud and Darwin as He had been with Luther and Calvin. He was with modern science, with the secular humanists, with the agnostics, and even in His own mysterious way with the atheists. So much was good about the world. So much was to be learned there—beyond the barriers erected by parochial schools, parishes, diocesan newspapers, Catholic bookstores, seminaries, colleges, and universities.

So the world was entered, tasted, and found to be sweet, and, as it was, questions were asked. Why were we so afraid before? What did we have to fear from *them*? What could the freely searching intellect discover that would destroy us? Did not the mind seek Truth? And was there not Goodness out here? And more: whence these eyes that made us see people only as Catholic or non-Catholic? How arrogant of us to think that only through our Church could these "outsiders" be saved! And who separated us from the God out here—the real God, not the commandant back there barking out orders and telling us to listen or be damned?

These questions, of course, came from those who were raised within the fort—surely not from their fathers who struggled to build the fort in the first place. And the answers were likewise those of the later generation. We were cut off from our secular brothers and their God by this very Catholic garrison, by these very Catholics maintaining it, and by this very Catholic part of ourselves that led us to distrust the world's aspirations for a richer, more complete humanity. The evil was not the open, trusting, and trustworthy world, but the narrow, defensive, restrictive ghetto. The enemy wasn't them, it was our very selves.

Such was the climate into which Andrew Greeley brought his apparently well-founded message of hope. His claims were not extravagant. The underachievement of American Catholics in the intellectual life was not being questioned. Nor did Greeley assert, at least until the evidence was in, that the Catholic graduates of 1961 would follow through on their scholarly aspirations. His strongest assertion was the unspectacular "We have become average." We—the products of these confining parochial schools—have come abreast of the rest of the American population. And this thoroughly unimpressive statement nearly always was juxtaposed with "average is not good enough" and a whole series of practical prescriptions for how to become better. As Greeley wrote in *Commonweal*, "We cannot be content until Catholic scholarship is better than any other kind; we can bear adequate witness to the Lord in the intellectual world only when we are the very best; and to be no worse than the average is a long, long way from being the best."[20]

But even a glimmer of hope, if its source was the ghetto, was too much. Heads were turned the other way, eyes dazzled by the undiferentiated aura of goodness just over the wall. That peculiar Catholic penchant for punishment had completed its tragic cycle: Catholicism itself was now the target. And perhaps something else was at work—something that Sigmund Freud called the narcissism of slight differences. People who are much alike often exaggerate the slight discrepancies that exist between them and do so to the detriment of the other (and to the increment.of the hostility between them). Greeley *was* a self-critic, a Church liberal, if you will, someone encouraging the young to fill the Catholic gap in American intellectual life, someone filling the void with his own person. Yet it was precisely the self-critical, liberal element of Catholicism that he found himself aligned against in the anti-intellectualism debate. And, on the other hand, there he was, "hailed by people with whom I could not possibly ally myself."[21]

Secular academia seemed much more receptive to him at this time. It harbored stereotypes of the Catholic that annoyed him, true enough, but there was a curiosity, an openness, even a warmth there that caught him by surprise. In a letter to *Commonweal* in March 1963, Greeley wrote of an "atmosphere of sympathetic curiosity about Catholicism to be discovered in many parts of the intellectual world, an attitude of interested friendliness which would have been impossible even five years ago."[22] Later he examined "The Catholic Message and the American Intellectual" for readers of the *Critic.* Despite the prejudices of intellectuals against the Catholic Church, he said ("When an American Bishop makes a statement, the WASP intellectual hears from the dim memory of childhood the voice of Innocent III or Cardinal Torquemada"), despite the ways in which Catholics often give substance to those prejudices, despite the fact that intellectuals are "liberal, pragmatic, empiricist, critical, and personalistic" while the Church of recent history is "authoritarian, dogmatic, deductive, conservative and often less than human," despite even the intellectual's shrug of the shoulders at the question of a Transcendent—despite all of these, Greeley said he had seen the beginnings of dialogue between the church and the university. "It seems that there has never been a time when intellectuals were more fascinated by the Church or more eager to hear about it."[23]

Oh, there were ironies in the events and feelings of the years of the "great debate." Their pattern would be repeated in the unfolding argument over Catholic education and in the year of God's death. And a decade later, Father Andrew Greeley, the emerging Catholic intellectual, would be turned around 180 degrees. No longer would his statistics demonstrate that Catholics were as good Americans (read now: as good Protestants) as everybody else, but that they were different from everybody else and that what mattered were precisely those differences.

4 The Education of Catholic Americans

"I believe in the Spirit," Andrew Greeley answered my query about his future. "I listen to what the Spirit is trying to tell me."

Whether it was the Spirit or sheer accident that brought Greeley to the National Opinion Research Center in June 1961, the consequences were enormous. Much of the feud over Catholic anti-intellectualism, in fact, falls into place when one realizes that one of the protagonists was engaged in survey research. National probability sampling is more than a sociological method; it is a pair of eyes. When faced with a confusing array of stimuli, the eyes center on the great American mean and then see everything in relation to it—not to set ideals, surely, but simply to determine one's location. Is one above average or below? To the left of center or to the right? Typical or atypical? To an elite group concerned with the ideal, the mean is too drab, too gray, too run-of-the-mill—too *real*. It jars the assumption that one's self is the microcosm of the world, that what is happening to *me* is also happening to *all of them*. The pollster, on the other hand, may forget that the modal is not the model; or worse, he may exaggerate the power of the mean to predict the future and use it as a cudgel with which to batter his ideological enemy.

Catholics had come abreast of the population economically and socially and were well on their way intellectually. That was an impressive accomplishment, Greeley asserted in *Religion and Career*, fully aware that the mainstream of intellectual life in America was not at all distinguished. "Not at all impressive—deficient, in fact," was the judgment of the Catholic self-critics, standing in the presence of the great Eastern universities, unaware of the countless lesser institutions that made up the texture of American intellectual life. In this case, in an argument where the mean was used for the first time, it *would* have mattered to ask again and again: impressive *compared with what?*

Religion and Career gave Greeley the skills and the eyes that would determine his position in a variety of battles to come. He was an empirical sociologist now, possessed of a certain style, with a new role in the Catholic intellectual community; and much of what he would produce would bulge with tables of percentages, coefficients of association, statements of probability, appendices—all the appurtenances of survey research "facts." His advice to the young, even when he tried to inspire, had always been realistic and down to earth. So now would be his sociology.

A book appeared in the early months of 1964, just a bit before Greeley placed his finger on the New Breed in the pages of *America*. Like the child puzzled by the emperor's lack of clothes, it asked an innocent question, and, like the child, it drew a bevy of gasps, cheers, and outright anger. A New Hampshire woman, Mary Perkins Ryan, wondered in the title of a book *Are Parochial Schools the Answer?*[1] And in its 176 pages she did more than wonder—she answered in the negative. The Catholic school system, she said, was an obstacle to the Catholic mission of witnessing to the presence and activity of Christ.

Would not the Church and the world be better served if the child-centered parish became an adult-centered Christian community? Ryan asked. If the home became (as it once was) the seat of religious formation? If all the resources poured into the Catholic school system were freed from "what is essentially an auxiliary service"? Think of the time, she mused, that a bishop would have at his disposal, "time now spent in attending commencements, laying cornerstones, opening new buildings, and giving awards for spelling bees." Think of 13,000 priests, 5,000 brothers, 103,000 sisters, 62,000 lay teachers freed for other work. What a witness the Church would make if its people came out and let their light shine, "if enough priests and religious worked on secular campuses so that they could come to be known by great numbers of young people, Catholic and non-Catholic!"[2]

"Mrs. Ryan's little book landed like a stink-bomb in the little old schoolhouse," one commentator observed; "the response was nearly a public relations panic."[3] The Brooklyn *Tablet* attacked it as a denunciation of the very idea of Christian education. An official of the National Catholic Education Association called it "incredibly naive" and "foolish." Though Ryan was not on the program of the ensuing meeting of the NCEA, she was a major topic of conversation and practically the only one discussed in the news. At a press conference four Catholic school superintendents "took strong exception" to the book, and three of the four predicted "immense harm and confusion" from it. Just as the case for federal aid to parochial schools was gaining momentum, Ryan's critics fumed, here was a book urging Catholics to abandon the fight.

The Catholic school system of which Ryan spoke (and the word "system" was really a euphemism) comprised, in the early sixties, more than 300 institutions of higher learning, 2,500 secondary schools, and 10,000 elementary schools. Nearly three-fifths of the Catholic parishes in the country had their own elementary schools. Catholic schools accounted for more than six million students, or about 14 percent of the country's student population. No other modernized country had a system of such extensive coverage financed by nongovernmental sources. The history of the schools went back to the middle of the nineteenth century when the Catholic minority began to feel uneasy about nativist America. At that time the country was committing itself to mass public education, but the nondenominational schools that sprang up turned out to be Protestant. Catholics, in response, became defensive, feeling they could survive only in the security of their own schools; and in the 1840s such schools began to appear in New York. Forty years later the American hierarchy decreed that a Catholic school be established in every parish and that every Catholic child be in a Catholic school. The necessity of separate schools was strongly defended at the turn of the century by Catholic immigrants, especially Germans and Poles, to whom Catholic schools were a way of preserving what was theirs in the old country. Begun, then, for reasons that were largely defensive, the school system flourished even when the need for protection was gone. In the period after World War II, for example, Catholic schools experienced a remarkable surge in growth.

But now, in the 1960s, were the schools necessary? Did Catholic parents really want them for their children? The questions were hotly debated by Catholic educators, and Ryan's book was merely the tip of the iceberg. Were the schools divisive? Did they tend to preserve ethnic solidarities, to prevent immigrant groups from being absorbed into American life? Did it not take *common* educational experiences to produce cultural consensus in the United States? These questions came from outside the Church—and, more recently, from within it. And behind all the polemics lay a most sensitive issue: Was it now time for parochial schools to receive financial assistance from the government?

Even before *Are Parochial Schools the Answer?* was on bookstore shelves, Greeley and Peter Rossi were in the pages of the *Critic* describing a study of Catholic education to be undertaken by NORC.[4] The two took note of the grim things Ryan had to say about Catholic schools in her forthcoming book—as well as of recent forecasts of trouble in *Look* and *Newsweek*. But they parted company with Ryan. All schools can do, they argued, was pass on knowledge—*in*form, not form. What Ryan wanted, no school could accomplish. Further, there was absolutely no sign that the Catholic school system was moribund. While only one-third of the Catholic adults in the country had been to parochial schools, more than two-fifths of the Catholic children were in such schools in 1963. It was hardly the sign of a dying system.

As readers of the *Critic* and the *School Review* were being advised of these optimistic data, NORC interviewers were knocking on the doors of more than 2,700 randomly selected Catholics throughout the country, asking for their cooperation in a study of the kinds of schools people had attended. Funded by the Carnegie Corporation, NORC Survey 476 was the first national survey ever made of the Catholic population in the United States. Greeley and Rossi were investigating three basic questions:

1. Were Catholic schools effective as religious educators? "Effective" meant different things to different people. To Bishop Ernest Primeau, who wrote the foreword to *Are Parochial Schools the Answer?*, it meant "forming a people acceptable to God." To the sociologists at NORC, however, it meant something more tangible. Did Catholic-school Catholics, they phrased the question, *adhere more completely to the norms of Catholicism* than public-school

Catholics? Did they attend Mass and receive the sacraments more frequently? Did they hold more orthodox beliefs? Did they accept more
completely the authority of the Church? Were they, therefore,
"better" Catholics?

2. Were Catholic schools divisive? "Divisive," too, had a multi-
plicity of meanings, but the researchers settled on these questions to
find their answer: Were Catholic-school Catholics isolated from
non-Catholics? Were they disinterested in secular community affairs? Were they intolerant of other groups? Were they prejudiced toward them?

3. Did Catholic schools impede the economic and occupational achievement of those who attended them? The question
concerned possible academic deficiencies in the schools and possible anti-intellectual, otherworldly orientations that hampered
their students in later life. It was another attempt to test the longe-
vity of the so-called "Catholic Ethic."

Despite its appearances, the study that would be written up as
The Education of Catholic Americans (1966) was actually historical
in nature. The sample surveyed were Catholics between 23 and 57
years of age. Thus, they had been in school sometime in the half century between 1910 and 1960, and the subject of investigation was
Catholic education of *that* period—with *its* methods and *its* conception of goals. That, of course, made the controversy over the
schools stickier, for the educators in Ryan's camp were arguing
that it was precisely the goals of the first half of the twentieth
century that had to be abandoned.

Nevertheless, given those goals (which were all the researchers
had to work with), did Catholic education produce "better" Catholics? Yes, wrote Greeley, Rossi, and Leonard Pinto in the October-
November 1964 *Critic*, but the differences between Catholic-school
Catholics and public-school Catholics were not that convincing.
"To confirm the undramatic is a pedestrian task, especially when
the researcher finds that the facts place him squarely between two
positions in a controversy."[5] To sample the results: 86 percent of the
All Catholic group (those whose primary and secondary education
was exclusively Catholic) attended Mass weekly; 73 percent of the
Some Catholic group (part of whose education was in Catholic

schools) and 64 percent of the No Catholic group (Catholics whose
education was entirely public) did likewise. The figures for receiving communion "at least several times a month" were 38 percent, 25 percent, and 17 percent, respectively, and those for con-
fessing at least once a month 51 percent, 38 percent, and 32 percent.
Catholic-school Catholics were more likely to accept the Church's
teaching role on such subjects as race, birth control, and education.
They also proved, on a brief test of religious knowledge, to be better
informed regarding the fine points of Catholic doctrine, and they
were more orthodox in their own acceptance of doctrine (89 percent
of the All Catholic group, for example, compared with 75 and 61
percent of the others, respectively, agreed that "Jesus directly handed
over the leadership of His Church to Peter and the popes"). They
showed greater assent to Catholic moral dictates, especially in
matters that set Catholics apart from other Americans (81 percent of
the All Catholic group, compared with 74 and 71 percent of the
others, disagreed with the statement "It is not really wrong for an
engaged couple to have some sexual relations before they are married"). They also were more likely to participate in the organizational activity of the Church and contribute money to it. Catholics from Catholic schools *did* adhere to the official norms of
Catholicism more than did their confreres from public schools.

But was not this apparent impact of Catholic education due to
selectivity, to the fact that those who enrolled in Catholic schools
came from "better" Catholic families? And, therefore, was not the religiousness of Catholic school graduates due not to the schools but
to the families that sent their children to the schools—one of the
points of Mary Ryan's book?

Those questions led to the biggest surprise the data held for
Greeley and Rossi (and also ensured that the data would be mis-
understood by the public). It *was* true that parents who chose Catholic education for their children were more devout than those who did
not. Far from duplicating what was accomplished at home, however, Catholic schools, it was found, had impressive independent effects on children from highly religious families. Indeed, for these
children, a multiplier effect seemed to be operative, so that "religiousness of home and school reinforce each other, and when they
are working in concert, the level of religious behavior increases in

some sort of exponential fashion."[6] The effect of Catholic schooling
was increased even more if a student went on to a Catholic college
and married a practicing Catholic. Those highly devout families
who were not able to send their children to Catholic schools simply
were not able to develop an adequate compensatory mechanism.

On the other hand, for students from less devout backgrounds—approximately three-quarters of the children in the
schools—Catholic education accomplished little in the area of religious and value formation. "Catholic school administrators could
reasonably assume that, at least in the past, they were wasting their
time with the vast majority of their students . . . . In theory
at least, there was not much point in admitting children who were
not from very devout families."[7]

Lest this result come as a surprise, Greeley and Rossi cautioned,
we must remember that most sociological inquiries have shown that
the intimate settings of home, neighborhood, and workplace are a
good deal more effective in the process of socialization than is formal education. With that in mind, the authors concluded that "the
Catholic experiment in value-oriented education has been a moderate (though expensive) success." *Given the goals* of the Catholic
schools from 1910 to 1960—to ensure participation at Mass and in
the sacraments, to accept the Church as an authoritative teacher
(especially in the area of sexual morality), to "keep the faith"—the
schools had done "a reasonably adequate job."[8]

Given the limited success of Catholic schools in religious and
value formation, it was not surprising to discover that they failed to
show the slightest trace of divisiveness—the second major concern of
the study. The divisiveness theory, in fact, remained "spectacularly
unproven." To be sure, Catholics from Catholic schools were less
likely to associate with non-Catholics while they were in school, but
in adult life they had as many non-Catholic visitors, friends, neighbors, and co-workers as public-school Catholics. Nor were they any
less interested than public-school Catholics in community affairs.
They were no more or less anti-Negro, anti-Semitic, or anti-Pro-
testant, no more or less "Manichaean," religiously extreme, or per-
missive. The only difference in cultural attitudes was that Catholics
from Catholic schools were more tolerant regarding civil liberties
than their co-religionists from public schools. Even when a battery

of controls was introduced, the answer to the question of divisiveness was a resounding no. Again, the results were not surprising.
"There is ample reason in social theory to expect that, just as
schools produce different values only with great difficulty, so they
will separate peoples only with great difficulty."[9]

The defenders of Catholic education would do well to moderate
their joy at this second finding, Greeley and Rossi commented, for
was not the goal of the schools, especially in view of Church
teachings on social justice, to produce adults not *as* tolerant as
others but considerably *more* tolerant? Why, the critics of the
schools would surely ask, did the products of Catholic education
show no more love of neighbor than fellow Catholics from public
schools? Still, there was a glimmer of hope in the data. The
youngest, best-educated products of Catholic schooling stood out
from their public-school counterparts in their degree of tolerance
and social consciousness.

The third question of the Carnegie study—whether Catholic
schools impeded the occupational and economic success of Catholics—yielded an even stronger negative answer. Far from ham-
pering their graduates, Catholic schools seemed to give them a
boost. Even with key social and demographic variables controlled,
Catholics who went to Catholic schools were more successful than
Catholics who did not. Again, a multiplier effect seemed to be at
work. Catholic schooling had the greatest effect in improved socioeconomic status on those students from impressive socioeconomic
backgrounds. To others it was of little or no help.

If one level of Catholic education had to be jettisoned, the researchers asked, which should it be—elementary school, secondary
school, or college? The question was simple enough and so was its
answer—none could be safely eliminated; the data showed the effects of Catholic education to be cumulative. And how important
was Catholic higher education in the entire process? The question
had not been asked to this point because so few in the sample had
been to college. But when those few were inspected, striking differences appeared between graduates of Catholic and secular universities, differences of 25, 30, and 39 percentage points on various
indices. It was not the colleges themselves that were so influential;
rather, the differences were the result of attending a Catholic college
after a Catholic high school after a Catholic grammar school. Not

only were those with sixteen years of exclusively Catholic education "better" Catholics, but they were considerably more tolerant— giving substance to the hypothesis that integration into one's own religious-ethnic community enables him to relate more openly to the rest of society, giving hope to Catholic educators concerned about the social awareness, the "charity," of their graduates. The effect of comprehensive religious education with college as its culmination was so strong that the authors concluded:

> If one wishes to prevent American Catholicism from developing through its school system an elite which is both religious and socially rather impressive, one would do all in one's power to eliminate Catholic higher education. . . . This would apparently deprive the Roman Church in America of many of its most fervent future leaders; it would also quite possibly deprive the larger society of a group of citizens who would be more socially conscious and enlightened than many.[10]

Finally, what was the future of Catholic education? Was it, as some journalists suggested, in its death throes, or was there continued growth on the horizon? Wrote Greeley and Rossi, "The data strongly indicate that growth is precisely what is going to happen."[11] Demand for Catholic education was high. In areas where a Catholic school was available, 70 percent had attended it. Furthermore, demand increased as socioeconomic status improved, and Catholics were rising in socioeconomic status. The prediction was simply an extrapolation of present trends. Expansion of the schools would (and should) not be unlimited, however; never had more than two-thirds of the Catholic population desired religious education for their children and, besides, the birth rate in the country was beginning to level off. The only danger to the schools, the authors concluded, "would be the teacher situation." (It was, in retrospect, an ominous phrase.) If the "vocation shortage" increased, more lay teachers would have to be hired, costs would skyrocket, and the system could be in financial jeopardy.

Greeley and Rossi were not arguing for or against continued growth in the Catholic school system. They were simply making a prediction that the expansion of the past quarter-century would not be reversed and might even continue:

> Our opinion, for what it is worth, is that discussion by Catholics
> and non-Catholics alike concerning whether there will be Catho-
> lic schools is quite irrelevant. . . . Being for or against a school sys-
> tem with over five million students is like being for or against the
> Rocky Mountains: it is great fun but it does not notably alter
> reality.[12]

And like the Rocky Mountains (or the Sahara Desert, depending on your point of view), *The Education of Catholic Americans* was there—sober, complex, comprehensive. It did not notably
alter the positions taken in the argument over the schools, but it did
lend a measure of precision—and a good deal of ammunition—to
both sides. *America* reported that the Greeley-Rossi study showed
that the schools made a substantial difference and editorialized that
yes, they were worth it.[13] The Brooklyn *Tablet* headlined its story
"Study Sees Significant Relationship in Catholic Schooling, Adult
Life,"[14] but the *New York Times,* in an article that infuriated
Greeley, said, "Education in Roman Catholic schools has been
'virtually wasted' on three quarters of the students."[15] And *Commonweal* called it the way the *New York Times* did.[16]

Other reactions to the Greeley-Rossi report were mixed. *Time*
summarized it well.[17] *Newsweek* said it was "mired in qualifications."[18] Robert Cross of Columbia University, a non-Catholic
specializing in Catholic church history, referred to the "skimpi-
ness" of parochial school success;[19] and Daniel Callahan let it be
known in *Commentary* that he still saw the future a different way:
"Sooner or later it is bound to dawn on more Catholics that the
much-desired reform of the Church cannot take place as long as so
much of its money is channeled into education.[20]

And Mary Perkins Ryan said the report really didn't answer her
question; or, rather, it had not affected her answer. The areas in
which the schools were successful were not exactly "the 'component
parts' of the Christian life as set out either in the New Testament or
the documents of Vatican II," she wrote in a review of the Greeley-
Rossi study. Where was the association between Catholic education
and charity. (One paritcularly infamous item in the study asked
whether it was more important to avoid meat on Friday or to love
your neighbor, and only 53 percent of the Catholic-school Catholics
chose love.) The institution for Christian socialization, Ryan said
again, must be the group of two or three, or ten or twenty, gathered

to celebrate the Eucharist. As for formal religious education, the study showed, it "can, by itself, have very little lasting effect even if given in a Catholic school."[21]

Overlooked in the controversy was Greeley and Rossi's documentation of the spectacular influence of the Catholic college—when experience in a Catholic college followed twelve years of all-Catholic education. Eliminate the Catholic college, concluded *The Education of Catholic Americans*, and you destroy what you have painstakingly constructed for twelve years.

Long before that conclusion reached the public, Father Greeley was off on another project, touring the United States for an eye-witness look at the level of Catholic education responsible for its most dramatic effects. With assistants William van Cleve and Grace Ann Carroll (and with more support from Carnegie) he logged two to five days at thirty-six schools, amassing fifteen hundred interviews with faculty, students, and administrators. His impressions of Catholic higher education in 1965–1966 were delivered in the Catholic press and in a monograph called *The Changing Catholic College* (1967).

Why had some Catholic institutions grown rapidly and others failed to grow in the previous decade? The strongest correlate of improvement, Greeley found, was not the market potential of certain geographic locations (though that was important), not school size, not the proportion of laymen in administrative positions, not any one of a dozen other variables. It was the competence of the top administrator, his independence from the religious order that "owned" the school, his overall charisma. It seems that Greeley and his colleagues chanced to visit Catholic colleges at a time when their presidents had immense power and the freedom to exercise it. The presidents were not as yet hemmed in by faculty organizations; the trustees were in their hands because they were members of the religious community (and the president was frequently their religious superior); the students were, by and large, cowed. Hence a president could make a substantial difference. "The great-man theory of history, if it applies anywhere, most assuredly applies to an institution of higher education": thus Greeley apprised readers of the *Critic* in the fall of 1966.[22]

Schools that Greeley classified as Rapid-Improvement had a

good deal going for them—size, resources, reputation, a national
image—but without top leadership, Greeley asserted, their growth
would not have been what it was. Charismatic leaders were on his
mind at this time (he was simultaneously digging into American
Catholic history and finding such leaders for a book to be called *The
Catholic Experience*), and when he found them in the flesh in those
presidents' offices, he was enthusiastic. One president, with his
Gaelic charm and wit, reminded Greeley and his colleagues of
Spencer Tracy playing Frank Skeffington in *The Last Hurrah.*
Another's assistant brought to mind "a powerful diesel locomotive
proceeding down an open track at full speed, spitting out ideas and
plans much as locomotive wheels spit out sparks." Had these men
not been priests, "it would be a safe guess to say that all of them
would be college presidents in any event (if they had not become
major political figures in the Kennedy administration)."[23]

What about Medium-Improvement schools? Had they the
leadership just depicted, Greeley claimed, they too would have been
on their way. But as matters stood, growth had occurred only by accident. "They are better than they were, but through no fault of their
own."[24] As for schools at the bottom of the list, not even a brilliant
president could have ended the stagnation. In some cases their geographic location was unfavorable; in one, concentration on physical expansion had overshadowed concern for qualitative improvement; in another, the ecclesiastical background was so conservative
that movement was impossible.

Faculty status at Catholic schools had improved considerably,
Greeley reported. Salaries were up, teaching loads down, research
competence developing. And there were the "new professors"—
young people with the best of credentials, oriented toward research
and scholarship, who turned down offers to more prestigious institutions because Catholic schools needed their help. "Their enthusiasm and willingness to make a fair amount of sacrifices for
Catholic colleges is one of the bright spots on the Catholic higher
education horizon."[25] On the debit side, however, were disil-
lusioning administrative policies likely to drive the new professors
away, the low morale of religious faculty, and the sorry state of departments of theology.

As for students, their plight could be summarized by revising a joke about the Taft-Hartley Law. "Higher education is heaven for faculty, . . . purgatory for administrators, and hell for students." Because of the tenacious influence of religious communities on the student life of "their" campuses, because religious communities think their role is to act *in loco parentis*, students are highly regimented—and in some cases their civil rights are even violated. Freedom of the student press is restricted; organizations are not free to invite speakers to campus; disciplinary boards, often fair and not arbitrary, still do not guarantee due process. The basic assumption is that one cannot trust people. "Even though Catholic theology takes a rather benign and optimistic view of human nature, by the time this theology is filtered down to the practical operation of student life in many Catholic campuses it has become highly Calvinistic."[26]

Greeley insisted that *The Changing Catholic College* was not, for all its realism, pessimistic. Still angry over the reaction to *The Education of Catholic Americans*, he warned that those who quoted this book out of context did so at their own risk. Nobody projected anything but a continued exponential increase in enrollment for Catholic colleges—and that set the stage for innovation. Yes, for all their problems, Catholic schools *did* have opportunities. There were charismatic leaders who did not suffer from inferiority complexes. There were model schools, too, the Johns and Nancys, the saving remnant, of academic institutions. Greeley closed *The Changing Catholic College* as he did *Strangers in the House*, describing one of the schools. Its name was changed to St. Mary's.

St. Mary's *looked* like a poor school—unpretentious buildings in the middle of a large American city, corridors lined with boxes, crowded offices and classrooms, the smell of a chemistry lab next to the president's office. But its budget was $1.3 million, with no deficit, and its library was recently ranked in the top 20 percent of all liberal arts college libraries. And something else was happening in its dilapidated halls:

> One member of the research team remarked after the first hour and a half in the school, "Everybody's laughing here—the sisters, the laymen, and the girls. They're laughing all the time. What in the world is the matter with them?" What is the matter with students, faculty, and administration at St. Mary's is something that is not

the matter with most other colleges in the country—Catholic, or
non-Catholic. The people at St. Mary's are happy. As a matter of
fact, they are happier than anybody has a right to be, especially the
students.[27]

What was going on? Imaginative, creative instruction from
well-trained sister and lay faculty, voluntary theology workshops to
which students swarmed, programs that brought a quarter of the
student' body to work in the inner city. A relaxed, playful atmosphere, "one that is difficult to believe even when one is in the midst
of it, and even more difficult to believe once one has departed (and it
is by no means easy to depart)."[28]

There was magic in St. Mary's past, one Mother Jeremia, the
former superior of St. Mary's religious order. "We believe, in this
religious order," she told Greeley, "that our function is to create
an atmosphere in which each of the nuns is able to develop her own
talents and personality to its fullest. We don't want to mold our sisters into any pattern. We want them to be themselves in the best possible way." Of the college she added, "We decided fifty years ago that
you could either build beautiful buildings or educate young women, and we chose to do the latter."[29]

So there *was* a great administrator in St. Mary's history. There
was also a spirit of flexibility on the part of the entire religious
order, a feeling that if they were going into the work of education
then they would do that work in the most efficient way possible.
Young sisters, therefore, were sent to secular graduate schools (long
before it became a practice of other religious communities) and laymen moved into key positions at St. Mary's (without the fear that
they would try to take the school away). Freedom and permissive-
ness were encouraged within the order and within the school. Pressure from outside ecclesiastical authorities was resisted. Here was an
instance in which the ownership of a college by a religious community did not deaden education but filled it with spirit.

The places and the people Father Greeley loves to describe have
much in common—intellectual curiosity, love of play, belief in the
potency of the person, of their own person. They are *brilliant*, not
awe-inspiring, but shining, sparkling (like diamonds in the rough,
not cut, polished, and well cemented in a setting). St. Mary's may
not have been the best institution, academically, of those he visited,

but, humanly, none was its equal. At the end of his visit Greeley facetiously warned the president against a plan to move the school to a campus with several non-Catholic liberal arts colleges:

> "You have too much going for you here, Sister," he [Greeley] noted, "don't take the risk of losing it by moving."

> "But," Sister President replied, "what is important here is not buildings; it's people, and the people will be the same out there as they are here."

> "Yes, but the people out there will be more than just your college, Sister, and a lot of them take higher education very, very seriously."

> The Sister President's eyes sparkled. "How much do you want to bet that we change them before they change us?"[30]

Sister President, in Greeley's opinion, had a lot more going for her than Mary Perkins Ryan—and so did the other charismatic leaders in Catholic education. When Greeley attended that infamous National Catholic Education Association meeting in April 1964 (in Atlantic City), he did not hear the death knell that certain journalists did. Though they described the convention as if it were a pitched battle between the Monsignori and Ryan, Greeley said:

> I came away convinced that there were profound and dynamic forces for growth in Catholic education. Despite all the weaknesses that are so patent, some of those in the Church who are most gifted with insight were at that convention, and the direction of their thoughts made the terms of the controversy between Mrs. Ryan and the Monsignori seem quite irrelevant.[31]

Were parochial schools the answer? Greeley thought *The Changing Catholic College* was a hopeful book, a photograph that revealed how far Catholic higher education had come, what possibilities were open to it, and how to seize upon them. But Doris Grumbach read the same book and reached a different conclusion:

> On every score the climate is seen to be dismal, the intellectual tone of these schools gray and discouraging, the student bodies of even the best schools "deficient in both social awareness and social commitment," the quality of campus religious life so poor that "most

alert, intelligent and potentially dedicated students at Catholic colleges are being turned against the organized institutional Church." Most pathetic is the resistance to innovation of any sort.[32]

Daniel Callahan, who earlier, in response to *The Education of Catholic Americans*, had still predicted trouble for the parochial schools, likewise turned Greeley's findings against him, but in a different way. Greeley made a convincing case, Callahan said, that the more "professional," the more "American," the more "secular" a college's leadership, the more successful that college would be. What Greeley's book *really* shows, he said in the *Saturday Review*, is that the secularization of Catholic schools is imminent. They soon *will* lose their distinctive characteristics—or at least they will if they wish to improve. Of Greeley's position that Catholicism and success in American higher education are compatible, he added, *"The Changing Catholic College* implicitly tears that case apart more effectively than any outside critic ever could."[33]

And so the battle wore on, the lines drawn as before: gloomy liberals from the East versus an optimistic nose-counter from the Midwest. For them it was either prolonged illness or death for Catholic colleges; for him it was an "explosion of college enrollment" and an unparalleled opportunity to innovate. *They* said the Church was a spiritual community that did not belong in "organized" education. *He* replied that an unorganized community was a contradiction in terms. *They* said a Catholic university was unecumenical. *He* insisted the Church had to do its own thinking before it could engage in dialogue. *They* said inquiry in a Catholic university could never be free. *He* countered that the free university came into being in a world overwhelmingly Catholic. *They* said Catholic universities would end up as Catholic as Harvard is Congregationalist. *He* rebutted: only if you despair of the vitality of the Catholic faith. Well, they said, we need more lay administrators and lay trustees. No, he came back, we need more great administrators, and the lay trustees we have are being co-opted by conservative boards. Even if you're right, they said, there is still no money for a first-rate Catholic university. He replied: organize the alumni; they are no longer impoverished. And he added: why do academicians in Catholic colleges have to ape all that is bad in American higher education? Just as the multiversities are trying to rehumanize themselves, the better Catholic institutions are trying to prove that they, too, can become multiversities. If we could experiment, if Notre Dame, for example, could stop trying to be a Catholic Princeton, "then we could conceivably see the day when Princeton will claim—God save us all—that it is striving to be a non-Catholic Notre Dame."[34]

If nothing else, Greeley's research opened up for him a career as a sociologist of higher education. He began to serve on national committees concerned with student life, became an editor of the *Journal of Higher Education*, and in April 1968 was named program director in higher education at NORC. The year before he had been approached by a committee in the Department of Education—a unit of the University of Chicago distinct from NORC—as a possible chairman of their program in higher education. He was interested. It was customary for NORC researchers to have tenured appointments in university departments; for one thing, such appointments eased the strain on the NORC budget. During the summer of 1967 he negotiated with the department, and they unanimously recommended his appointment. But by September the offer had not come and the matter was closed.

What, and/or who, had killed his appointment? Greeley became curious. Was it his close association with Jack Egan and Peter Rossi that did him in? (Father Egan had fought the university's plans to "redevelop" surrounding neighborhoods in Hyde Park, and Rossi had justified Egan's role in *The Politics of Urban Renewal.*) Was it even, just possibly, his Catholicism, his priesthood? The answers did not come in 1967, but seeds of suspicion about the "free" and "open" University of Chicago were already germinating in Greeley's mind.

Nevertheless, he continued to concentrate his scholarly activity on higher education. His description of the New Breed brought an invitation from the Hazen Foundation of New Haven, Connecticut, to join Yale's Kenneth Keniston, Stanford's Joseph Katz, Wisconsin's Joseph Kauffman, and a half dozen others to examine higher education from the students' point of view. Greeley came to the committee's deliberations with Grace Ann Carroll and memories of John Henry Newman. The influence of both was evident in the final report, which Greeley authored and entitled *The Student in Higher Education* (1968).

The students who were the subjects of the book were not leftists dedicated to tearing down the established power structure nor rightists trying to reestablish the simplicities of the past, not the senior at Harvard looking ahead to a career in nuclear physics nor the freshman at Michigan State crying to herself at night because she is homesick, but rather the large numbers of ordinary students in between. These students were searching for purpose, but were skeptical of formal ideology. They believed in "flower power," in open, trusting, and undemanding relationships. They were poised and sophisticated on the exterior but hesitant and uncertain below the surface. It was rare for a middle-class youth, subject throughout his life to evaluations, rankings, and comparisons, to have experienced unconditional acceptance as he grew up. "Under such circumstances, self-doubt, self-rejection, self-hatred, and self-punishment become almost endemic to the collegiate culture."[35]

When such a student, filled with doubts about himself, suspicious of organizations and their administrators, arrives at college, it takes only a few months for his expectations to plummet and his curiosity to be extinguished, the report went on. During orientation week he learns where the bookstore is, where his laundry goes, where he collects his mail. If he feels lonely, there is a counseling center. If he gets sick, there are student health services. Should he have academic difficulties, he has been assigned an advisor. If he has religious doubts, there is a chaplain somewhere. All his needs have been seen to, but somehow he gets the impression that they have not been taken care of but disposed of, and in such a way as to make life as easy as possible for the faculty and administration.

He will probably be forced to take several introductory courses taught by fledgling teaching assistants in lecture halls that seat from 100 to 500 students. The assistant will want to communicate a "body of knowledge" which the student must master. If the student fails (and it is secretly hoped that the less "qualified" students will fail), he will drop out of the system before the coddled full professors (who, by virtue of their lengthy list of publications lend "distinction" to the school) have to deal with him. It is an efficient process, but it has precious little to do with education, which must, in plain English, begin where the student is and build on his inherent curiosity.

The Student in Higher Education advocated a "developmental" college experience, one that integrated the student's cognitive growth with that of his entire personality. To be sure, the primary task of universities was to develop the intellect. But "to split 'intellectual' from 'other' development seems highly analytic, for in practice, when dealing with an individual, it becomes virtually impossible to separate intellectual from moral and emotional growth."[36] The cognitive and the noncognitive had to be integrated.

In the face of predictions from the quantitative experts in higher education (those who spoke of growth in body counts and provided a dollar figure for each body), the Hazen Foundation committee was speaking *qualitatively*. Their recommendations were numerous: Do not "pass on knowledge" in the first year, but rather, orient the student toward learning; leave the material that must be "passed on" to teaching machines and use faculty in as many tutorials and individual seminars as possible; make grades optional; hire only those Ph.D.'s (and there will be a surplus to choose from in the early seventies) interested in the developmental experiences of their students and pay them as much as—or even more than—their research-oriented colleagues; increase student participation in policy-making; democratize the making and enforcing of rules; create new physical structures (especially housing and eating facilities) that promote the formation of intimate communities; make room for volunteer student service outside the universities instead of treating it as a burden; bring liberal education to Everyman, not simply to elites with IQs of better than 120. Above all, experiment:

> The university should say to a handful of its more gifted faculty and administrators, "Find some students who are interested in the experiment you want to try and then go ahead and do it. We will guarantee to do all in our power to get the students into graduate schools, and we will keep the accrediting agencies at bay. Go ahead and experiment to your heart's content and don't worry about the lamentations of administrators and the wailing of faculty colleagues. You may have to work outside the structure of the guild-dominated regular course of instruction, but don't worry about the guilds. We'll protect you from them too."[37]

In 1969 it seemed there would be a chance for Greeley to do some experimenting of his own when he became a full professor (on a joint basis with NORC) at the Chicago Circle Campus of the University of Illinois. He was to create a graduate program in higher education, but three weeks after he signed the contract of appointment, the dean with whom he had been negotiating resigned. Left in the lurch, Greeley found that the massive bureaucracies of the state universities were simply beyond him. In March 1971, having accomplished nothing, he resigned the position.

There followed three years on the board of trustees of Rosary College in River Forest, Illinois. Again, none of his dreams came to fruition. In the early seventies, Rosary, like so many colleges, was fighting for its life. "Innovative education" was in another world now, far from the day-to-day realities of enrollments and finances. Greeley realized that the opportunities of the middle sixties had disappeared. The schools had "blown it"; campus unrest diverted attention from educational experimentation and caused alumni and legislators to back off from financial help for universities and support for educational research. There were signs as early as 1968 that the bright expectations for education would come crashing down, and by 1970, after Cambodia and Kent State, Greeley recognized that it had "all gone down the drain."

So his career as a researcher in higher education would be no more than a costly interlude. Before it ended he produced two other books on the subject, both of them resulting from his longstanding relationship with the Carnegie Corporation. *From Backwater to Mainstream* was published in 1969 (Clark Kerr had asked him to write it) and *Recent Alumni and Higher Education* (which he co-authored with Joe L. Spaeth of NORC) in 1970. The former re-iterated much of what Greeley said in *The Changing Catholic College* (indeed, it contained entire passages from that book), but this time Greeley named names. "Spencer Tracy," we learn, was Father Michael Walsh, and his university, Boston College. Along with Notre Dame and Holy Cross, it was one of three Rapid-Improvement schools profiled. "St. Mary's" was Immaculate Heart College of Los Angeles, soon to join the Claremont College Group. Greeley described the history of Catholic higher education in the United States as one of serendipitous founding, helter-skelter expansionism—and high mortality. Two-thirds of the colleges for men founded before 1956, for example, were no longer in existence.

The schools that survived were being, for weal or woe, "secularized" (Callahan's forecast had been correct after all)—the great leveling force of the accrediting agencies was seeing to that. And in the feverish debate over the existence of Catholic schools, stark financial realities were looming larger, in some cases even deciding the question. Catholic schools, Greeley reported, were no worse off than the typical private institution—which placed them in plenty of trouble. Several years earlier he had forecast two decades of rising demand for desks at Catholic colleges; now the picture was different—unstable enrollments and the prospect, with increasing tuition, of severe decline. Contributed services of religious faculty were diminishing, the salaries of lay faculty increasing. Fund-raising was often inept; besides, "it would seem that American Catholics are not as generous in contributions as Jews or Protestants." The church-state issue made government help uncertain in some areas of the country. "It is safe to predict that many of the smaller and weaker Catholic schools may not survive into the 1980s; the larger and better schools probably will, but it will be a perilous adventure."[38]

Recent Alumni and Higher Education reported on the fifth survey, in 1968, of the class of 1961. Greeley had already used some of the findings in the anti-intellectualism debate, telling readers, Catholic and non-Catholic, that alumni of Catholic colleges *had* fulfilled their ambitions of combining scholarship with Catholicism. In an article for *America* he worked on another "dogma to which many Catholic liberals cling despite all proof to the contrary." Catholic alumni in 1968 were *not* dissatisfied with their schools. They were critical of them, true; they knew the curriculum, the library, the professional standing of the faculty were something less than perfect. Yet the Catholic alumnus was still more likely to be strongly attached to his college than the typical alumnus and to say he wanted his children to attend the school that he did. "One might even go so far as to say that the alumni seem to be more confident of Catholic higher education in the future than do many Catholic educators."[39]

The reason for alumni loyalty was not that they thought they had attended quality schools. To the contrary, only 14 percent of the Catholic college graduates rated their alma mater in the top quartile of American colleges. This contrasted with 52 percent of the alumni of private universities and 53 percent of those from liberal arts colleges—a finding Greeley did not emphasize in the *America* article. No, the alumni were loyal for a different reason. They esteemed their alma mater's role in value formation, and to a greater extent than alumni from all other types of institution. *The Education of Catholic Americans* concluded that experience in a Catholic college, following experiences in Catholic elementary and secondary schools, had a significant impact on value formation. The alumni of Catholic institutions saw it the same way.

Alumni expect a lot from higher education, Greeley said in a postscript to *Recent Alumni and Higher Education*. Colleges are supposed to be "parent, priest, psychiatrist, master craftsman, confidant, charismatic leader, prophet, social reformer"—but they cannot be all of these, and it would be well if society, and the colleges themselves, recognized this fact.[40] Reflecting on the class of 1969, Greeley offered some farewell advice to higher education. First, beware of "relevancy"—a year in the inner city does not guarantee sensitivity or sophistication; it may produce "narrow, bigoted zealots" and "romantic revolutionaries." The new "urban studies," he warned in *Educational Record*, are probably doomed before they start, if they are merely a response to guilt feelings, to a vague sense that one must "do something."[41] Watch out, he added, for the "T-Group temptation," which says "the college must 'swing'; it must 'turn on'; it must be 'hip,' " and which leads one into "encounter groups, marathon groups, sensitivity groups, affinity groups, white and black caucuses, and could even embrace astrology, witchcraft, divination, contemplation, drugs, rock music, and the whole psychedelic bag." The new enemies were the "devotees of feeling" among the student body, the "faculty barbarians" who ape the students, and the "losers" who "expect the demise of American higher education by no later than the second quarter of next year."[42]

Greeley was backing off now from the notion of education that developed the total personality (that had been prostituted by "relevancy" and "group therapy") and was asking again for an emphasis on the intellect. He told me several years later, "I thought with the Hazen report I'd made some contribution to the beginning of higher educational reform, and I was appalled by some of the things that were claiming to be higher education." The advocates of feeling had taken over; *cognition* was on the run. Greeley still included the noncognitive in his outlines of the ideal educational experience, but (as he wrote in the *Journal of Higher Education*) he no longer wished to give "aid and comfort to the pop psychological kooks who currently abound in the land."[43] Though higher education was in a critical period, he wrote in the conclusion of *Recent Alumni and Higher Education*, the barbarians and losers could still be defeated.

The barbarians and losers could be defeated: a sad, sour note to end enormous amounts of work—committees, books, reports, articles too numerous to mention. Greeley had invested heavily in higher education, and now the market had crashed. There was nothing to do but quit and lose touch with the schools, such as Immaculate Heart College, that had so inspired him. In 1974 Greeley's only connection with higher education was his presence on a reconstituted Hazen committee—that and nothing more. As he looks back on a time of hard, hard work that never paid off, he can only say, "I was glad to get out of it."

If the picture in higher education had become bleak, so had that in the Catholic elementary and secondary school system. What *The Education of Catholic Americans* confidently predicted would never happen *did* happen; five million students attended 13,000 parochial schools in 1967, but only four million attended 11,000 such schools in 1973. Between 1963 and 1974 the percentage of Catholic children in parochial elementary and secondary schools dropped from 44 to 29, most of the decline occurring at the elementary level. The Greeley-Rossi report was correct in its assessment of *demand* for the schools—the decline was not due to parents' removing children from the schools—but it failed to foresee that few schools would be built to accommodate a Catholic population moving to the suburbs. Costs were soaring; there was an acute vocation shortage among teaching nuns. Catholic administrators, asking themselves whether parochial schools were the answer, were not about to take a chance on new construction.

Greeley's thoughts on the about-face of parochial schools were contained in a book on which he collaborated with a Milwaukee lawyer by the name of William Brown. The book was about the size of Mary Ryan's and, like hers, it asked a simple question: *Can*

Catholic Schools Survive? (1970). Principal author Brown said yes, they can and should—and without public assistance. To Catholic parents he said, calculate the cash difference between voluntary contributions to Catholic schools and the involuntary tax increases sure to come if Catholic schools close down, and you will quickly discover that the price of having one's own schools, and being able to do what one wishes in them, is small indeed.

Brown's figures were preceded by Greeley's analysis of the decline of parochial schools. Lack of demand was not the cause—70 percent of Catholic parents have steadily expressed a preference for Catholic schools. Nor was a hostile culture out to do in the schools. No, the problem lay with Catholic educators themselves, they and the journalists who criticized old models but failed to provide new ones. On the brink of success, everybody lost their nerve. They lost confidence, faith, morale, enthusiasm. They suffered the self-hate characteristic of any immigrant group in the later stages of acculturation. The shift from the mentality of the Counter-Reformation to that of the Ecumenical Age, from immigrant slum to professional suburb—both of them peaking in 1960—was too much. There was no new vision, no new theory, to replace the rigid certainties that had propped up Catholic education in the past. And so the fight for the schools was given up even before it began.

Cemented in Greeley's thinking now was a distinction between a Catholic *population* (as he knew it from opinion polling and from life in the parish) and a Catholic *liberal elite* overpowered, as he put it, by a death wish. Catholics in the neighborhoods were enthusiastic about the schools. They wanted them in 1963, and they wanted them when surveyed again in 1974. But liberals in Catholic education and in the media could not hear the voices from the neighborhoods. Should the schools fail to survive, said Greeley, historians will say "not that Catholic education was crushed by a hostile non-Catholic society, nor that it was abandoned by an uninterested Catholic population, but rather that it committed suicide."[44]

5 The Wake of Vatican II

One morning in the summer of 1964, when the analysis of the parochial school data was in a particularly acute stage, Father Greeley received a phone call. "You've been transferred," the voice said.

"Oh?" replied Greeley. Immediately he called the rectory at Christ the King and found that a certain letter *had* come in the mail. He asked to have it read to him. It was true; he had been transferred to St. Thomas the Apostle parish, just across Fifty-fifth Street from the University of Chicago. No more than that—the letter contained no explanation, no mention of the future of his work at NORC.

Greeley hastened to St. Thomas for a talk with the pastor there. He knew the man well, for he had been a curate at St. Angela's during Greeley's seminary years and toastmaster at the banquet following Greeley's first Mass. Greeley asked about his work at the university. His new pastor hesitated; then he pointed out that the parish had three hospitals to take care of, that it wouldn't be fair to the other priests, that he couldn't make an exception for Greeley. The university work would have to go.

"I spent twenty-four pretty bleak hours," Greeley recalls. It seemed he had no choice but to comply, but then he thought of Archbishop (by then Cardinal) Meyer, the man who, after all, had sent him to graduate school and encouraged him to stay on at NORC He called Meyer's office.

The cardinal was not available, but a short time later Cletus O'Donnell, chancellor of the archdiocese, returned Greeley's call. "You're not upset about the change, are you?" he began.

"Well, yes I am. I've got these commitments . . ."

"Oh, we want you to keep those up. We moved you to the university parish so you would be closer. We just wanted to make it

more convenient for you. Everybody knows we want you to continue at the university."

"Oh yes? My pastor doesn't."

"Well, we'll straighten that out."

The matter was taken care of quickly and in the fall of 1964
Greeley left Christ the King (a parish which, for all his ambivalence, he hated to leave) and moved to St. Thomas. Another curate
at Christ the King, Father John Hotchkin, was leaving too—to do
graduate work in theology. "Father H" had arrived in 1960, fresh
from the North American College in Rome. "He taught me theology," Greeley says, and it's true. The books of letters to John and
Nancy are full of references to the theological ideas of John Hotchkin. The two of them had great times during their years together
and, with all their enthusiasm for projects, gave their pastor a run
for his money; but it seems that by 1964 the pastor had had enough.
He wanted a full-time curate, not one who spent most of his hours at
the university or writing in his room. "The pastor got rid of us,"
Greeley recollects. "I'm sure he did."

Life at St. Thomas quickly became unbearable. Greeley was tied
down to the rectory by a hospital call system and had to dash off at
all hours on a moment's notice; the pastor resented the fact that Cardinal Meyer's office had "straightened out" the matter of Greeley's
university work; the payoffs in friendships with parishioners were no
longer present. In March 1965, just six months after he moved to St.
Thomas, Greeley wrote the cardinal asking to be released from
parish work. I cannot do both, he explained, either the parish work
or the university work has to go. The problem was especially difficult because Greeley was about to embark on his national tour of
Catholic colleges—a plan devised to help extricate him from St.
Thomas.

Meyer granted Greeley's request—and then he died. His reply to
Greeley's letter, it turned out, was his last official act.

The loss of the cardinal was staggering. Here was a man who
actually encouraged Greeley to write, to develop his skills in graduate school, to continue on as a research scholar after graduation. If
Greeley had a problem putting together the roles of parish priest
and NORC researcher, the cardinal's door was open for consulta-
tion and support.

In the summer of 1965, after Greeley left St. Thomas for a room in the rectory of St. Dorothy's parish, Chicago received a new archbishop, John Cody. Greeley phoned for an appointment to report on his work and arrived one day with the galley sheets for *The Education of Catholic Americans*. When Cody came into the office, Greeley remembers (bitterness coming into his voice) he began to criticize. You write too much—everybody says so. What kind of arrangements do you have for censorship? You're drifting away from parish work, you know. I'm not going to leave you at the university for very long. "By the way, how much do they pay you?"

"Not very much," Greeley replied. But he wouldn't specify the figure.

Their conversation soon reached an impasse. "So there I was with the galley sheets of *The Education of Catholic Americans*. I brought them in under my arm. I walked out with them under my arm. And that was the end of me and the archdiocese of Chicago. I've been an un-person ever since."

It had all happened suddenly, dramatically—from Christ the King to nothing, from a supportive archbishop who said "write more" to a hostile one who said "you write too much." To this day Greeley's anger has not abated. Greeley never asked to leave Christ the King, never wanted to be a priest without a parish, never imagined a superior like John Cody. But suddenly, as total surprises, these were *faits accomplis*. "I got out one step ahead of the sheriff. If Meyer hadn't released me from parish work just before he died, I would have been defenseless. Even then, if Cody had moved on me, he could have gotten away with it." By 1966 it was too late. *The Education of Catholic Americans*, the first survey ever of the American Catholic population, had made Greeley a national figure.

More was happening to make the summer of 1965 a "horrendously hellish" one. Some of the young people Greeley had known at Christ the King kept coming to see him, first at St. Thomas and then at his new home at St. Dorothy's. Their relationship was different now—he was a friend, not a man of authority. Barriers came down, and Greeley saw and heard for the first time things that shook him to the core. "I was appalled to see how much some of these people were suffering. I can't talk about young people today, but at that stage of the game there was just an immense amount of self-hatred and self-loathing. I guess later on in the decade they were able to take it out by being angry at society but these kids weren't able to do that. All kinds of people were dangerously close to suicide."

These were the children "spoiled" by their parents (that was what he was told a decade ago)—children, Greeley realized now, who had been given everything but love. Now the feeling began to drown them. *I*—not just my products or my accomplishments—am worthless; *I* am no good. Greeley finds words difficult as he thinks back, but notes, "I sent an awful lot of people off to therapists that summer."

Just before that fatal season hit, in May 1965, Greeley published "The Temptation of the New Breed" in *America*.[1] A year had passed since his original article, and one could sense the discomfort that would soon explode. The New Breed, he complained, is increasingly handicapped by a lack of ideology. They have *no* specific goals, can make *no* critical social analyses, are capable of *no* systematic commitment to work. Talented, yes, but disdainful of the grubby, day-to-day work of building an organization—or even working within an organization.

> We ask the New Breed what they want of us, or what they want of society, and they say: "We want you to love us, we want you to permit us to make something of the world where you have failed." But then if we ask: "How have we failed, and how do you want us to love you?" their words become vague. They tell us simply that we have failed because there is not enough love or freedom in the world.[2]

Freedom and love are not enough, Greeley argued. The New Breed "must abandon the cheap cliches and slogans of the books of existentialist philosophy and become hard-nosed and practical. . . . The basic problem is that the very best young people we have are not sure *who* they are, *where* they are going, or *what* they want out of life." He had soured on the New Breed.

> I cannot help feeling that, for all their rejection of "phoniness," the New Breed's emotionalism has just a bit of phony about it, too. The problems they have can be solved with intelligent effort; it is possible for the New Breed to take counsel, to put their life in

order. What I find almost inexcusable is the tendency of so many of them to drift. It seems to me that in their lives there are, indeed, just too many "great big hairy deals."[3]

A year later the lesson of the summer of 1965 had sunk in; they were crying for *love*, no more, no less. In June 1966, two years after he baptized the movement, Greeley wrote "A Farewell to the New Breed." He was wrong, he said; the young do not need an ideology and a practical program as much as they need encouragement and love—come to think of it, just what they were asking for. "They do not have enough faith in their own goodness, their own dignity, their own value, their own promise." They despair, not of reforming society, but of their own value. Greeley himself failed to encourage them, he added. "I admit in all honesty that it will be a long, long time before I am able to excuse myself for this failure." And he asked anyone who was listening to "love them with a love that does not require them to fit into his patterns or do what he wants them to do, to progress along the path he has chosen for them or adopt the values he thinks they ought to adopt."[4]

Greeley tried to follow his own advice with the New Breed, tried to put together lives that had shattered almost overnight. He did it by forming a parish (in view of his difficulties with the cardinal, something *he* needed, too) of twenty-five or thirty New Breeders. It was a floating, experimental, "underground" community that began to come together at a summer home he had acquired on the eastern shore of Lake Michigan. Greeley purchased the house, located in the community of Grand Beach, in the fall of 1965. He was to discover that many of the South Side Irish (including the mayor of Chicago) had second homes there. To Greeley, the house at Grand Beach came to be what Twin Lakes was when he was a boy. To fellow priests, it became to focal point of envy and resentment, a visible sign of a substantial, independent source of income.

Greeley's new parish found Grand Beach an ideal place to gather—the lake, the sand, the wind, the friendship, the unity in belief, all of it an hour from Chicago. Greeley was on his tour of American Catholic colleges when he purchased his new home, and often he would fly into Chicago and head directly for Grand Beach for a weekend with his young parishioners, returning on Sunday to his basement room at St. Dorothy's. As the community developed, it had days of recollection and discussion intertwined with the liturgy—often, in the beginning, very moving and very exciting experiences.

The community prospered and Greeley wrote about it and about other underground churches that were developing along with it. He wrote with the same combination of hope and practical advice that had ushered in the New Breed just two years before. The New Community, he said, is a term for "nothing more than groups of friends periodically meeting to discuss their life, their work, their faith." Members of communities like his simply do not find what they need in their urban parishes, even in the most dynamic of them. At home they participate in a madhouse of parochial activities and remain committed to their parishes, but they are on the trail of something else, something closer, something more meaningful: "a place where a person is able to be himself because he loves and is loved, . . . where he is able to speak his mind because it is safe to do so, . . . where he does not have to impress others with his brilliance, or his wit, or his success, . . . where he need not be afraid to speak of his hopes and his fears, or of his joys and his failures."[5] The New Community was a response to the anguish of the New Breed.

The New Community was also part of something more extensive than Christ the King parish or even the American Catholic Church. Rural communes were being formed almost daily in remote parts of the western United States; "educational villages," composed of tightly knit groups of younger faculty and students, were appearing on university campuses; the cursillo and pentecostal movements were creating small, intense religious communes; Orthodox Jews had banded together on the fringes of Harvard. And there were Zen monasteries, Meher Baba groups, intimate fellowships of believers in astrology or the *I Ching*. Quasisacred attempts at intense interpersonal fellowship were sprouting all over the landscape.

One could sense Greeley's hope for these ventures—and especially for his own community—in his litanies of advice. *Do* require hard work, he said; *do* tolerate diversity; *do* be patient with each other as you gradually unmask yourselves. *Don't* force honesty, openness, love. These grow slowly, organically, and cannot be sped along by gimmickry. Let no one become the amateur psychologist of the group; it would be better to have a professional one, even an outsider. Though it is not especially easy, try "to steer a middle path between pressure, manipulations, and covert aggression on the one hand and distrust, fear, and insecurity on the other."[6] Above all, have no newsletter, no national secretariat, no national conventions, no national chaplain, no national program committees. That, after all, is what we are trying to avoid.

At the beginning, Greeley thought the New Community to be terribly important:

> It may well become a revolutionary development of the Church. It may represent a major step forward in the Christian life comparable to the appearances of the communities of hermits in the fourth century, the monastic communities of the sixth century, the friars in the twelfth and thirteenth centuries, and the congregations in the seventeenth and eighteenth centuries.

The young of Christ the King, a few of them already priests and nuns, others coming together and thinking of marriage, were being *healed*. Perhaps parishes like his actually did "mark the beginning of an entirely new era in the history of Christianity."[7]

But then, slowly at first, and almost inevitably (it seems in retrospect), the community began to teeter, and Greeley's new hope, like so many previous ones, began to disintegrate.

Memories of the downfall of his parish are most painful to Greeley (this is, perhaps, the hardest topic for him to talk about). He was their priest, he recalls, not because he wanted to be, but because he was older, the center, in a way the reason for its existence. They began to define him in ways he could not accept. "You're trying to dominate my life," they said, and for a while he believed them. Those that he had sent to therapy began to consider *him* the source of their problems. "I became conscious of being an object of transference." He became uncertain, hesitant—so many of them were saying it that they might be right. Perhaps the problem *was* psychological, perhaps it *did* lie with a need of his to dominate, to have disciples (rather than with a mission to preach, to be loyal to, a demanding gospel), perhaps he *was* creating a mold for them (rather than simply challenging them), perhaps the problem *was*, after all, interpersonal (rather than religious). It was another difficult period for Andrew Greeley. After he had an opportunity to sort things out, he said no.

No—he was not engaging in some kind of countertransference. No—he was not trying to dominate their lives. No—he did not have an insatiable craving for disciples. No—the problem was not psychological. "At least at that stage in their lives," Greeley looks back now, "they were either unable or unwilling to make the kind of religious commitment I was challenging them to make. To pretend that we had a common faith was a mistake, and to sustain the pretense for a year or two years after was causing needless anguish—for me in any case." The problem was *religious*, he insists. "At some stage you say, 'Either you are going to respond to this or you don't need me as a priest. I m here to preach the gospel.' *That* broke the community—that challenge."

The community ground to an end slowly, perhaps because of Greeley's own stubbornness in wanting to make it work. "My big mistake was in not quitting earlier," he says. Many of the experimental churches ended the way his did, only more abruptly. As his New Community broke up, the pain sparing no one, he sorted out his feelings in "The Risks of Community," an article that appeared in the July–August 1970 issue of the *Critic*. It had been four years since his speculation that the Church might be witnessing a revolutionary development in lifestyle and six years since his landmark description of the New Breed.

Now he was a psychoanalyst performing an autopsy. What had happened? Without anyone's realizing it, a group of close friends who immensely enjoyed each other began to recreate their familial pasts. Every one became a caricature of the weakest dimension of his personality, analyzing and reanalyzing who was responsible for what, who said what injurious things to whom, needing to blame someone for what was happening, directing the blame to the parent figure in the group. The only way out of the mess would have been to acknowledge it for what it was—a regression to familial patterns of behavior. No one, however, wanted to make the admission. No one dared make the suggestion that some (those who could not see what was happening) ought to leave the group. There was nothing left but self-destruction.

This time the destruction was so great that the New Breed could not be put together. Adolescents who seemed so open and malleable, as Greeley phrased it, were closed off to him by the whole burden of their family experience. By 1971 the community was completely disbanded. In 1974 only two of the original group remained close to Father Greeley. One was Nancy Gallagher of *Letters to Nancy*, and the other was her husband Bill McCready, a close associate of Greeley's at NORC. The vast majority—among them, John of *And Young Men Shall See Visions*—simply vanished. The New Community, it turned out, was not the salvation of the New Breed but a stopping-off place on its exodus from the Church.

And the man who had hoped so much at the outset of his public life, whose career intersected American Catholicism as it seemed on the verge of enormous success, sustained another loss. The reaction of the liberal elite to his "optimistic" data was one thing, but the abandonment of these young people was of a different order altogether. "The pain of separation is not diminished by the observation of one psychiatrist who has spent a considerable amount of time studying such patterns: 'When will they forgive you? Some of them may perhaps be reconciled with you on their deathbed—some not even then.' "[8]

And what of the Catholic Church at large, following in the wake of a pope and a council that were, in their own way, just as much of a new breed? All through the sixties Greeley wrote about institutional Catholicism, beginning in 1964 with "We are but one step away from greatness; and before the rest of the world knows it, we are going to take that step,"[9] ending in 1969 with "For the first time in my life, I am profoundly worried about American Catholicism."[10] He produced furiously during this time, dictating most of his material, writing one weekly column for the *National Catholic Reporter* and another for local Catholic papers, creating articles of diagnosis and prescription and exhortation for the *Critic, Sign, Commonweal, America, Overview,* and *Homiletic and Pastoral Review.* The titles of his books expressed his ambivalence: *The Hesitant Pilgrim* (1966), *The Crucible of Change* (1968), *A Future to Hope In* (1969), *Life for a Wanderer* (1969), *Come Blow Your Mind with Me* (1971). Early in the game he indicated the basis of his hopes:

I am optimistic enough to expect, *in the long run*, an increase in
religious and priestly vocations. I think the quality of books published by Catholic firms will notably improve. I foresee a much
greater reliance on social science and planning in ecclesiastical decision-making. I see the collegial principle becoming operative in
the Church once again, with bishops acting in much more intimate cooperation with their presbyterate, and priests in much
more intimate cooperation with their *laos*. The fraternal use of
authority will gradually replace the paternalistic, and even the
curate will cease to be the "nonperson" he so often is.[11]

He was realistic enough to identify problems—the mass of
Catholics were apathetic, a theoretical perspective on the American
Catholic phenomenon was lacking, lay intellectuals were becoming
alienated from the main body of Church structure, educational institutions needed reform, power had to be decentralized—but he felt
these did not threaten the existence of the Church, and he felt they
could be overcome. Besides, *American* Catholicism had a special
genius to see it to success.

For one thing, said Greeley, the American Church was im-
bedded in "virtually the only industrial country in the Western
world where the vast majority of the population maintains a formal
religious affiliation and goes to church with some frequency." Nor
had the working class left the American Church as it had, say, the
French. "American Catholicism has never been identified with an
Old Regime which stood in the way of social progress; on the contrary, it has to a considerable extent succeeded in identifying itself
with the aspirations of the immigrants to gain acceptance in American society." The clergy has always been similar in background to
the laity, so much so that, twenty years ago, Cardinal Cushing could
remark with pride that no bishop in the country had come from a
family in which a parent had gone to college. Consequently, there
has been little anticlericalism (so he said in 1966)—or its equally
pernicious opposite, clericalism—in the American Church. Because
the church has been independent of state support, the laity has had
to pay for churches and schools, developing a keen sense of participation by doing so. Independence has meant that the Church has
been free to experiment. Experimentation has produced excesses, of
course, but "if unfounded enthusiasms are a price that must be paid
for a relatively open Church, then I think we will be ready to cheer-

fully pay the price." Finally, and perhaps most important, America
and American Catholicism have believed in freedom. A man like
John Courtney Murray spent a lifetime advocating freedom for the
universal Church, and he lived to see his life's work justified in the
final session of the Vatican Council. Indeed, in many ways it seems
that the entire Church is finally catching up with values that have
been part of the American experience—"openness, flexibility, organizational efficiency, freedom, ecumenism, cooperation between
clergy and laity, public opinion, incarnationalism, technical progress."[12] There *are* things wrong with the American Church, Greeley said, but its principal weakness is no more than a fear of living
up to the best in its own experience.

If America had its own genius, so too did the Midwest. "Catholicism Midwest Style," Greeley wrote in 1966, meant openness, flexibility, and creativity—more of these were to be found in Chicago
than on the red plains of Oklahoma, on the banks of the Missis-
sippi, or in the towers of Manhattan Island. The midwestern
Church "has been much less threatened by American society than
has the Church in other regions. It could afford to relax, experiment, innovate; there was no one to make fun of its mistakes."[13]
When Catholics arrived on the eastern seaboard, they found themselves threatened by a well-established WASP aristocracy not particularly eager to have them as neighbors. In Chicago, St. Paul, and
St. Louis, however, Catholics were on the scene in large numbers
from the very beginning. It was *their* society as much as anyone
else's. Everyone was an immigrant, and there was little discrimination against Catholics *qua* Catholics. Catholic colleges did not
have a Harvard or a Yale hanging over their heads. The midwestern
Church was provincial, unsophisticated, inarticulate, true enough;
Greeley was chagrined to admit it was "willing to let its reflecting be
done by journals of opinion from the East." But still, he felt, there
was confidence and vitality in the nation's heartland. "You can become alienated in the midwest if you want to, but, by damn, it's
harder."[14]

In *The Catholic Experience* (1967) Greeley elaborated on the
genius of the American Church with a "sociological interpretation" of its history. The book sketched the lives of great "Americanizers" and "anti-Americanizers" in the Catholic Church, the for-

mer rejoicing in American culture, seeing opportunity rather than
danger in her democracy, going so far as to believe that the American experience had much relevance for universal Church, the latter
worried about anti-Catholic bigotry, wary of materialism; secu-
larism, and paganism, fearful that becoming thoroughly American
meant becoming less Catholic. There was no doubt in 1967 where
the author's sympathies lay. As the Americanizers performed on his
pages he marveled at their brilliance and applauded loudly. And
when the anti-Americanizers took over, he buried his head in his
hands.

First to take the stage were the Carrolls, Charles and John—
Charles, a signer of the Declaration of Independence, a distinguished ally of George Washington throughout the Revolutionary
War, a member of the United States Congress; John, a cousin of
Charles and the first bishop of the United States. The Carroll clan
belonged to the Maryland aristocracy, and were active participants
in the social, economic, and political life of the colony, proof
to anyone with an open mind that Roman Catholics in the emerging
United States were patriotic, and evidence, centuries later, that
the liberal Americanizing tradition in American Catholicism was
truly the first born.

John Carroll, like many of the brave figures of *The Catholic
Experience,* was ahead of his time—indeed, ahead of our time. He
insisted that the Church organize itself in a manner suited to the
American environment. When it seemed certain, as the eighteenth
century came to a close, that Rome would make him America's first
bishop, he demanded that the American clergy *elect* their bishop and
that Rome be limited to confirming that election. Rome agreed, and
Carroll was thus chosen by the vote of his fellow clergy. Carroll also
supported the system whereby Church property was owned by
boards of lay trustees elected by members of the parish—a system
that worked well in many places but still was subject to abuse. And
he called for a vernacular liturgy, asking, "Can there be anything
more preposterous than an unknown tongue" which insured that
"the great part of our congregations must be utterly ignorant of the
meaning and sense of the publick office of the Church."[15]

No one could have been more American in his dealings with the
government than Bishop John Carroll. "He would congratulate

public officials when they were elected, he would offer prayers for them, and he was friendly with them on a personal basis . . . . He was a patriot and would support the War of 1812 even though his Federalist background certainly must have made him less than sympathetic with it."[16] In his communications with Rome he backed the American position on the relationship between church and state—a position almost inconceivable on the other side of the Atlantic.

To judge from *The Catholic Experience*, John and his cousin Charles were earlier incarnations of those talented presidents of Catholic colleges whom Greeley was meeting face-to-face. They were "calm, confident, competent men who took leadership positions for granted and whose self-assurance was so immense that no one dared question it." John might have been a more ancient manifestation of that Spencer Tracy of college presidents, Michael Walsh. A young man who knew him wrote of his spirit and cheer, of his dignity, of the respect he commanded: "The Archbishop in fact was a thoroughbred, and a polished gentleman who put everybody at their ease in his company while delighting them with his conversation."[17]

The likes of John's cousin Charles would not appear again until John Kennedy. Charles may not have been a devout Catholic, "but he in fact was the one who persuaded his fellow Americans that it was possible to be a sincere practicing Catholic and at the same time an unquestioned patriot."[18] By their influence, the Carroll cousins set the tiny American Church (only one percent of a population of three million) on a carefully charted, confident course between loyalty to Rome and a fiercely independent American spirit.

The problems of Bishop John England, the next figure to take the spotlight in *The Catholic Experience*, were more complex than those of the Carrolls. He arrived in Charleston, South Carolina, on December 28, 1820, with twenty-two years of life ahead of him, "twenty-two years in which he would shake the American church as it had never been shaken before and has not been shaken since."[19] America at the time of England's arrival was being swamped by waves of immigrants, most of them Irish like himself. When John Carroll died in 1815, the Catholic population in the United States was 90,000. When John England died in 1842—only twenty-seven years later—the figure was moving rapidly toward two million.

Would the mass of immigrants, and the religion they brought with them, become insecure, defensive, rigid, and parochial, or would they become open-minded and generous? History would say the former, but John England still stands as testimony that it could have been the other way.

> John England was a man bigger than life; indeed, there were oc-
> casions when he seemed twice as big as life . . . . His performance
> in the first year in Charleston was sufficient indication of what was
> to come. Two weeks after his arrival, having issued a lengthy and
> eloquent pastoral on the nature of the bishop's office, England set
> out on a visitation of his huge diocese. During the winter and
> spring as he traveled at breakneck speed around the southland, he
> also found time to make plans for the construction of a cathedral,
> to found a Catholic book society, write a lenten pastoral, publish
> an English catechism, put the skids permanently under the rebel-
> lious trustees in Charleston, preach in Episcopalian and Presby-
> terian churches, write a letter to Maréchal suggesting a national
> council, prepare for publication and translation of a missal with
> an introduction and explanation of 120 pages that he himself had
> penned, make plans for a new translation of the Bible into English,
> and begin to lay the groundwork for a weekly Catholic newspaper
> and for a constitutional convention in his diocese.[20]

England continued at the same pace for the rest of his life (and even delivered a stirring oration on his deathbed). He published a constitution, subscribed to by clergy and laity, by which his diocese would be ruled, founded a national newspaper, the *United States Catholic Miscellany*, established a seminary with a revolutionary educational scheme, battled for collegial government in the Ameri-can Church. His respect for the United States was "passionate." He was indeed, in the chapter's title, the "Super-American from County Cork."

England failed to leave his mark on the American Church be-cause, although he succeeded in his relationships with non-Catho-lics, he could not gain the support of his fellow bishops. His enemies in the hierarchy blocked the appointment of men he named as successors in the Charleston diocese, and Rome sent instead a man to "clean up the mess" that England had left behind him.

The heroic England was followed in *The Catholic Experience* by a villain, John Hughes, archbishop of New York, a "fearsome man." At precisely the time when the crises of the immigration experience were most severe," Greeley wrote, "Hughes's influence can only be considered a major disaster."[21]

In retrospect, it was easy for Carroll, presiding over a small native American church, and England, whose Charleston diocese was not terribly affected by immigration, to adopt a stance of Americanization. However, "for John Hughes in New York two decades before the Civil War, the Americanization of the immigrant, at least as it was described by the native Americans of New York City, seemed more frequently to mean that the immigrants must become Anglo-Saxon Protestants or they would not be welcomed in this country. John Hughes was not prepared to let this happen."[22]

It was not without reason that native Americans were troubled, and even terrified, by Catholic immigrants. The immigrants were uneducated and often unruly. They lived in slums and worked for lower wages than did native Americans. Their votes could be captured by a corrupt political machine. Their political and religious leaders were often demagogues. They threatened to undercut the existing social and economic structure of the city. It was even said that they were of racially inferior stock.

It is also understandable that immigrants would become defensive in a culture growing more hostile by the day. The Know Nothing Party had come into existence; churches were being burned; inflammatory literature was being circulated; convents were being stormed. But John Hughes, argued Greeley, was not the man for this time. He served only to make a bad situation worse.

Possessed of a fierce temper, the man thrived on controversy. He saw himself as the protector of a flock not able to take care of itself, surrounded by ravenous wolves. He read every newspaper he could get his hands on and let no attack on the Church (or on John Hughes) go unanswered. He was devastating, had amazing powers of ridicule, and could win arguments, but he could not compromise and gain friends. Hughes managed to destroy New York's Public School Society and railed against the double tax Catholics had to pay for the education of their children. When nativists burned Catholic churches in Philadelphia in 1844, Hughes told the government of New York that if the same thing happened there "the city would become a Moscow." He was prepared to have armed forces of

Catholics in New York's churches ready to take lives in defense of their property. The churches, it turned out, were never burned.

John Hughes was an ineffective administrator and a poor financial planner. He was, simply, a warrior—one, unfortunately, who reinforced the prejudices of the nativists against immigrant Catholics and helped set the Church on a course of anti-Americanization that lasted until the end of the nineteenth century.

The Americanizing trend returned to reach its peak in the 1890s. In the previous decade immigration had reached close to its all-time high, the Catholic population doubling from six to twelve million. The mood in the country was one of optimism: the Civil War was becoming a distant memory, industry and commerce were expanding at a fantastic rate, the United States was becoming a great power. The nation's optimism rubbed off on Church leaders like John Ireland, John Keane, John Lancaster Spalding, and James Gibbons. For the leaders by this time knew that the church could survive in America, knew that it could handle immigration and expansion, knew indeed that it was on the brink of spectacular success.

Said Ireland: "I can truly say that my Catholic heart and my American heart are one, and I am delighted to say that the free air of America has cheered the soul of Leo XIII, and that he has not been without guidance from our institutions. When the question is asked, 'Do you put Church before country or country before Church?' I say that one is not to be put before the other. They are in different spheres altogether."[23]

Said Keane: "During the past few years, my duty has compelled me to cross the ocean four times, and I have never visited the old countries abroad that I haven't come back thanking God that I am an American."[24]

Said Spalding: "We have shown that respect for law is compatible with civil and religious liberty; that a free people can become prosperous and strong . . . ; that the State and the Church can move in separate orbits and still cooperate for the common welfare; that men of different races and beliefs may live together in peace."[25]

Said Gibbons (in Rome): "For myself, as a citizen of the United States, without closing my eyes to our defects as a nation, I proclaim, with a deep sense of pride and gratitude, and in this great capital of Christendom, that I belong to a country where the civil government holds over us the aegis of its protection without interfering in the legitimate exercise of our sublime mission as ministers of the Gospel of Jesus Christ."[26]

These were men of radically differing temperaments, but men with much in common—incurable optimism (with the exception of Spalding in his moody moments), confidence, expansiveness, belief in democracy and the separation of church and state, social consciousness, eagerness for friendship with non-Catholics, pride in the American Church, concern for education, an active rather than a contemplative orientation, loyalty to Rome. They were cultural assimilationists, too. That fact hardly detracted from Greeley's enthusiasm for them when he wrote *The Catholic Experience*, though it would make a considerable difference in just a few years.

The enthusiasm of the Americanists of the 1890s came to an abrupt end. Pope Leo XIII issued an encyclical, *Testem Benevolentiae*, in which he condemned the "Americanism heresy"—a heresy, it seemed, that existed more in the preface of a French translation of the life of Isaac Hecker (another of the heroes of *The Catholic Experience*) than it did in America. While the encyclical did not name names, while it did not even affirm that certain condemned doctrines were in fact held in the United States, it took the élan from the 1890s. "Gibbons, Ireland, and Keane, even though they argued with some conviction that they had not been condemned, were deeply hurt by the letter, and some of the joy and verve went out of their lives."[27] The encyclical alone did not undermine the development of more men like Ireland, Keane, and Gibbons in the United States. The establishment there of an apostolic delegation (the Curia's man could now keep a watchful eye on the Americans), the training of future bishops at the American college in Rome (where they could be socialized into the appropriate ways of thinking), and the Modernist controversy all played a part as well. But it is eminently clear to the author of *The Catholic Experience* that bishops like these have not appeared in America since.

There were others heroes and villains in *The Catholic Experience*, Americanizers like Orestes Brownson in the nineteenth century, bigots like Father Charles Coughlin, the "radio priest" of the

postdepression years. The last man to capture Greeley's imagination, however, was John Fitzgerald Kennedy; and, writing in
1967, the author had a unique proposal in his regard:

> Canonize John Kennedy? At first such a suggestion surely seems
> facetious, and unquestionably would bring laughter to the lips of
> the aloof, witty, ironic man who was the first Catholic President of
> the United States. Yet in another age, when the manner and pur-
> pose of canonization were different, John Kennedy would cer-
> tainly be hailed as a saint. In the early years of Christianity, canon-
> ization was . . . the popular acclaim which the Christian
> community gave to someone who had become a hero. Great politi-
> cal leaders, especially those who died in the service of their country,
> were quite apt to become such heroes and be hailed as saints. Eng-
> land has its Edward, France has its Louis, Hungary has its
> Stephen. John Kennedy would certainly fit the qualifications be-
> cause one wonders if any man who has ever lived has ever been so
> much of a hero to so many people in so many different nations of
> the world.[28]

If we cannot make him a saint, Greeley continued, "perhaps the
most appropriate title would be 'doctor of the universal Church.' "
When Kennedy spoke as a candidate for the presidency before the
ministerial association in Houston, Texas, "for the first time in the
history of the American Church, a Catholic preaching the Church's
doctrine on the relationship between religion and society was believed, believed at least enough to be elected President of the United
States."[29] Anti-Catholic nativism did not die easily in 1960 (Kennedy's religion is estimated to have cost him five million votes) but it
was, albeit by the skimpiest of margins, defeated. For his role, for his
ability to make Catholic doctrine clear and credible, Greeley offered
Kennedy the unofficial title of "doctor of the Church."

On Inauguration Day 1961, American Catholicism, in the person of John Kennedy, had come full circle. For the first time since
Charles Carroll the most powerful American Catholic was not a
member of the hierarchy. The Catholic Church, having survived the
immigration trauma, was once again a legitimately native American Church; and within it the liberalizing tradition was victorious.

The triumph of the 1960s, however, would last no longer than
that of the 1890s. In the spring and summer of 1968 the nation's

emotions were grated by a series of shocks and surprises. The bombing of North Vietnam, and Lyndon Johnson, were on—then off. Martin Luther King, Jr. and Robert Kennedy, bearers of hope, were gunned down. In Europe the Russians took possession of Czechoslovakia, and in Chicago police and people battled in the streets as Democrats attempted to nominate a presidential candidate. Few people noticed when Paul VI issued "The Credo of the People of God" on June 30, but many were genuinely stunned a month later when he promulgated *Humanae Vitae*, the encyclical forbidding the use of "artificial" contraception.

Greeley's response to the document was to advise "cooling it." Data indicated that many Catholics were ignoring the pope's directives anyway—if not practicing even *more* birth control. Don't confront the issue, he said; the best strategy was "staying away from crisis wherever feasible and working out compromise solutions,"[30] all the time, of course, protecting one's own conscience.

But even that advice seemed like a band-aid to cover a ravenous cancer. In January, 1969 *Time* passed on to its readers predictions Greeley had made in *Overview*, a monthly newsletter of Chicago's Thomas More Association. Priests and nuns were going to abandon their vocations in increasing numbers, and new recruits were going to become scarce; more laymen and priests would refuse to accept the Church as authoritative teacher, especially in matters sexual; tensions between priests and bishops would grow; the Catholic educational system was in deep trouble because of a collapse in the morale of educators and, consequently, more and more schools would close. "Many of the auxiliary institutions of American Catholicism will suffer. Diocesan papers, publishing houses, book stores, and magazines, will be hard hit, and many will disappear from the scene."[31] Five years before, a "golden era" had been on its way.

Precise documentation of the American Church's abrupt setback did not come until 1974, when NORC replicated its 1963 study of parochial education. In the elevan years between the two surveys, weekly Mass attendance by adult Catholics dropped from 71 to 50 percent. In 1963, 70 percent thought it "certainly true" that Jesus handed over the leadership of the Church to Peter and the popes, but in 1974 only 42 percent believed likewise (and only 32 percent subscribed fully to the doctrine of papal infallibility). This decline in

Church authority was particularly evident in the matter of sex. In 1963, 45 percent approved artificial contraception; in 1974, despite *Humanae Vitae*, 83 percent did. Remarriage after divorce was accepted by 52 percent in 1963 and 73 percent in the new survey, sexual relations between an engaged couple by 12 percent in 1963 and 43 percent in 1974. In 1974, 36 percent felt that legal abortions should be available for married women who did not want more children (27 percent would consider one for themselves in such circumstances).

Later data were more chilling. Between 1965 and 1975 the number of seminarians decreased from 50,000 to 18,000. Religious sisters dropped from 180,000 to 135,000 religious brothers from 12,000 to 8,6000. Among the general population of Catholics, apostasy rates doubled from 7 to 14 percent. And all of this in the aftermath of such promise.

When Greeley was invited to More House, the Catholic Center at Yale University, to present a series of lectures in March, 1970, he attempted to set the dizzying sixties in perspective. Why the sudden disaster? Greeley began with a portrait of the 1950s, the years in which he was ordained a priest and was exhilarated by the enthusiasm of Christ the King parishioners. "Organizationally the church of the 1950s was prospering," he said. "It represented the finest flourishing of immigrant Catholicism, and in some ways was extraordinarily impressive. The immigrants and their children had built the most extensive and elaborate religious institutional structure in the world. It was John Courtney Murray who remarked, 'Good, very good, but not good enough.' "[32]

In 1960 two wheels that had been turning in the Catholic Church—slowly, independently, each at its own pace—happened to strike the twelfth hour simultaneously. In America the immigrant era ended, and the Church of cap-and-sweater people like the parishioners at St. Angela's was now the Church of suburbanites like those at Christ the King. And in the universal Church the era of the Counter-Reformation came to a close as Pope John ushered in the Ecumenical Age. Two defensive postures that had reinforced each other were being abandoned. "The lid was about to blow off."[33]

Within an all-too-brief period the reversals predicted in *Time* were facts of life. There would have been turmoil even without the Vatican Council, but when Pope John opened his little window, pent-up forces blew into the Church and were legitimized. There was an opportunity for a rapid reform of Church structure, and renewal seemed on its way—at least until John died and Church leaders lost their nerve and tried to put on the brakes. Most important, however, all those Catholics who had learned to question and criticize the old Church, who dismantled it with abandon, gave not a moment's thought to constructing something to replace it.

There were four major areas of destruction, and the first of them was the schools. As the 1960s opened, Catholic education could look back on the two most impressive decades in its history, but ten years later schools were closing and enrollment declining. The schools' *clients* had not done an about-face, but a handful of educators who read a few tiny books questioning the protectionist rationale of Catholic education lost confidence in what they were doing. They suffered from self-hate, too: "The grandson of the immigrant has to be out of the ghetto for a while before he does not have to feel defensive about his origins and is freed from the necessity of validating himself in the eyes of the outside world by attacking that from which he came."[34]

Ecclesiastical authority was in even more trouble than the schools by the end of the 1960s. Its legitimacy and credibility were under direct, even contemptuous, attack—something unheard of a decade before. Eighty percent of the Catholic population did not take seriously the Church's teaching on birth control, and substantial proportions of elite groups did not believe any of its teachings on other matters. Greeley explained the sudden shift with his "Meat on Friday" hypothesis: fiddle with even the smallest part of an ossified symbol system—repeal the ban against meat on Friday—and the entire apparatus is likely to fall apart. *That* was the weakness of the 1950s: beliefs and organizational patterns so rigid that even the slightest change, the barest breath of fresh air, could not be accommodated. All the structure could do was come down.

The decline of the clergy—the third disaster area— was more surprising than that of the schools or of ecclesiastical authority, for most of it occurred after 1965. The crashing of expectations that soared after the Vatican Council along with increasing uncertainty about their role created "a near-panic among the younger clergy and religious." The value system of the old Church specified that the priest was the leader and protector of the immigrant population, but with that clear delineation gone, what was the priest to do? Younger clergy "are disillusioned about renewal; they do not believe their leaders; they lack a sense of participation in decision making; they do not know what to do with the new freedom they have found; and they are very much afraid of the future."[35]

Sexuality was a fourth area in which the old had deteriorated without something new to take its place. "Sex is certainly the most corrosive issue facing Roman Catholicism at the present time . . . , the only subject on which the mass of the population is as disaffected as the elites." The Church's stance on birth control was questioned in private even in the fifties, but in the sixties younger clergy were willing not only to express their doubts publicly, but to act on them in the confessional. Again, the finger was pulled out of the dike. "If the birth-control theory can be questioned, then there seems to be no reason—at least in the minds of many—why the Church's position on divorce and, indeed, premarital and extramarital sexuality, and even homosexuality, cannot also be called into question."[36]

The story of the sixties, then, was the destruction of the old Church. A new one could have been built as the old came down, but "American Catholicism failed to respond to the challenge in the 1960s because neither the hierarchy nor the clergy nor the intellectuals were able to respond."[37]

There was no concealing Greeley's depression at the fate of an American Church that had ripped itself apart while he stood powerless on the fringes. His enthusiasm for John Kennedy would diminish in the years to come, and so would his support for the Americanizers on the issue of ethnic enclaves. In 1970 he was unwilling to say that *Humanae Vitae* was the *cause* of the turnabout in the fortunes of the Church (as *Testem Benevolentiae* had been in the 1890s), but data collected in 1974 would leave him no choice.

Those data were released in *Catholic Schools in a Declining Church* (1976). Not only did they alter Greeley's earlier "Meat on Friday" theory, they also proved false the claim of right-wingers that American Catholics were "turned off" by changes initiated by the Vatican Council. The Vatican Council, first of all, alienated only a minority of American Catholics: 19 percent thought that "changes in the Church" were for the worse; 14 percent were indifferent to them; and a full 67 percent thought they were for the better. Nor did the decline begin when Catholics were allowed to eat meat on Fridays. No, practically all the blame for the deterioration in American Catholic religiousness—the kind of religiousness sociologists can measure, at any rate—could be placed squarely on the doorstep of *Humanae Vitae*. The encyclical on birth control was far more important than Greeley had thought earlier.

According to Gallup data, Catholic Mass attendance dropped only two percentage points between the end of the Council in 1965 and the publication of *Humanae Vitae* in 1968, but it declined eight percentage points in the three years following the encyclical. Apostasy rates, which had remained at 7 percent from 1953 to 1967, doubled after the encyclical (no change was observed in the same period in the Protestant rate of 9 percent); the same thing happened with rates of resignation from the priesthood and religious orders. The young were particularly susceptible. Between 1967 and 1974 approximately a quarter of college-educated Catholics under 30 left the Church. In the decade bracketed by the two NORC surveys financial contributions to the Church from Catholic families declined by 31 percent, and three-fourths of the loss (which totaled $1.7 billion in 1974) was directly attributable to a negative reaction to the birth control directive. On practically every measure of religious devotion and loyalty to the Church, the largest chunk of variance was related to subjects' acceptance or rejection of *Humanae Vitae*.

In the words of Greeley, "The Vatican Council appears to have been one of the great religious successes in human history. Many of the fundamental practices and structures of the Catholic Church, unchanged for over 1,500 years, were transformed in the space of a few years, months, or even on a single Sunday morning."[38] American Catholics were uplifted by the changes and seemed eager for more. Then came July 29, 1968.

We know now that by that date, most Catholics had already made a decision about the morality of the Pill. They were *for* it, and when Pope Paul denounced it (let it be said, against the advice of a commission appointed to study the matter), Catholics discredited him and the institution he represented. If he could be so patently wrong on such a critical issue, one affecting what goes on in the beds of married people three times a week, he could be wrong about anything. Catholic people felt disillusioned, betrayed— is *this* what the council and the "changes" were all about? Most did not leave the Church, and Pill-users continued to receive communion as often as other Catholics. But the damage to institutional Catholicism was profound, and all that Vatican II might have become was prematurely aborted. "I have no doubt," Greeley said, "that historians of the future will judge *Humanae Vitae* to be one of the worst mistakes in the history of Catholic Christianity."[39]

As the 1960s came to a close, the waves of Greeley's dream were striking with fury. A leader of an intimate community that was tearing itself to pieces, Greeley saw similar self-destruction throughout the American Church. His investments, like those of his father, were disappearing in a great spiritual crash. At the time Greeley told a group of friends:

> The things I wanted to accomplish have all been failures. I think I'm realistic enough to know that I am not responsible for the failures, but failures they were just the same. I dreamed of training a new Catholic lay elite in Christ the King and this did not happen. I hoped my decade of research on Catholic education would make a contribution to the rejuvenation of this battered but important institution, but it did not. I wanted to be a sociologist to help plan the future of the Chicago Archdiocese and I shall never do this. I hoped that the post-Conciliar renewal would lead to the emergence of a stronger American church, simultaneously Catholic and American, and to this effort devoted much of my writing for many years; and it is now clear that the post-Conciliar renewal has turned from a rout into a disaster. I had high hopes for the Association of Chicago Priests and wrote most of the draft which led to the personnel board; I now know that the ACP is a failure. I was deeply involved in the higher educational reform movement, particularly by authoring the Hazen Report which is now considered a landmark in higher education literature; but this reform is now as dead as the students at Kent State. I thought that community of young people with whom I associated might become a center for a new style of religious dedication and I now have little expectation that it will ever get much beyond a pleasant study group.[40]

"I despair," he told them, "about the future of American Catholicism. I think that very little of it will be saved." And of himself: "I conclude that I am not a man for this season."

Despair in Father Greeley, however, always manages to evoke its opposite. Even as the disastrous sixties reached their denouement, a leprechaun, down but not out, found its way to the tip of his pen. Greeley reported on the first papal press conference ever held in the English language. The pontiff was an Irish-Italian raised in Brooklyn and a graduate of the Harvard School of Business:

(Kevin Cardinal Orsini was elected Pope by "inspiration" on the forty-third day of the conclave; ninety-six-year-old Cardinal Antonelli leaped from his throne in the Sistine Chapel and shouted in his feeble voice, "Orsini Papa!" With varying degrees of weariness, surprise, dismay, and joy, all the other cardinals echoed the shout: "Orsini Papa!" It was then pointed out by several of those present that this was indeed a legitimate and definitive way of selecting a pope, even though it was one that apparently had not been used in the history of the Papacy. Almost without realizing it, the cardinals had selected their youngest member, the forty-six-year-old Orsini, as the new Pope. There were some, later on, who claimed that Antonelli had been sound asleep, and in his sleep had had a nightmare of Orsini becoming Pope. His cry of "Orsini Papa!" it was alleged, was not an inspiration from the Holy Spirit, but the result of a bad dream. In any case, Orsini's supporters had seized the opportunity to proclaim their man the victor, and after forty-three days of a conclave in which nine cardinals had already died, no one was prepared to dispute his claim to the Papacy.)

Kevin I, attired in a gray Savile Row suit, light blue shirt, and Paisley tie, finally arrived at the Monte Mario for his press conference, a transcript of which appeared the following day in the New York *Times*:

Q. (*Times* of London) Your Holiness, the whole world is wondering—
A. Please don't call me Your Holiness. I don't know that I'm all that holy, and it's sort of an old-fashioned name. You can call me Pope or Mr. Pope, but please don't call me Your Holiness.
Q. Well, yes, sir. The whole world is wondering what your position will be on the birth-control issue.
A. I think it's a very complex issue and one that I certainly wouldn't want to address myself to in any specific detail this morning. We have really messed up this sex business in the Church for a long time and I don't think we're going to be able to make any coherent Christian statement on family planning until we do a lot of thinking and talking about the whole question of sexual personalism. . . .

Q. (St. Louis *Post-Dispatch*) There has been considerable talk of restoring the practice of popular election of bishops to the Catholic Church. Would you care to comment on this possibility?

A. Oh, I'd be happy to comment. Two of my predecessors of happy memory—I can't quite remember what their names were, but they were back in the sixth century—said that it was sinful to choose a bishop by any other methods besides popular election. Being at heart a very conservative fellow, I agree with them. . . .

Q. (St. Louis *Post-Dispatch*) Then, am I to understand, sir, that you are in favor of limited terms for bishops and perhaps even for the Pope?

A. Well, if you think I'm going to stay in this office until I die in it, you're sadly mistaken. This may be a fine job for five or ten years, but after that I'm going to want to retire someplace where it's peaceful and quiet. . . .

Q. (*Wall Street Journal*) Are we to take it, sir, that you are going to make public the financial status of the Vatican?

A. Well, I'm going to try and do it as soon as I can figure out what the financial status is. As far as I can understand, nobody but God exactly understands the finances of the Vatican, and unfortunately he's not about to make a private revelation on the subject.

Q. (*Triumph*) Most Holy Father—

A. I'm not Holy, and I'm certainly not Most Holy, and I'm also certainly not your father or anybody else's, so call me Pope, or Mr. Pope, or Bishop, and drop the rest of that nonsense.

Q. (*Triumph*, again) You will, of course, maintain the papal diplomatic service?

A. I will most certainly do no such thing. . . .

Q. (Manchester *Guardian*) What do you intend to do about *Osservatore Romano*?

A. I wish to heaven I knew what to do about it—would you like to be editor of it?

Q. No, sir, I wouldn't.

A. Yeah, that's what they all say. Next question, please. . . .

Q. (Frankfurter *Zeitung*) Do you expect there to be any heresy trials in your administration?

A. Good God, no! . . .

Q. (Frankfurter *Zeitung*) But what do you think of the case of Reverend Dr. Hans Küng?

A. You mean do I think Hans is a heretic? Why, don't be silly. Hans is basically a conservative. I never could understand why people thought he was dangerous or a radical. How in the world can anybody who owns an Alfa-Romeo be a radical?

Q. (*Il Messaggero*) What, your Holiness—I mean, Pope—what is your opinion on the forthcoming Italian elections?

A. I hope everybody votes in them.

Q. (*Il Messaggero*) But what party are you supporting?

A. We've got a secret ballot in this country just like most other countries, and who I vote for is my secret.

Q. (*Il Messaggero*) But are you going to take a stand in Italian politics?

A. What's the matter? Do you think I'm crazy? . . .

Q. (Milwaukee *Sentinel*) Do you intend, sir, to continue the practice of censorship of books that are written by Catholics?

A. I think it would be a good idea to take every imprimatur in the world and throw it in the furnace, and we ought to throw half of the book censors in the furnace, too. The basic thing to say about censorship is that it didn't work, it doesn't work, and it's never going to work, and the quicker we forget about it, the better off we're all going to be.

Q. (Washington *Post*) From all you've said so far, sir, it would seem that you are really anticipating a very notable decline in papal authority. I wonder if you could tell us whether you think that this is a drastic change in Church doctrine?

A. Well, I don't know where you got that idea; I must say, as a matter of fact, I think what I'm talking about is a rather notable increase in papal authority. . . .

Q. (*Seventeen*) Do you have anything to say for young people?

A. Well, I'd say to the young to be patient with us older people because we're going to try and learn how to listen to you, and that we'll try, in our turn, to be patient with you while you try to learn how to listen to us. I don't think there's much wrong with young people that a little bit of experience won't cure—and there's not much wrong with older people that sharing the enthusiasm of the young won't cure.

Q. (New York *Times*) Thank you, Mr. Pope.

A. You're quite welcome, Scotty.[41]

I once asked Father Greeley about the muse who created that piece: "What *is* a leprechaun?"

His face brightened. "A fun spirit—the Holy Spirit when he goes to Ireland. He's always serious, but so serious that he's a playful, laughing spirit. He wheels and deals and whirls and swirls and dives and dances and claps his hands." A bubbling yet hardened old sprite, bouncing on the surface, yet knowing the depths, knowing, in fact, something that we do not about life and death, about sustaining loss. Greeley smiled and hit upon the spirit's essence: "He plays tricks."

"You mean he pokes fun?"

"No. Plays tricks."

I knew from his tone that "plays tricks" said it all and said it perfectly. Somehow, some part of Andrew Greeley was able to view all that had happened to him in the 1960s as a leprechaun-like spirit having fun with him, surprising him, making jokes at his expense. Some Holy Spirit, though, I thought later. He whispers in Greeley's ear to *challenge* the young, knowing full well that *love* is what they need. He tells him the good news about future Catholic intellectuals and chuckles as he fails to add that good news is bad news. He gets Greeley wildly enthusiastic over a new church and a new school but doesn't mention the cracks in the basement. And, as a matter of fact, he steers him right to the top of the roof (where he can take in the broad view of a sociologist) so he'll be sitting in just the right spot as the buildings come crashing down.

That's like calling someone over for a look at the dike and then pulling your finger out of the wall.

Or inviting him to a wedding and then throwing a wake.

6   And Then God Died

When Harvey Cox published *The Secular City* in 1965, it did not take long for Andrew Greeley to ignite a crackling debate over the very premise of that widely acclaimed book. To Cox, "secularization" meant "the loosing of the world from religious and quasi-religious understandings of itself, the dispelling of all closed world-views, the breaking of all supernatural myths and sacred symbols." It meant, simply, the aging and eventual passing away of religion, a peaceful end, to be sure, but a death nevertheless. Secularization, he argued, was the by-product of urbanization, a structure of common life increasingly characteristic of rural villages as well as cities, in which impersonality, tolerance of diversity, and anonymity have replaced traditional moral sanctions and long-term acquaintanceships. "The urban center is the place of human control, of rational planning, of bureaucratic organization—and the urban center is not just in Washington, London, New York, and Peking. It is everywhere."[1] When man moved from tribe to town, he changed his gods, and as he now migrates from town to technopolis, he alters his deities once again, this time finding them no longer necessary.

Do not attempt to stem the tide of secularization, preached Cox—a Baptist theologian—in *The Secular City*, for you will be sure to lose. Let us, rather, welcome the new metropolis, celebrate its arrival, and discover the spiritual possibilities within it.

> Secularization rolls on, and if we are to understand and communicate with our present age we must learn to love it in its unremitting secularity. We must learn, as [Dietrich] Bonhoeffer said, to speak of God in a secular fashion and find a nonreligious interpretation of biblical concepts. It will do no good to cling to our

religious and metaphysical versions of Christianity in the hope
that one day religion or metaphysics will once again be back. They
are disappearing forever and that means we can now let go and
immerse ourselves in the new world of the secular city.[2]

We are liberated, he declared, from the religious and metaphysical
tutelage of the past; we can now turn from a preoccupation with
other worlds to the salvation of this one, we have at last—praise the
(secular) lord—"come of age."

In stepped Andrew Greeley. Was religion itself (not just the
American Catholic Church) in a state of decay? Greeley thought not
and said so in a *Commonweal* symposium edited by Daniel
Callahan.

The trouble, Greeley said bluntly, is that Cox's secular city just
does not exist. "The question at issue is not whether the unsecular
city is better than the secular one, but whether the secular city actually exists and whether secular man is very common." What proof
does Cox offer for his theory of faceless modern man? "Cox quotes
T. S. Eliot, Sören Kierkegaard, Ortega y Gasset, [Rainer Maria]
Rilke, Franz Kafka, and Ferdinand Tönnies; and this, my friends,
is the sociological dimension in contemporary theology. We argue
to an anonymous, mobile, secularist society on the grounds that
everyone knows it exists (including sophomores) and that theologians, philosophers and the literati know it more than anyone
else."[3]

Greeley acknowledged that Tönnies did describe a shift in
lifestyle from peasant society to industrial society, from *Gemeinschaft* ("community") to *Gesellschaft* ("association"). And Greeley
found the distinction illuminating: *Gemeinschaft* man living a life
that was traditional, intimate, family-centered, static, having relationships that were few in number but face-to-face and of lifelong
duration; *Gesellschaft* man, on the other hand, mobile, anonymous, unhampered by roots, relating to others in impersonal,
rational, contractual ways; *Gemeinschaft* man constrained by the
very closeness of his ties to tradition and to others; *Gesellschaft* man
"liberated" (or so Cox claimed) by the anonymity of his urban life,
"liberated" enough to divest himself of God.

Greeley had no quarrel with Cox's claim that *Gesellschaft* had
made its appearance, but he adamantly refused to concede that it had

replaced its opposite. Secular man exists, all right, but side by side with unsecular man and, if the evidence is to be believed, in far smaller numbers than unsecular man. *Gemeinschaft* communities still flourish amidst the anomie of urban life; indeed, in some strange way, they crop up in the most bureaucratized segments of the city. The metropolis, Greeley argued, is not anomic, but symbiotic, "made up not of atomized individuals, but of hundreds of tightly organized and competing local neighborhood communities," often defined along religious and ethnic lines. Real-estate men planning developments know as much. So do politicians drawing up tickets. So do journalists, community organizers, and civil rights leaders. So does the Chicago Commission on Human Relations. So does the federal government. So does everyone, it seems, except those "at the upper levels of university life" (that was for Cox) "or in the mass media" (that was for Daniel Callahan and *Commonweal*).[4]

Cox was given a chance to reply to Greeley's remarks, and reply he did. He did not, he answered, say that unsecular, *Gemeinschaft* man has disappeared from the city. "Even today," he had written in *The Secular City*, "we find residents of New York City with a tribal mentality"—but perhaps Father Greeley forgot to read that page.[5] The real differences between Greeley and himself, Cox went on, concern the future. How can Father Greeley, pledged to the most sophisticated kind of sociological analysis, be so sure about what is coming? Greeley's position belies "an unarticulated but operative theory of social stasis," an assumption that things will basically remain the same. This orientation is common in contemporary sociology, but is not without its critics. Even the patriarchal Max Weber assumed that society's change was linear and directional, not cyclic or homeostatic.

When Callahan gathered the arguments together in *The Secular City Debate* (1966), he wanted to leave out Greeley's reply-to-the-reply, but Greeley raised "blue bloody hell" and so he—Greeley—was given the last word. The last word consisted of respect for Cox ("In a world where it is difficult to find anyone who will engage in an honest argument, Mr. Cox is only too willing to argue, and for this I salute him") but none for Callahan ("Mr. Callahan clearly does not want to argue and so I will not argue with him").[6] He then pinpointed the essence of his quarrel with Cox. If we agree, he said, that the city is both secular and unsecular, we must be arguing about the future—will the secular prevail? And the burden of proof, said Greeley, is on Harvey Cox (the reverse, of course, of what Cox had told Greeley). Greeley would believe it when he saw it. Nor, said Greeley, did he espouse a static theory of society; he believed that society is changing, but the change is one of "differentiation" and not "secularization."

"Differentiation," Greeley later told readers of *The Hesitant Pilgrim*, is a concept of Talcott Parsons, who sees society moving toward greater and greater complexity. As it does, multipurpose institutions of the past abandon some of their functions to newly emerging institutions. Religion and society, in Parsons's view, were at one time practically identical; but now many of the functions performed by religious organizations—such as medical care, education, and social welfare—have been taken over by secular ones. This does not mean that religion has become less important, but rather that its function has become more focused—to provide meaning and a sense of belonging. An analogy is the family, once the seat of such activities as manufacturing, education, and entertainment that have progressively become removed from it. Their removal, however, has not diminished the importance of the family. It still provides a center of intimacy in a society becoming more impersonal by the day. In a similar way, said Greeley, religion has *retreated* from society's institutional life—and Cox is correct in this sense—but the retreat is a manifestation not of secularization, but of differentiation. The religious dimension of man's life is as important as it ever was.

So the debate came down to predictions about the future. Would secularization and *Gesellschaft* come to dominate man's manner of association, or would they follow the pattern of differentiation, falling into coexistence with religion and *Gemeinschaft* bonding? In 1966 the argument took a bizarre turn when theologians Thomas Altizer and William Hamilton tossed into the fray the proclamation that God had died. "We must realize that the death of God is an historical event, that God has died in our cosmos, in our history, in our *existenz*,"[7] they wrote in *Radical Theology and the Death of God* (1966); and in no time at all the American public was being informed of, and even propagandized about, their theological "breakthrough." When *Catholic Digest* asked Greeley to comment on data collected for them by the Gallup organization in 1965, he saw his chance to cut down this "mad offspring" of the secularization hypothesis. The Gallup data were replies of a national sample of adults to questions concerning religious beliefs and practices—questions identical to ones asked of another national sample in 1952 by Ben Gaffin and Associates. Despite the fact that the 1952 data cards had been lost, one could still make broad comparisons between 1952 and 1965—a rare opportunity, at that time, in sociological research. In *What Do We Believe?* (1968) the 1952–1965 differences were analyzed by Protestant historian-theologian Martin Marty (who saw an erosion of distinctive theological positions among Protestants, but no evidence of secularization), Jewish rabbi-scholar Stuart Rosenberg (who complained about the small number of Jewish respondents and insisted the questionnaire was inappropriate to the Jewish experience), and Catholic priest-sociologist Andrew Greeley.

Greeley began by commenting on "the God who would not stay dead." The God-is-dead outburst, he charged, is nothing more than a "public relations gimmick," touching "what apparently is an important aspect of the American personality, the willingness, even eagerness, to believe that everything is rapidly going to hell." Well, everything is not going to hell, he said, nor does God "even seem to be appreciably ill."[8] In 1952, 99 percent of America's adult population believed in God and was at least "quite sure" about that belief. In 1965, the percentage was 96—an insignificant change. The only noticeable decline in belief was among the small number of Jewish respondents, from 97 percent in 1952 to 75 percent in 1965. Figures for Protestants were 99 percent in 1952 and 98 percent in 1965; for Catholics, 100 percent in 1952 and 100 percent in 1965. Even 75 percent of those who professed no religion or a religion other than the major three—they were 7 percent of the total sample—were "quite sure" of God's existence in 1965 (this compared with 83 percent in 1952). None of the data gave the slightest hint that a religionless society was on its way.

Other variables in the survey told the same story. Belief in the divinity of Christ, in the Trinity, in life after death showed only negligible changes from 1952 to 1965; nor was there any difference in the number of respondents who said they prayed or considered themselves active members of a church. The only question that yielded results in any way compatible with the secularization hypothesis was "How important would you say religion is in your own life?" In 1952, 75 percent said "very important"; by 1965, the percentage had dropped to 70. But this was only the most meager support—especially in view of the fact that in the same period church and synagogue attendance had actually taken an upswing.

And what of young people—those whose beliefs and behaviors were likely to give an indication of what was coming in the years ahead? "The Future of God," Greeley reported (cautioning that the young were a dubious basis for prediction), looks about the same among those between 18 and 25 years of age as it does among those over 25. Catholic youth in 1965 were as likely as older Catholics to believe in God and more likely to believe in life after death. Protestant youth were somewhat less likely to pray and to believe in life after death than were Protestants over 25, though more of the younger generation (100 percent, in fact) said they believed in God. (The comparison could not be made for Jews because of the small numbers of respondents.) Greeley concluded that "young American Protestants and Catholics are, if anything, more likely to believe that God is not dead than are their parents."[9]

Religion had not declined appreciably in the United States between 1952 and 1965. That conclusion was consistent with the best data available on the subject, data that were admittedly tenuous. It was hardly a spectacular finding. As the authors wrote, "The reality which we are describing, alas, in this volume tends to be very gray, very complicated, and relatively dull."[10]

The year 1969, however, was not so dull. Pentecostalism and the Jesus movement gained strength. Harvey Cox, the high priest of secular theology, joined the ranks of renascent supernaturalists in *The Feast of Fools*. And more, wrote Greeley:

> During a recent unpleasantness between the University of Chicago and its SDS, the normal, decorous quiet of the Social Science building was rent one fine afternoon by ear-piercing shrieks. Secretaries, research assistants, and even a few faculty members dashed to their office doors to discover who was being murdered. Three young women dressed in shabby and tattered garments were stand-

ing in front of the Sociology Department office shrieking curses: "Fie on thee, Morris Janowitz! A hex on thy strategy!"

WITCH (Women's International Terrorist Conspiracy from Hell) had come to put a curse on the Sociology Department.

So far, nothing seems to have happened to Professor Janowitz or the Sociology Department. But if it does, there are going to be an awful lot of frightened people along the Midway. (I offered as a matter of professional courtesy to sprinkle holy water on the departmental office, but, while social science is ready for witch-craft, it is not yet ready for exorcism.)[11]

WITCH was just the tip of the iceberg. Across the land, Greeley told readers of the *New York Times Magazine* in June 1969, "There's a New Time Religion on Campus." Asian philosophy, meditation, yoga, Zen, the *Bardo Thodol*, tantra, the kundalini, the chakras, the *I Ching*, karate, aikido, the yang-yin, macrobiotic diets, Gurdjieff, Meher Baba, astrology, astral bodies, auras, UFOs, tarot cards, parapsychology, mysticism, sorcery, spiritualism, magic—and, of course, psychedelic drugs—all had appeared on campus. A Catholic university had a coven of warlocks. On the West Coast, semimonastic cults subsisted on vegetarian diets and spent long hours in contemplation. "What (you should excuse the expression) the hell is going on?"[12]

What was going on, Greeley answered his own question, was something funny yet quite serious, a put-on that was not a put-on, a strange admixture that in days long past was called *liturgy*—or sacred play. "To put a hex on the Sociology Department is comic, but it is also a tentative assertion that there are powers in Heaven and on Earth that may transcend sociology departments." Though the bizarre return of the sacred is limited to a minority of students, it is curious that the resurgence is taking place among elite groups at the best universities—at precisely those places, in other words, where secularization ought to be the most effective and the most complete. "One repeats the question: What the hell is going on? God is dead, but the devil lives?"[13]

What was going on? When Greeley asked students in his Sociology of Religion class, they began to talk immediately about the failure of science. "Let's face it," one graduate student said, "science is

dead. While the newspapers and magazines were giving all the attention to the death of God, science was really the one that was dying."
The science he was speaking of was rational, positivistic, empirical
science—precisely the kind at which Greeley was spending a career.
"Imperialistic" science had not ended war or injustice, had not
responded to men's needs. Nor did the "rational" faculty and
administration at the university live up to their own scientific principles. "One may disagree with such an indictment of science,"
Greeley commented, "and yet when Berger, the hero of *Hair*, says,
'Screw your science, screw your rationality,' he speaks for many of
his generation."[14]

Religion at least recognizes that man is more than reason; so the
students explained their feelings to Greeley. Religion does something about a sinking sense of alienation and unimportance. Why
use the *I Ching* when the IBM 360 is available? Because, one student
said, "The *I Ching* says that there are powers that stand beyond and
are more powerful than the 360, powers with which in some way
you can enter into a meaningful relationship when you can't do it
with the 360." And the cults are something to which their members
can *belong*: "If you get into a group like that, you at least know that
somebody will notice the difference if you're murdered. Around the
university, you could be dead in your room for days and nobody
would even know the difference." Religion offers *meaning*, too, the
beginnings of an interpretive scheme. In the words of a young
woman, "The sacred is even better than drugs because when you're
on drugs the world looks beautiful to you only if you're on a trip
and ugly when you're not on a trip. But religion has persuaded some
people that the world is beautiful most of the time, despite the ugli-
ness we see."[15]

It would not be fair to say that these neo-sacralists "believe in
God"—at least in the one they left in their parish congregations—
but, in Greeley's judgment, they are experimenting with the
"experience of the sacred" and are authentically religious.
"Personal efficacy, meaning, community, encounter with the ecstatic and the transcendental, and the refusal to believe that mere
reason can explain either life or personhood—all of these have traditionally been considered religious postures."[16] God might have died

down the street in the faculty lounge of the divinity school, but He had just popped up among students at the heart of a "secular" campus.

The year 1969 also saw another Greeley assault on the secularization hypothesis. Is religion on the wane? he asked in *Religion in the Year 2000*. If we cannot answer that question with good longitudinal data (and that contained in *What Do We Believe?* was far from the best), we can at least make use of comparative data. How, for example, would the vitality of religion compare with that of the American political system?

> ITEM: Approximately 60 percent of the American electorate votes in national elections. Approximately 68 percent of the adult population attends religious services in any given four-week period.

> ITEM: 27 percent of the electorate reports it discussed politics with others prior to an election; 90 percent of the people in the Detroit area, the only geographic source of data on this point, reports discussing religion with others during the month just past.

> ITEM: Approximately five families in every 100 made a financial contribution to a political party or candidate in 1956. At least 40 in every 100 made a financial contribution to a religious body; three in every 100 tithe.

> ITEM: Only 7 percent of all respondents says it has no strong feelings about its religious beliefs. . . . the proportion of the electorate that declares itself indifferent to political positions and issues is always greater than 7 percent.[17]

The comparisons could be multiplied at great length, according to Greeley's source, Guy A. Swanson, but there would be little point in going on. If we juxtapose data on religion with data on contemporary politics, we must be cautious indeed—and that's putting it mildly—with assertions of the present irrelevance of religion.

In *Religion in the Year 2000* Greeley for the first time presented sociological evidence in opposition to his own—presented it, that is, so that he could proceed to demolish it. Sociologists Charles Glock and Rodney Stark, for example, had discovered (especially in liberal

Protestant denominations) that substantial numbers of respondents to their questionnaires said that the existence of God was only "probably"—not "certainly"—true. And, when asked to describe how they thought of God, surprisingly high percentages failed to say He was a person—a concept at the heart of their Christian tradition. Glock and Stark concluded that there were large numbers of doubters, and large numbers of unorthodox believers, within the boundaries of the traditional religious denominations.

Greeley rebutted by saying that a response of "probably" true to the question of God's existence did not indicate doubt but a high degree of religious and theological sophistication. Respondents were aware that the existence of God could not be demonstrated with the certainty of a mathematical theorem; yet they still remained religiously committed. The same could be said of their concept of God. Ambiguity did not reflect doubt but an appreciation of the complexity of the question of God.

Another argument advanced in support of the secularization hypothesis was that America's degree of religious participation was an exception to the norm for nations in the industrial West. "One need only visit European countries"—so the argument ran—"or look at the European survey data to realize that Church membership and Church attendance are very low in these countries and that in some of them, such as England, comparative figures from the preceding century indicate the extent of the decline in religious practices."[18]

This was an impressive argument, Greeley conceded, yet he had answers. First of all, belief in God was not at all that low in Europe. Surveys in Scandinavia, Italy, the Low Countries, Czechoslovakia, and Great Britain showed that between 80 and 85 percent of adults believed in God. And surveys were ambivalent as well. In one West German poll, only 68 percent of the respondents said they were certain of God's existence, but 86 percent admitted to praying! Furthermore, a lack of overt practice need not mean that religion has disappeared from the personal lives of people. David Martin looked at apparently religionless individuals in Great Britain and noted:

> Of the doubters and agnostics and atheists, over a quarter say they pray on occasion to the God whose existence they doubt; one in twelve went to church within the past six months. . . . Over half

the nonbelievers consider that there should be religious education in the schools. . . . Nearly a quarter tend to think that Christ was something more than a man.[19]

Greeley's interpretation of these and other of Martin's data was that "Church membership and Church affiliation in England may be less striking than in the United States" (perhaps because England's working class can only view the Anglican parson as a squire from the seventeenth century) "but basic religious convictions still seem to persist in great masses of the population."[20]

Why, then, does the secularization hypothesis prevail?

It seems to me that there are any number of reasons for this; all kinds of people—journalists (particularly those writing for religious journals), religious leaders, professional viewers-with-alarm, and other insecure types—have a considerable amount of emotion invested in the proposition that the world is going to hell in the proverbial hand basket. Secondly, theologians feeling very much in the backwaters of the university world are frequently almost pathetically eager to prove that they are as enlightened as are their colleagues in the "real" sciences, who apparently are the people they have in mind when they speak of modern man. . . .[21]

The most important reason for the current strength of the secularization hypothesis, however, is the belief in many sectors of academia that religion and science are incompatible. Often religion "is dismissed with the facile agnostic answer that one can neither prove nor disprove the existence of God or of the Transcendent"—a dismissal more likely to occur in social science and humanities departments than in the physical or biological sciences. "Perhaps the physical scientists and the biologists are less likely to be so certain about incompatibility because they realize what a chancy, uncertain, unpredictable thing the scientific quest really is."[22] Instead of predicting the demise of religion, however, it would be far more useful to sort out the complex relationship between religion and science—a relationship which has not produced unbearable tension for the overwhelming majority of people.

If religion is not going to fade away, what will be its shape in the year 2000? Greeley's forecast was not at all startling: religious denominations would not yield to the ecumenical movement;

doctrinal orthodoxy would remain; people would still worship in local congregations; the religious masses would not abandon the churches (nor, on the other hand, would they cease to be passive); despite an increase in part-time or limited-term clergy, full-time clergy would continue as the majority of religious functionaries; the Low-Church liturgy of the underground would not replace other forms of worship. Against this backdrop of revolutions that would never come to pass, Greeley saw "a number of very dramatic changes in North Atlantic and American religion." Religion and social science were about to enter into a dialogue from which both would profit immensely. Religion, in particular, would come to appreciate the essential link between religious development and personality development, to understand the central role of sexuality in the entire developmental process. There would be more tolerance of diversity within and between the various religious traditions, and there would be democratic structures capable of managing that diversity. Individual responsibility would continue to be stressed, and greater concern would be shown for small, intimate, fellowship congregations. By the end of the century clergymen would clearly understand that their role was to be that of an expressive and affectionate leader. Finally, there would be a continued decline in Puritanism and substantially more emphasis on the nonrational, "both the ecstatic and Dionysian nonrational and also the reflective and the contemplative and mystical nonrational."[23]

Above all, religion in the year 2000 would still *be*.

"Death-of-God" theology burned itself out as quickly as it had been ignited. By 1970 the media were discovering a religious revival in America, and sociologists and theologians were describing it as "counter-secularization." Ridiculous, said Father Greeley in an issue of *Social Research*. "Society was never really 'de-sacralized' in the first place."[24] The secular city was born in Selma and died in Watts, and (he added in the *New York Times*) "the only place God might really have been dead was in the divinity schools and I have a hunch that all he actually did was to go on a sabbatical."[25]

Greeley was less concerned now with the *statistics* of belief in God, more inclined to search for an *explanation* of the reasons for the persistence of religion. He was under greater pressure to "utter theory" and cut down those critics from sociology who dismissed him as nothing but an empiricist out to destroy the conventional wisdom. His emerging views on religion would show the influence of many social scientists (and he would quote them all at great length), but none was as important as Clifford Geertz, a colleague at the University of Chicago and a former student of Talcott Parsons. Greeley and Geertz often had lunch together at Chicago and frequently attended each other's seminars. Greeley would never tire of acknowledging his debt to Geertz, describing it in one book as "immense," saying in another that Geertz was "the most distinguished social scientist of religion currently practicing."[26]

The seeds of Greeley's sociology of religion were sown in *What Do We Believe?* when he pinpointed two functions of religion—to provide senses of belonging and meaning. In 1972 a book was devoted to each of these. The first was *The Denominational Society*, a textbook in the sociology of religion, not "very high-level theorizing" to be sure, but "an attempt to use the theories of other men to understand the complexities of American religious phenomena."[27] The second, *Unsecular Man*, went to the heart of Andrew Greeley's understanding of religion.

The Denominational Society contended that the United States was one of only four societies in the western world (the others were Canada, Holland, and Switzerland) in which there was neither a single established church nor a variety of protesting sects, but denominations, a unique organizational adjustment to the fact of religious pluralism. Why did religion in America take on denominational characteristics? For one reason, the religious pluralism of the original colonies inhibited the development of an established church. For another, the "belonging vacuum" created by immigration from Europe to America, by the transition from peasant village to industrial metropolis, insured that religion in this country would provide not only meaning but also a sense of social location and social identity.

It was Emile Durkheim who emphasized the integrative function of religion in society; indeed, for him, the collective and the religious were practically coterminous. Anthropologist Bronislaw Malinowski took objection to Durkheim's identification of society and religion, yet he agreed that religion was "the very cement of social fabric. . . . Its function is to hold society together in face of the stress and strains brought to it by disasters and threats that are both internal and external."[28] Since Malinowski's time social theorists have argued that religion can fractionate society as well as unify it—and their arguments are cogent indeed. Nevertheless, it remains true that religion, in the variety of its manifestations across the globe, has proved capable of bringing the people of a given society together.

In America it brought together wave after wave of immigrants landing on a strange and alien shore. Religion in this country has always been an ethnic phenomenon. In *Protestant, Catholic, Jew,* Will Herberg described how immigrants *became* ethnics—Poles and Russians and Slovaks and Greeks—*after* arriving in this country, and he noted how integral to the process were the various churches. By providing places where they could meet and be with their own kind, churches helped bewildered immigrants sort out who they were in a complex and confusing society. The religious institutions that emerged were not churches in the European sense, for none aspired to become *the* national ecclesiastical institution; nor were they sects because they were socially established, normative, nuclear to the society.

Denominationalism explains the unusually high level of religious observance in America. In Europe there was simply no "belonging vacuum" of the magnitude that the immigration experience created here, no need for people to search for a place where *their* language was spoken and *their* customs carried on.

One thing more: it would be a mistake to make the facile assumption that America's pluralistic political structure set the stage for the pluralism of its religious denominations. An equally strong case could be made for the reverse of that proposition, that the multidenominational nature of the original colonies was a *fait accompli* that the framers of the Constitution had to deal with. Delegates to the Constitutional Convention came as representatives of denominational states, as Congregationalists, Friends, Presbyterians, Anglicans. Their milieu was one of pluralism, and the document they created outlined a political structure able to deal with pluralism, able to absorb the variety of immigrants who came in later years.

Unsecular Man, the hub of a constellation of other Greeley volumes, opened with characteristic bluntness. "Let us be clear at the beginning: this is a volume of dissent. It rejects most of the conventional wisdom about the contemporary religious situation"—wisdom perpetrated by popular journals, divinity schools, self-defined "relevant" clerics and laymen, pop sociological-religious analysts, sociologists who do not specialize in religion but feel free to pronounce upon its state. Greeley not only saw to it that his enemies knew who they were; he also made sure that he himself was standing out in the open, that his position would not be misinterpreted: "the basic human religious needs and the basic religious functions have not changed very notably since the late Ice Age."[29]

Greeley ticked off the list of opposing views. Religion is *not* in a state of collapse, he said, contrary to the declaration of Eugene Fontinell in his book, *Toward a Reconstruction of Religion*. In opposition to Martin Marty in *The Modern Schism*, Greeley argued that liberalism, evolutionism, socialism, and historicism have been extremely unsuccessful rivals of religion. John Cogley stated in *Religion in a Secular Age* that modernity and religion are antonyms for millions in the West, but Greeley contended that vastly more millions are able to harmonize religion and modernity. Ramon Echarren argued in an issue of *Concilium* that mankind is changing profoundly; Greeley said it is not. In *A Rumor of Angels* Peter Berger expressed the belief that the supernatural is today more remote from the lives of people than at any time in the past; Greeley countered that primitive societies, too, had their equivalents of atheists and agnostics and that enthusiastic religious commitment is no more unfashionable today than it was among neolithic man.

After displaying the data contained in *Religion in the Year 2000* to show that the supernatural is very much with us, Greeley turned to the most elementary assumption of the "conventional wisdom," that of organic social evolution. The assertions of Bonhoeffer and Cox that secular man had "come of age" were "rooted in the faith— and here I use the word advisedly—that secular man and technological man are the inevitable result of an evolutionary process which cannot be resisted."[30] But the version of mankind moving forward in a single direction through crisis and change is precisely that—a vision, something in the eye of the beholder, not in social events themselves.

In *Social Change in History* and *The Social Bond*, Robert Nisbet put together a devastating case against the evolutionary perspective. "Change," he wrote, "cannot be deduced or empirically derived from the elements of social structure." Though we may prefer to believe otherwise, fixity is the true characteristic of human institutions. Nisbet analyzed a number of them: the family (where monogamous marriage has remained the norm despite the continued presence of deviations and evasions); the calendar (it took the Protestant world several centuries to adopt the vastly superior Gregorian calendar); science (which, according to Nisbet, "can suffer from the kind of conventionalism of the old and hostility to the new that we are more accustomed to thinking of in areas of politics, religion, or life styles"); and literature (the supposed haven of the creative, change-inducing mind; in actuality the abode of "routinization, conventionalism, and downright conservatism").[31] Even the university, that place where, given its commitment to openness and curiosity, one would expect the most dramatic changes—even the university is characterized by the persistence of basic structures. The norms of academic consensus, the criteria for faculty and student advancement, for example, are much the same today as they were at the University of Bologna in the thirteenth century.

Change *does* occur (Greeley concurred with Nisbet), but rarely in the basic structures of society—and certainly not in the basic human needs to which religion responds. Mankind—Greeley meant most men at many times in their lives—has needed and will continue to need some sort of ultimate explanation, some sort of *meaning*; and religion is a symbol system that provides just such a meaning.

According to Clifford Geertz, religion is one of several systems by which men order and interpret their lives. Religion differs from *common sense* (another of the cultural systems that provide understanding) because it goes deeper. Common sense is "a simple acceptance of the world, its objects and its processes, as being just what they seem to be."[32] Common sense, however, does not answer all man's questions. It did not explain, for example, why a large toadstool grew up in the house of a Javanese carpenter in the space of a few days. It does not explain why the just suffer and the unjust prosper. Common sense, as a Javanese image has it, is like a water buffalo listening to an orchestra.

Science penetrates more deeply than common sense. Science could have told the carpenter why the toadstool made its sudden appearance in his living quarters. But science is not religion, for its attitude toward underlying realities is one of rational, detached, questioning impartiality. Religion, on the other hand, seeks to produce commitment to the underlying reality, to encounter and become involved with it, not simply to analyze it. Religion tells its adherents what the structure of the real is *and* how one is to live in harmony with that structure.

Neither is religion *art* (for the artist attempts to dwell on appearances and to disengage himself from the question of factuality, while religion attempts to go behind surfaces and create an aura of utter actuality), nor is it *ideology* (which is an attempt to explain—and produce commitment to—political reality alone). The symbols of religion are unique; they tell truths about phenomena beyond man's analytic capacity, about moral evil, about human suffering. And they tell them not in abstract schematic propositions but in concrete, often poetic, stories that invite the hearer to become emotionally involved and committed. The religious myth "is a comprehensive view of reality; it explains it, interprets it, provides the ritual by which man may maintain his contact with it, and even conveys certain very concrete notions about how reality is to be used to facilitate mankind's life and comfort."[33]

When we moderns wish to explain why a drought breaks and rain comes, we describe certain changes in atmospheric conditions; not so the ancient Babylonians, as Henri Frankfort points out in *Before Philosophy*. The same facts were experienced by them as the gigantic bird Imdugud coming to their rescue. "It covered the sky with the black storm clouds of its wings and devoured the Bull of Heaven, whose hot breath had scorched the crops."[34]

Childish fantasy? Or contact of the *entire* person with an existential reality? The Babylonians wished to understand a natural phenomenon, to be sure, but they were after more: Why should there be powers in the world hostile to us, and why should there be powers on our side? And why should the thunderstorm save us in the nick of time by ending the drought? These were questions that involved the Babylonians at the core of their existence, sources of bafflement to be grappled with. The myth of Imdugud was not mere fantasy—not legend, saga, fable, fairy tale. It was true myth, and true myth, Frankfort tells us, "presents its images and its imaginary actors, not with the playfulness of fantasy, but with a compelling authority. It perpetuates the revelation of a 'Thou.' "[35]

Is modern man, who can give a scientific explanation for drought and rain, beyond religious myth? No, Greeley replied, for there is no less mystery today than in years past:

> We understand thunder, lightning, storms, the movement of heavenly bodies, but a case could be made that even in physical science a good deal of bafflement remains. . . . and as Monsieur Piccard remarked after his submarine journey in the Gulf Stream, "The more we learn about the mysteries of nature, the more unfathomable these mysteries seem to be; because the more we understand, the clearer it is to us how much we have yet to understand and how much we probably never will be able to understand."[36]

Besides, human relationships have expanded in number and kind, and their increasing complexity has rendered them more puzzling. And even though we understand more about the depths of human experience, what we have discovered has served only to raise more difficult questions.

> For archaic man, the dimensions of human existence were relatively limited, the complexities of his life relatively few, and the mysteries of his relationships relatively uncomplex. He may have been baffled by the signs in the heavens, but he was less baffled by himself and his fellow man. We may understand more than he did about the heavens, but the mystery of man is far more convoluted for us than it was for him.[37]

The question of ultimate meaning is further intensified for modern man because, as Thomas Luckmann points out in *The Invisible Religion*, he inherits no *single* meaning system from his society. There exists, rather, a supermarket of such systems, and modern man, that "consumer of interpretive schemes," must shop for and select the components of the meaning system according to which he wishes to live. He has the freedom of choice (though in actuality he may not exercise it), but along with that freedom comes the burden, and the pain, of responsibility. Delivered from the constraints of community, he is also deprived of the support of community. Thus, "modern man is *more* religious than his predecessors precisely because now he must interpret and choose and his predecessors did not have to do either."[38]

Unsecular Man, a book that sold out twice in the hard-cover edition and is now available in Dutch, German, Italian, and Spanish, was far removed from the battles of the late sixties over the death of God. With it Greeley identified his understanding of human religious needs and wrote a preface for many books to come, among them *The Jesus Myth; The Sinai Myth; The Devil, You Say!; The Mary Myth; Sexual Intimacy;* and *Love and Play.* Greeley argued in *Unsecular Man* that theology must reinterpret myths "broken" by the criticism of modern science. Myths are "broken" when science—as it should—questions their description of what literally happened in the past. Far from demythologizing religion because of science's review, however, we should use science, as well as our own mythopoetic instincts, to penetrate to the heart of religious myths. "The relevant point is that the myth-makers were far more interested in conveying an interpretive scheme about the nature of ultimate reality than they were in telling a story that would measure up to the strict scientific canons devised only centuries in the future." Thus, what matters about the Sinai myth is not how many days Moses spent on the mountain, but rather "that the Sinai story conveys to those who heard it a world view, an ethical system, a sense of mission and hope rooted in the conviction that God has entered into a covenant with the Israelite people." And the basic issue in the Jesus myth is not the literal fact of His resurrection—the truth of that will never be known with certainty— "but the existential truth conveyed in the Resurrection story: through Jesus mankind triumphed over sin and death."[39] Greeley insisted—and near the end of *Unsecular Man* he preached—that the organized Church has to engage in this kind of creative interpretation of mythological traditions if it is to meet the religious needs of technological man.

> It is late at night. A man has driven many miles to a house on the shore of a lake. He parks his car, walks down the steps to a pier jutting out into the water. On this moonless night the man looks up toward the great black umbrella of stars over his head and a feel-

ing of unspeakable peace comes over him. In the next instant of
awareness it is morning; he has no idea what happened to all the
hours in between.

A young woman has just made love with her husband. They have
snatched an interlude together in the middle of the afternoon. It
was the best sex they ever had, and she lies exhausted in his arms.
Suddenly, a new and very different kind of pleasure takes possession of her. She smiles first and then laughs; her entire body takes
on a peculiarly delightful glow. This new pleasure makes intercourse seem mild in comparison. The whole of the universe has
somehow flooded her being.[40]

So began another Greeley effort in the sociology of religion, this
time a primer on mysticism. *Ecstasy: A Way of Knowing* (1974) was
originally written for the Catholic readership of the Thomas More
Association but was eventually published by Prentice-Hall. Why
mysticism? Surely nothing in the spiritual life of the author steered
him in that direction.

I am scarcely a mystic myself in any ordinary sense of the word;
indeed I am not even very meditative or contemplative. I don't
disapprove of either; on the contrary, I respect and admire those
qualities. The lack of them in my own personality and character I
account as a failing. But for reasons of nature and nurture I am a
hard-nosed rational empiricist skeptic. By temperament and training I am one of the least mystical persons I know, and while my
preconscious intellect may occasionally take over when I am
writing a prose essay, most of my life is marked by strong vigorous
control of the "reality principle," which means that for me
deautomatization is virtually impossible. Again let me insist that I
am not saying this is necessarily a good way to be; it is simply the
way I am.[41]

No, what turned Father Greeley on to ecstatic experience (as
much as a "rational empiricist skeptic" could be "turned on") was
his reading of the poetry of John of the Cross and Gerard Manley
Hopkins. These were men who articulated in a compelling way
those things that Greeley believed; and more, they were men who
"clearly had had direct and immediate contact with a reality Out
There whose existence I accepted as a matter of abstract intellectual
principle."[42] Mysticism, too, was part of the religious revival that

greeted death-of-God theology; it was a kind of knowledge that stood in stark contrast to the positivistic science under attack from Greeley's students. And Greeley had met some "natural" mystics— or, in some cases, had discovered them among people he already knew. None of the mystics were prigs, or madmen, or misanthropes, as he had been led to believe by social science research and his own "dreadfully academic" seminary training in mystical theology. On the contrary, they were some of the most attractive people he knew. Some, simply assuming that everyone had experiences like their own, did not realize they were mystics. Others, like Nancy Gallagher McCready, wrote of their experiences, and their poetry made its way into Father Greeley's book:

> *Start with my toes,*
> *you old Ghost*
> *Spirit the soles of my shoes*
> *and teach me a Pentecostal*
> *Boogaloo*
> *Sprain my ankles with dancing*
> *Sandal around my feet,*
> *to roam with me in the rain*
> *and feel at home in my footprints.*
>
> *Oh! look at me spinning,*
> *Sprinkling, tonguing teaching*
> *Winsoming wondrous steps*
> *lift me, how!?*
> *We'd better quit now,*
> *too all dizzy down giggly*
> *Stop—you're tickling*
> *(my funnybone's fickle for you)*
> *Stop—I'll drop.*
> *I'm dying, I'm flying*
> *with your winding my feet and*
> *legs and waist*
> *Lassoed*
> *Stop chasing fool—I'm racing from you*
> *Don't catch me*
> *Do!*
> *I'll drown!*
> *Oh, drown me—most*
> *For I love you so,*
> *You Old Ghost!*[43]

Ecstasy contained what was now a familiar sight in Greeley's books—long quotations from writers in the field, in this case from mystics like St. Augustine, the Sufi poet Jami, Simone Weil, Teresa of Avila, Teilhard de Chardin, from the few psychologists and sociologists who had bothered to study mysticism. William James's description of the mystical state appeared early in the book, and it was followed by Marghanita Laski's brief empirical confirmation of James's observations and the list of "triggers" of ecstatic episodes—nature, sexual love, childbirth, exercise—which were reported by her subjects (mostly friends and acquaintances). The heart of *Ecstasy*, however, was the realization that there are large numbers of "natural," everyday mystics, people who do not consider themselves such, people leading otherwise normal, unextraordinary lives. It was *their* experience—that of a young man on a pier losing track of time, that of a woman overwhelmed by a presence after making love, that of a young man relieved of worry by the Ode to Joy—that introduced and set the tone for the entire book.

Mystics may well know what we do not. Though Greeley did not feel he had to postulate some special intervention by the divinity to explain a mystical interlude, he wished to take very seriously the mystic's claim—one documented as well in Abraham Maslow's study of "peak-experiences"—that in ecstatic experience one sees things *the way they are.* According to the mystic,

> . . . the experience is more one of knowing than of feeling. If anything is heightened in the ecstatic interlude, it is the cognitive faculties of the mystic: he knows something others do not know and that he did not know before. He *sees*, he *understands*, he *perceives*, he *comprehends.* The occasional mystic who has perused the psychological and psychiatric literature becomes impatient with the insensitivity of the writers: "They really haven't been listening" is the most common criticism. They don't realize that, above all, the mystic *knows* cognition is at the core of his experience.[44]

Thus, mystics are to be taken seriously—not uncritically, of course, but with the admission that "there is both a confidence and authenticity about their description that is persuasive."[45] Ecstasy, in the words of the book's subtitle, is a legitimate and valid *way of knowing.*

If Greeley could not join the ranks of the ecstatics, could not *know* the way they knew, at least, good sociologist that he was, he could *count* them. How many mystics were there in America? How did they get to be the way they were? Were they psychological misfits or were they well adjusted? Greeley would write later, "There may be a certain madness—or at least unmitigated gall—in using survey instruments, computer analysis, and log linear models to deal with what is the ultimate, if not The Ultimate, in human experience,"[46] but when the Henry Luce Foundation agreed late in 1971 to commit $150,000 to a NORC survey of the "Fundamental Belief Systems of the American Population," he and Bill McCready threw caution to the winds and included in their questionnaire items dealing with mystical—as well as psychic—experiences.

What proportion of America's adult population had had some kind of extraordinary inner experience? In 1973, 59 percent said they had experienced the *deja vu* phenomenon at least once in their lives; 58 percent had felt a sense of contact with someone even though that person was far away; 27 percent had felt in touch with someone who had died; and 24 percent said that they had "seen events that happened at a great distance as they were happening." On the item concerning mystical experience ("Have you ever felt as though you were very close to a powerful, spiritual force that seemed to lift you out of yourself?") 18 percent said "once or twice"; 12 percent said "several times"; and 5 percent said "often." At least a third of America's adult population, then, had had some experience of the ecstatic—and perhaps as many as ten million had had such experiences frequently. When asked to describe what the mystical interlude was like, most of those who had had one checked "a feeling of deep and profound peace." Listening to music and prayer were the most common "triggers" of ecstatic episodes, and their most frequent duration was "a few minutes or less" (though a surprising number of respondents said "a day or more").

Who were the mystics? There were as many in their late teens and twenties as there were in their sixties and seventies, but slightly more in the forty-to-sixty age bracket. A higher percentage of blacks than whites, of males than females, of college-educated than non-college-educated, of Protestants than Catholics reported having mystical experiences. Mystics were more optimistic and much more likely to believe in personal survival after death. They were, in general, more satisfied with their lives and "happier" than the population at large (the .40 correlation between frequent mystical experience and "balance affect" on the Bradburn Psychological Well-Being Scale was the highest NORC had ever seen in connection with that scale, and the correlation reached .60 for mystics of the "classic" type). White mystics were less racist than whites who reported no ecstatic episodes in their lives. The picture of the mystic as a frustrated, rigid, maladjusted, unhappy freak could not have been more thoroughly discredited by the replies of the nearly 1,500 participants in the study.

And how did mystics get to be the way they were? Greeley and McCready identified distinct patterns in the backgrounds of blacks and whites. White mystics tended to come from families in which mother and father were close to each other and joyous in their religion (the attitudes of the father were more decisive than those of the mother), while the dominant childhood experience of black mystics was closeness to the mother in a family where father and mother were not very close. (Black mystics, incidentally, were not disproportionately poor members of fundamentalist congregations, which one might hypothesize if he believed mysticism to be a response to deprivation.) The Greeley-McCready data were written up for the *Journal of Social Research* and the *New York Times Magazine*, where they drew an enormous response. They also appeared in monographs entitled *Reconnaissance into the Sociology of the Paranormal* (1975) and *The Ultimate Values of the American Population* (1976).

Mystics would hardly be impressed with these findings, the authors concluded. "Neither of us is mystical, and those we know who are find our efforts diverting but hardly profound."[47] But at least mysticism could no longer be written off as deviant behavior, as something "like" schizophrenia or "like" a regression to infantile relationships with reality. No, hard as it might be for psychologists to accept, the evidence indicated that mysticism was good for you.

Andrew Greeley's work in the sociology of religion, then, has moved from skirmishes over the death of God and secular theology to a theoretical analysis of the functions of religion and, finally, to an empirical investigation of extraordinary religious experiences. If he was on the winning side in the debate over secularization—and the years since the "death of God" show that he was—his victory won him no friends among his colleagues in the sociology of religion. In March 1974 the *Journal for the Scientific Study of Religion* took up his life work—supposedly, everything he had written—and subjected it to the review of four critics—Jeffrey Hadden, Patrick McNamara, Martin Marty, and Samuel Mueller. Greeley described their treatment as "absolutely vicious."

Mixed with the comment that Greeley was "both interesting and important to our discipline" were references to him as "the Howard Cosell of the Catholic Church" and "the man we all love to hate." Hadden said Greeley provided "more raw data than any living sociologist," yet his work was clouded by value presuppositions. McNamara praised Greeley's work on the Protestant ethic hypothesis and said *The Hesitant Pilgrim* and *The Crucible of Change* were "among the finest contemporary examples of applied sociology"—but why didn't he take on a *serious* theoretical analysis of the Roman Catholic Church? Martin Marty, a friend, thought Greeley's sense of history "routine and lifeless" and found in *What Do We Believe?* and *Religion in the Year 2000* "a kind of nostalgia for a static universe." And Samuel Mueller warned of misspellings in Greeley's work, straightened out some of his "sloppy" data analysis, and said Greeley simply produced too much.[48]

No one, individually or collectively, came to grips with the Greeley *corpus*. McNamara apparently had not read Greeley's analysis of American Catholicism presented at Yale in 1970, nor was he aware that that theoretical endeavor was being expanded into a book. Marty must have passed by the historical drama of *The Catholic Experience*. And Mueller—no doubt about it—missed the forest for the trees: his rectifying of Greeley's "sloppiness" only made Greeley's data more convincing. Hadden, at least, was aware of the problem of dealing with the sheer amount of information that Greeley had processed, the sheer quantity of his output. "Encountering the products of Greeley's' pen, typewriter, and dictaphone," he wrote, "is something like encountering New York City for the first time. One stands awed, inspired, and overwhelmed."[49]

In the next issue of the *Journal* Greeley came out swinging:

There is, of course, no escaping the assumption that quantity precludes quality, an assumption which all four of the commentators seem to share. So be it, although it is a judgment that is a little hard on Agatha Christie, Mozart, and G. K. Chesterton. Yet I must confess I find the suggestion that my work can't be careful because there is so much of it a little graceless when it comes from writers whose own work seems marked by neither quantity nor quality. . . . . And let me rub it in a bit more, fellows: I've got three more articles coming out in the AJS and the ASR this summer and fall. I will take seriously the criticisms of those who are able to match that measure of professional competence.[50]

Greeley was angry. He included in his reply to the critics not a word of the positive things they had to say. Hadden was "patronizing." Marty engaged in "an ever so small omission that makes me look like a naive and innocent clerical Pollyanna." McNamara stacked the deck so Greeley couldn't win. Mueller was "snide," "dreary," "small-minded," and represented "the worst kind of mean, vicious, academic pettiness."

But I guess it is all my fault. There must be something wrong with me if I have led four such honorable scholars to depart from the narrow ways of truthful discourse. I am sure that if I wrote less and less broadly, if I were less of a loudmouth Irish priest (to use Professor Janowitz's endearing phrase), they would not find in me so much cause for anger.

Maybe I ought to reform my life, change my ways, settle down and concentrate on one thing, stop being an obnoxious Irishman and become respectable, stuffy, and dull. Maybe I ought to become sober and serious, and listen to papers at professional meetings.

Maybe I ought to marry and work out my problems in bed instead of at a typewriter.

Don't anyone hold his breath.[51]

7   Sacerdos

Early in my conversations with Andrew Greeley there came a quiet moment of surprise. I realized (or was it that for the first time I noticed?) that at the center of all those Greeleys I had been in contact with—beneath the puckishness, the despair, the hatred, the joy, the ambition—there was a simple, integrating self, so straightforward and so obvious that, like the air around me, I had easily overlooked it. This self, I learned later, was the one that raised its hand in the second grade when a teacher asked how many of her students were going to be priests. It was a natural act, raising one's hand, full of ease, a reflex set in motion without a moment's hesitation. As simply and readily as that, Andrew Greeley slipped into his life's work and expressed the basic stance toward reality that he would carry, unchanged, into his adult life.

Sacerdos, a priest: no memorable religious experience beckoned Andrew Greeley into the priesthood, nor have any extraordinary inner events cemented a decision to remain a part of it. Father Greeley has never doubted that the priesthood is his calling, has never struggled through a "vocational" or a "celibacy" crisis, either before or after ordination. He will tell you that his understanding of the priesthood has matured but not changed radically. The same can be said of his fundamental world view, of his understanding of the way things are. He has always believed in God and talked to God— no more, no less. "I don't exactly climb up Mt. Carmel, but neither do I descend into the dark night of the soul." His idea of God has evolved, but not with the terror of loss and the joy of rediscovery, the incredible depths and the dizzying heights, of souls troubled—and stimulated—by periodic revolutions. There has been an overwhelming sense of organizational chaos, of uncertainty, of conflict in his *public* life, but nothing like a *personal* crisis that shook his being to the core (the closest to that, he said, was the disintegration of his New Community). Much anxiety has occurred over *what he should do next* but none over *who he is* or *what he believes.*

I sense now that the presence of this self—set and secure in its location in the cosmos—explains the remarkable capacity of this man to sustain the anxiety, the nastiness, the hatred, the *evil* (he would use the word, for this is what he sees) swirling in and about him. His personal identity clear, his energies focus on the battle to be won, the enemy to be destroyed. He always has something left, something *they* cannot take away, when the inevitable results of building risk upon risk, having stalked him down, finally come to rip away his investments. Rooted, he has strength. Peripheral selves whip about in the wind, never fearing the change, because they are certain of contact with the earth.

If this simple inconspicuous self, this priestly self, helps one understand Greeley's capacity for conflict, it also lifts some of the mystery from his role in the secularization debate. Persistence, fixity, continuity, evenness, sameness, basic religious functions that "have not changed very notably since the late Ice Age"[1]—these were the themes at which he hammered with his statistics and his polemic, these the targets that drew fire from critics like Cox and Marty. Mankind's conditions of living may have changed, Greeley held, but not his fundamental orientation toward the universe; there have been no crises in the latter, no revolutions, but the same eternal needs for meaning and belonging. *At its core, the world has not changed—* nor, at his core, has the man who insisted time and again on the truth of that very proposition. Greeley's "feel" for a personal God at the base of the universe has been a constant in the midst of extraordinary upheavals on the periphery of his being. One needs certain eyes (and certain *I*'s) to see certain phenomena, personal crisis to see mankind in revolution, personal constancy, in the case of Father Greeley, to see the evenness of mankind's development.

From as far back as one thinks of such things, then, Andrew Greeley has thought of himself as a priest; and all through the sixties, all through that decade of hope ushering in despair, he wrote about the priesthood: a long pamphlet entitled *Priests for Today and Tomorrow* (1964), articles brought together in *The Hesitant*

Pilgrim (1966), retreats for priests written up as *Uncertain Trumpet* (1968) and *New Horizons for the Priesthood* (1970). Greeley's memories of life in the seminary and the rectory were not always pleasant—they honed the scalpel he used to dissect the structure of priestly life.

First to come under diagnosis was the seminary, a virtual breeding ground of immaturity. "Those who supervised us both in the seminary and after ordination feared strong men, men who knew who they were and what their priesthood was and who would not permit, under any circumstances, their basic human dignity to be violated." Hence seminary training was geared to keep the students (and "I shall include myself near the top of the list") docile and obedient. No program could have been more successful. "We had to suppress so much, pretend so often, simulate so frequently, that deep down inside, most of us, I fear, had every reason to suspect that we were phonies." Nor could the seminary students relate authentically to one another. "Because the seminary authorities did not trust us, they created situations in which we were really unable to trust our fellows; hence, we all built defense mechanisms which kept a hostile and suspicious world at bay."[2] The seminarians were warned that human affection was dangerous, that their goal was to become as detached as possible from the people with whom they worked, that "particular friendships" (that meant homosexuality, but the men didn't know it then) were to be scrupulously avoided:

> We were, of course, to be friendly, equally friendly, to everyone (though less friendly to women, of course), but deeply friendly to no one, deeply involved with no one, deeply attached to no one . . . . The result was not some superhuman who towered above the mundane relationships of ordinary men; the result was rather a non-human or zombie who was incapable of entering into any meaningful relationship with anyone.[3]

After ordination, the distrust, suspicion, and fostering of immaturity continued in the rectory. More than that, one would have to say that the relationship between pastor and curate was very often *evil*. It may have been "the greatest single obstacle to the spread of the people of God in the United States"[4] and was "surely one of the most depressive and degrading relationships that has survived from the feudal ages . . . . Even if it were not a violation of Christian charity, it would still have to be abandoned because of its consummate inefficiency."[5]

Analyze the roles of pastor and curate. The one has unlimited power; the other is completely expendable. The one becomes isolated because of his power (and, as Lord Acton noted, corrupt because of his isolation); the other puts as much distance as possible between himself and his pastor, ingratiates himself with the people of the parish, and becomes the middleman between them and his superior. The pastor, in turn, becomes jealous of his curate's popularity and reasserts his authority, causing the curate to lose more initiative and withdraw even further. The initial positing of roles could only lead in this direction, could only spiral a difficult relationship into an abyss. And while there is conflict in abundance between pastor and curate, it usually remains latent. The curate continues on as nice guy, a "mouse in training to be a rat."[6]

The immaturity engendered in the seminary and rectory was no more painfully and embarrassingly evident than in priests' relationships with women. It took a layman at a group discussion retreat to raise the issue for Andrew Greeley, and once raised, neither he nor the other priests present could turn to another topic for the duration of the conference.

> Most women find that our approach of supermasculinity makes us awkward, rude, boorish, and ill-mannered. We are frightened by them and have exploitative, domineering attitudes toward them . . . [We] leave most sensitive women wondering at the end of their conversations with us whether we will now go back to the rectory and, like other late adolescent males, reassure ourselves of our masculinity by reading the latest issue of *Playboy*.[7]

Whence this fearful yet exploitative attitude toward women? From family backgrounds with inflexible, Jansenistic attitudes toward sex, from fathers afraid of their sons' mothers, from high school and seminary experiences that objectified women, making them either lofty, unattainable idols or lowly objects of pleasure. "The fact that we got close neither to the goddess nor the prostitute merely reinforced our semiconscious fantasies." Would not marriage for the clergy be an answer, then? Absolutely not, Greeley countered, were one to judge from the behavior of the typical American male, married or single—he is as domineering in his attitudes toward women as is the celibate. Frankly, "I am not altogether sure that for many of us the problem is even soluble."[8]

Not that Greeley was opposed to relaxing the celibacy regulation for priests. Ideally, he argued, celibacy should be optional; nothing else would be consonant with the demands of human freedom. But sex is not a panacea for immaturity nor a guarantee of fulfillment:

> Human beings are closed up within themselves in fear and loneliness, not because they are not loved by a member of the opposite sex, but because they are not loved by themselves. Self-rejection, self-loathing, self-hatred will be solved neither by sex nor by marriage, but only by an understanding of what the factors were in our emotional background which make it impossible for us to accept our own goodness and virtues.[9]

Besides, because of the woeful state of theory about sexuality and celibacy in the western Catholic Church, optional celibacy would lead in no time to compulsory marriage. A modern rationale for celibacy simply has not evolved because the regulation has been taken for granted for so long. In the absence of such a rationale, subtle but strong pressures would deprive priests of the freedom to be celibate; and that loss would be tragic, not because celibacy is a good thing in itself but because it frees a man to build up the people of God. For himself, Greeley said, "celibacy seems to leave me freer to worry more intensively about more people, to put myself in the loving service of a far greater number of people—and in a far more intense way than I would be able to if I had a family of my own."[10] Not that priests, and Greeley included himself, have taken advantage of the freedom celibacy offers—their lives offer no more love than anyone else's, but that is their fault, not that of the celibacy regulation.

Greeley dealt with other problems, too, in these books: "the persistence of anti-intellectualism," which he spoke about with his colleagues at home while holding up the class of 1961 to the gaze of outsiders; that "familiar black book with the red-edged pages," read daily out of a sense of duty but contributing in no way to an attitude of prayerful contemplation; uneasiness over the meaning of poverty in an era of affluence; the lack of professional standards.

Worst of all were "friendly" priests in the recreation room, good-natured and charitable on the surface, jealous and resentful down below, their whole being geared to holding you down, keeping you in your place, asking "Who do you think you are?" "Passive aggression," Greeley called this attitude scornfully; it was no less devastating for being hidden behind the smile of "the good Father."

In these books Greeley never hesitated to *prescribe*. Perhaps his most important advice was the simplest: delegate power. Do so in the seminary to create the opportunity for responsible decision-making and risk-taking. Do so in the rectory: curates are not to be regarded as servants but as professional colleagues; they should refuse to be expendable; they must communicate to their pastor that they are as concerned about *their* parish as he is.

Power must also be delegated in the diocese as a whole. As he made the point, Greeley reassured the reader time and again that he was not out to destroy order and authority in the Church but only to make them more effective. He was, he said, arguing for collegial authority, an essential part of Church tradition, to replace paternalism. The Church needed senates made up of clergy and laity elected by their parish and supplemented by a selection of professional people, whose role would be to provide upward communication to the bishop. It needed semipermanent research organs within the diocese to provide a reliable information base for the bishop. These bodies would not engage in decision-making—that was the bishop's prerogative—but they would provide the advice on which sound decisions could be made.

Characteristically, Greeley reduced all the problems in the priesthood to *theory*, to a set of assumptions about the nature of men and organizations, to a set of models outlining goals and exemplifying how the goals were to be reached. And the marketplace was well stocked with theories of the priesthood. There was the apostolate-of-kindness theory (in which the priest is basically a nice guy) and the temporal-order theory (in which the priest is excluded from doing anything a layman could do just as well). There was the liturgical-functionary theory (here the priest presides over the Eucharist and then is free to do what any other human being would do) and the builder-of-community theory (in which the priest's goal is to mold the people of his parish into a community of worshipers).

Discarding each, Greeley opted—as he continues to—for the "old notion of the priest as a leader of his people." It was the theory, after all, that was most compatible with the spirit of the Vatican Council. The priest does preside over the Eucharist each morning, but then he moves on to "serving the people of God, whether it be in the parish, in community organizations, in social protest, in academic work, in editing newspapers, in administering ecclesiastical institutions, in educating the young."[11] This model is like that of priest-as-liturgical-functionary, except that work beyond the liturgy also is seen as appropriate to the priestly role. The priest-as-leader is much like a senior colleague in a research collegium. He "influences the minds and hearts of men by permitting their minds and hearts to influence him." His function is not to give orders but to obtain commitment and consent. He does "everything in his power to encourage the charisma of the various members of the community. Indeed, it is primarily by serving his people in such a way that they are encouraged to develop their own talents and charisms that the priest contributes to the upbuilding of the Christian community."[12]

Throughout all his commentary on the priesthood Greeley showed an overwhelming concern for the practical. Theory was important because, in the final analysis, there was nothing as practical as good theory and nothing as damaging as bad (which usually meant unexamined) theory. And when basic theory was not essential to an issue being discussed, practical diagnoses and practical prescriptions peppered the text like so much buckshot. All the copy written in the mid-sixties was replete with examples, illustrations, and how-to's, with judgments about anything and everything, from Florida vacations (they may be all right) to tape recorders (not so good because we don't use the ones we buy). To an audience long accustomed to look for the practical, Greeley's work was cast in the right form.

To readers who agreed with him, his diagnoses and prescriptions were welcome; "incisive," · "clear," "down-to-earth," "refreshing," "responsible," "candid," "stimulating" were the words they used. By others—and I have spoken with them—they were deeply resented. What priest would like to be told that he was a zombie, "an amorphous blob of behavioral variables rocked about on a current of confusion and uncertainty,"[13] or that he was immature, afraid of women, exploitative, manipulative, superficial—a mouse? What member of the new breed of priests would care to be denounced for showing up at a party clad in a sweater instead of a Roman collar ("ashamed of the collar," said the author), for frequenting bars ("he thinks it is part of the humanism of the priesthood"), or for trying to make it with his parishioners as a teeny-bopper? And what authority, his critical readers ask, does this man have to *pontificate*—a kind, fair-minded Carmelite used that word—on the problems of the priesthood? Who appointed him spokesman? Who gave him the right to make such caustic and sweeping generalizations? And what makes his experience—and while we are at it, what makes that national whatever-it-is research organization at Chicago—so important that he is offered as an exemplar for all of America's priests? Does he *do* parish work or just hide behind his pen in his Lake Michigan home attacking those in the "secure Catholic ghetto" who do? Such questions were spoken or merely hinted at, but all were indicative of resentment. Prophet or not, many priests in his own archdiocese, in his own country, did not welcome him.

It was not until March 1969 that Greeley rolled in the heavy machinery of empirical sociology for a look at the American Catholic priesthood. On the first of that month NORC received a contract from the National Conference of Catholic Bishops to execute a national survey of active and resigned priests. The country's hierarchy, headed by John Cardinal Dearden of Detroit, was aware of trouble in the priesthood. Resignations were increasing; the cry for optional celibacy was becoming more strident; the media were devoting more time and space to disgruntled priests. Deciding that serious study was needed, NCCB committed $500,000 to investigations of priestly life from theological, historical, psychological, and sociological perspectives. Of the money, $300,000 found its way to NORC. During his negotiations with NCCB, Greeley had pressed for a study of the laity, too, for they were the priests' clients and the ones who ultimately paid the bills. But NCCB said no; their half million dollars was to be spent entirely on the priesthood.

What would the priesthood look like at a time when organized American Catholicism was in a state of chaos? During the year and a half following the start of their contract, NORC worked hard on the answer: 7,500 questionnaires, each 46 pages long, were mailed to carefully prepared samples of America's diocesan and religious priests and bishops; 1,500 of them were accompanied by the Personal Orientation Inventory, a measure of personal maturity. By the end of September 1970, 79 percent of the priests sampled had responded, 71 percent providing usable data. Curiously, only 59 percent of the country's 276 bishops—the persons who had authorized the study—returned their questionnaires.

A preliminary report on the findings was delivered in October of 1970 to the Ad Hoc Committee for Study of Priestly Life and Ministry, the NCCB unit (chaired by Cardinal John Krol of Philadelphia) with which Greeley's NORC team was in direct contact. It was a gathering that seemed harmless enough in advance. The relationship between the Krol committee and Father Greeley's staff had been entirely cooperative, and there was no reason to anticipate a change. And when it convened at Chicago's O'Hare airport, the meeting got off to a beautiful start, as well it might have. To the relief of those present, America's priests showed up in the data as psychologically well off, even above college-educated males of the same age in their morale. Greeley, in fact, had been surprised by the good shape the priesthood seemed to be in. Priests, by and large, were not accurately represented by the frustrated malcontents parading in the media. Nor were they any less mature or "self-actualized"—at least insofar as these traits could be measured—than comparable population groups. They were reasonably satisfied with their jobs and with the quality of their relationships with superiors, colleagues, subordinates, and lay associates. Furthermore, the overwhelming majority were still committed to the priesthood and interested in continuing their education. They accepted the fundamental doctrines of Christianity and acknowledged the need for papal and episcopal authority in the Church. There was restlessness, to be sure, and serious problems that could be clearly defined, but the clergy were not out to demolish the organizational structures of the Church or to rebel against the bishops.

And then the data on birth control were passed around the table. The participants took a look at the findings—and the air turned frigid. There could be no mistaking the meaning of those columns of figures. Only 40 percent of America's priests (and only 13 percent of those 35 and under) assented to the official teaching of the Church as outlined in *Humanae Vitae*. This compared with 83 percent of the bishops—a mammoth, unheard of difference. If that were not enough to stagger the committee, the tables also showed that Pope Paul's encyclical of July 1968 had actually boomeranged and driven priests even further from the official teaching of the Church. The handful of bishops present could only be stunned; these were *their* priests disregarding papal pronouncements—and disregarding *their* pronouncements, too, for the vast majority of bishops had lined up publicly in support of the papal position.

Greeley remembers well the reaction of those present. "The response was deafening silence. After the presentation one Cardinal left the room and did not return. When the presentation was complete, not a single question was asked, not a single word said. All the faces around the table were grim and stony."[14]

The findings on birth control were not the only ones to shock the bishops. Only 40 percent of the priests (and only 19 percent of those 35 and under) were willing to exclude all possibility of divorce for Catholic couples. Only 29 percent (and 8 percent of those 35 and under) felt that deliberate masturbation was a mortal sin. Despite a number of pronouncements from the hierarchy that there would be no change in celibacy regulations, priests still thought one was on the way: 65 percent (88 percent of those 35 and under), compared with only 18 percent of the bishops, expected a change. Priests did not uniformly reject the Church's stance on matters sexual—for the most part, they supported Church teaching on premarital sex and abortion—but they showed enough discrepancy to indicate that the power of the hierarchy to gain the assent of its priests to Church doctrine had disappeared, and that it had done so, seemingly, overnight.

Later analysis would reveal subtler, but equally profound, differences between priests and bishops. There was the matter of their contrasting spiritual orientations. While many priests agreed with formulations of orthodox doctrine, their values emphasized, as Greeley put it, "process rather than substance, existence rather than essence, open-endedness rather than immutability."[15] Did faith mean essentially "belief in the doctrines of the Catholic Church?"

Only 45 percent of the priests (but 69 percent of the bishops) thought so. Or was faith "primarily an encounter with God and Christ Jesus rather than an assent to a coherent set of defined truths?" Such a definition was preferred by a majority of priests (69 percent) but not of bishops (46 percent). So-called modern values (for example, "For me, God is found principally in my relationships with people") were more manifest in priests than in bishops, and the difference could not be explained solely by age. In their descriptions of the spiritual life, bishops were simply more "conservative" and less "modern" than priests of comparable years (although, curiously enough, they were more "liberal" regarding ecumenism and several social issues).

Most revealing, and lying at the core of other differences, was the split between hierarchy and clergy in their feelings about authority and the distribution of power in the Church. Both groups saw the *actual* distribution of power in the same way—bishops were the single most influential force in the diocese, and chancery officials were next in line. And both agreed that this is the way a diocese ought to operate in the *ideal*. Other groups such as priests and laity should have more power, granted, but the bishop still should be the single person with the most authority. When the survey questions narrowed down to the specifics of who ought to have decision-making power in concrete situations, however, glaring differences appeared in the replies of bishops and priests. Two-thirds of the bishops said *they* should determine where a priest is assigned, but only 41 percent of the priests agreed. Nearly three-quarters of the bishops felt it was up to them to decide where a priest has his living quarters—just 36 percent of their priests felt likewise. Over half the bishops said it was their prerogative to authorize Mass in homes or apartments—only 29 percent of the priests agreed. In short, priests wanted a considerable decentralization of power in practical matters and bishops did not.

But such decentralization was not occurring, and the resultant behavior of priests must have been disconcerting, if not outright galling, to the bishops gathered to hear the NORC data. Nearly one-third of America's priests, according to those data, never said the breviary. Over two-fifths had modified the rubrics of the Mass to fit certain occasions; one-third had said Mass without the proper vestments; one-fifth had given Communion to non-Catholics; a sixth had given sacraments to those who were divorced and re-married—all this despite clear injunctions to the contrary. And the future did not look promising; more priests wanted these preroga-tives, and it was the youngest of them who were going ahead and simply acting on their own. Indeed, it was the youngest priests who were most at odds with the position of bishops throughout the en-tire study.

As he drove home from that ill-fated O'Hare meeting Greeley had the uncanny feeling that the entire priesthood study had dead-ended even before any of its findings had been made public. "From that moment on, I am convinced that some of the members of the committee were determined to put as much distance as possible be-tween them and our report. I could have done two things. One was just sit back and let them destroy the study. Or I could have chosen to fight them—which I did. In either case they were through with me."[16]

Events passed quickly after the meeting. At NORC Greeley was "dazed" by staff dissension that had been building up over the months. It had never happened before, but then never before had his staff been made up of graduate students who were priests like him-self. He had been stunned a month before when Father Richard Schoenherr, the man responsible for the day-to-day direction of the project, announced his decision to leave the priesthood. Worried that the report might be read as a justification of that personal deci-sion, Greeley took over control of the project. Then the president of the National Federation of Priests' Councils asked Greeley for data tapes so the results could be analyzed from the priests' viewpoint—not from that of the bishops, as Greeley was sure to do. Greeley re-fused. In the meantime, Cardinal Krol decided to get an outside pro-fessional evaluation of the study. He asked Greeley if he objected, and Greeley said no. Later Krol informed him of the names of the re-view panel—sociologists Everett Hughes, Sally Cassidy, and John Donovan. Then Greeley protested. Hughes was all right, but Cas-sidy and Donovan were "enemies" sure to tear the report apart. His complaints, however, were wasted on the cardinal, and the evalua-tion team remained intact.

Greeley had no idea what conclusions the evaluators were reaching until he opened a copy of the *New York Times* one day in

July 1971. Then he learned that their report, hostile to the NORC survey, was being secretly distributed to the nation's bishops. Greeley had not merely been denied a chance to read the evaluation of his work, but it had also been leaked to the press without the opportunity for him to comment. He wrote NCCB protesting this treatment and asked for a copy of the evaluation. He was never sent one. When he finally obtained a copy through a friendly bishop, his worst suspicions were confirmed. The criticisms of Hughes, Donovan, and Cassidy concentrated not on the results reported by Greeley but on questions he failed to ask, approaches he neglected to pursue, avenues of analysis he passed by. *They* would have done it differently. "Vicious, dishonest, unfair," is the only way he can describe their review.

Feelings became more intense. Greeley complained directly to Cardinal Dearden, insisting now that the evaluation not be released in the same volume as the NORC report. It would serve only to discredit the study. Why not have a neutral party, skilled in survey research, evaluate the comments of the evaluators? Why should the evaluators exempt themselves from the forums provided for criticism by the sociological profession? And why were outside evaluations not commissioned for the theological, historical, and psychological investigations of the priesthood? "What is the reason for the NCCB having less confidence in our professional competence than in the competence of other scholars?" he wrote Dearden. In October 1971, the cardinal, attending a Synod of Bishops in Rome, replied: Take up the matter with Cardinal Krol. "Dearden let us down," Greeley said. A friend and a confidant in the beginning, he vanished when the going got tough. "I'd never trust him again."

In December Greeley protested again, this time to the entire Krol committee. Not only was the evaluation to be bound in with the NORC report without any reply from Greeley, but Greeley would not even be allowed to make revisions or check the galley proofs before publication. His protest did little good, although he was subsequently permitted to make a statement at the forthcoming meeting of the Ad Hoc Committee on the Implementation of the Priesthood Study, a five-bishop body that had replaced the Krol committee.

For all too long it had been painfully obvious what was going on. The $300,000 of bishops' money, invested in "objective" scientific research, had told them exactly what they did not want to hear, what they *could* not hear. You are operating in a vacuum, the data said. While your priests are not rebelling against you, they are ignoring you, dismissing you, "cheating" on you. If you do not believe, look at their scientifically assessed attitudes on birth control. And the responses of the bishops, in such circumstances, was inevitable: Shoot the messenger (scientist or not), discount and discredit the message he brings.

But at the February 1972 meeting of the Implementation Committee Greeley decided not only to duck but to shoot back. "I have no desire to be directly involved with the U.S. Catholic Conference at the present time, because as that body is now constituted, it is impossible for a scholar to work with it and maintain any standards of professional self-respect . . . . Honesty compels me to say that I believe the present leadership of the church to be morally, intellectually, and religiously bankrupt."[17] To the surprise of Archbishop Philip Hannan of New Orleans, chairman of the committee, Greeley released his comments to the press, and soon the entire text of his remarks was in the *National Catholic Reporter*. They revolved around his assertion that the fundamental crisis in the Church derived from a mistaken theory of leadership.

What does leadership mean—especially in the United States of America, 1972—if not the ability to gain the confidence of one's people, to establish one's credibility with them, to build, however slowly, a consensus among them? Whatever may have been the case in the past, said Greeley, real authority no longer comes automatically with an office, by some divine right; it must be earned. "All the reassertion of the authority in the world will not by itself recapture confidence, credibility or consensus."[18] The only answer is representative governance. John Carroll, America's first bishop, saw that. Why not today's hierarchy?

Why not? Again, because of a theory, because of a particular way of viewing their role in the church that justifies for the bishops the concentration of decision-making power in their own hands. Greeley had spelled it out in *America*: "As humble as they may be about their own personal inadequacies, they are confident that the charism of their office provides them with special inspiration from the Holy Spirit"[19]—an inspiration, by the way, not granted to priests and lay people. Bishops find themselves in a lonely, difficult position. Being "successors to the apostles," they, like the pope, inherit authority of divine origin, and if the authority is God's, how can they give it away, delegate it, share it? Much as they might *like* to do so, the power is simply not theirs to give. They feel their role is to remain true to the tradition of the Church and loyal to the promptings of the Spirit. Credibility? Consent of the governed? The concepts are meaningless according to the theory by which the bishops govern.

The dilemma confronting the organizational Church, and particularly its priesthood, said Greeley, is that one cannot have it both ways. If the bishops continue to operate under *their* theory—and most of them will—they will continue to lead in a vacuum. And priests in increasing numbers will continue to disregard them. In many dioceses,

> it must be said in all honesty, the only power the bishop has left is the power of the pursestrings, and unless the present erosion of authority is arrested, it is no apocalyptic prediction to say that by 1980, there will be no such thing as ecclesiastical authority in the American Church (except over the checkbook) save in those dioceses where bishops have been able to overcome the skepticism, not to say cynicism, of their priests by their own efforts.[20]

On the other hand, should bishops become aware that authority rests on the consent of the governed, that one leads by building confidence, credibility, and consensus, then their theory of divine governance will have to go. That would be nobody's loss, Greeley wrote later, for much of it is

> absolute nonsense theologically, historically, psychologically, and sociologically. Father Raymond Brown has pointed out in his book, *Priest and Bishop*, that bishops are not really the successors of the apostles in the way most of them would like to imagine, and whatever the theological explanation of "infallibility" may be, such infallibility has not prevented the papacy from all kinds of disastrous mistakes both in the past and in the present.[21]

Greeley had recommendations aplenty for Archbishop Hannan's Implementation Committee; but the most important, fusing his anger with the inescapable meaning of the data, was for repre-

sentative governance in the Church, and in particular for the democratic nomination of bishops. Nothing else was tolerable in the
United States of America in 1972. Nothing else would recapture for
the bishops the confidence, the credibility, the consensus—the
power—they had lost.

Though Greeley refused to believe his analysis would have any
impact on the hierarchy, he did achieve two minor victories. First,
he published his own commentary on the priesthood study, *Priests
in the United States: Reflections on a Survey* (1972), even before the
appearance of the official report he had authored for NCCB, *The
Catholic Priest in the United States: Sociological Investigations*
(1972). Second, the administrative board of the NCCB decided at the
last minute to publish its report without the discrediting evaluation. "They had to go to the bindery and separate it out," says
Greeley with obvious relish.

Both of these volumes tried to unravel the perplexing question
of attrition from the priesthood. Though no reliable data existed
prior to 1966, it did appear that the resignation rate was on the upswing. From 1966 to 1969, nearly 5 percent of the diocesan clergy in
the United States resigned, and that rate grew from 0.4 percent in
1966 to 2 percent in 1969. Three percent of the NORC sample—or
approximately 2,000 diocesan priests—said they "probably" or "de-
finitely" would leave. Another 10 percent were "uncertain" about
their future. While these rates of actual and planned resignation
were probably low compared to that of Protestant denominations,
the increase was alarming. Why were men leaving the priesthood?

Greeley was able to study that question from two perspectives,
that of priests thinking about resigning and that of priests who already had done so. The major NORC sample provided data on the
former, and a special sample of resigned priests, interviewed from
July to December 1970, supplied answers for the latter. Priests
planning to leave did so for a variety of reasons; and Greeley, using
the recently developed technique of path analysis, summarized the
interplay of explanatory variables. The desire to marry was itself a
cause of resignation, but even more, it was a channel through which
other causes—principally, frustration with the structure of priestly
life—expressed themselves. The implication was clear: no one was

to take the easy way out and think that modifying the celibacy regulation would magically revitalize the priesthood.

The view from the other side of the fence was essentially the same. The most common explanation for leaving given by ex-priests was the desire to marry, but almost as important was the feeling that they could not live within the institutional structure of the Church. Eighty percent of the resigned priests, incidentally, were married, four-fifths of them to Catholic wives, and an astounding 43 percent to former members of religious communities. These men seemed to be on a "binge of health" following their agonizing decision. They scored higher than active priests on measures of self-actualization, and those recently married had marital adjustment scores *higher* than those of college-educated males (but these scores diminished with each added year since resignation). Two-fifths of the resigned priests considered themselves active Catholics and attended Church weekly; another two-fifths identified themselves as Catholics who were not a part of the official Church; and one-fifth said they were no longer a part of the Church. Forty percent were interested in a return to the active ministry, but only 10 percent wished to do so on a full-time basis.

Greeley had a strong personal reaction to the question of resignation from the priesthood. He insisted, first of all, that the resignation process be modified to ease the burden on the man who wishes to leave. "I think former priests should be treated with dignity and respect, and that options ought to be open to them to serve the Church either as priests or as laymen." When a friend of *his* leaves the priesthood, Greeley feels a sense of abandonment, loss, and tragedy—for the man who leaves, for himself, for the priesthood, for the Church. Yet if a man's only option is to resign, then "as the Irish politicians would say, 'Do what you have to do.' "[22]

But why, for all that, do the media and "some liberal Catholic lay people" make folk heroes of priests who leave, and why do they do so to the detriment of those who stay? Greeley deeply resented the implication "that the best priests are leaving or that the normal and healthy males are leaving the priesthood . . . . I am particularly angered at those resigned priests who argue (as James Kavenaugh has) that it is only sexual immaturity that keeps us in the priesthood. If I am expected to respect the decision of a man to leave, then

I expect him and all his friends to respect the decision of the over-whelming majority of us who elect to stay."[23]

Further, the argument that one reforms an institution by leaving it is "politically absurd. The folk heroes of the present time ought not to be those who quit—however good their reasons for quitting—but those who stay to fight. In the words of John L. McKenzie, 'Why quit? Stay and bother them.' And in the words of Hans Küng, 'Why should I quit? Let the pope quit.' "[24]

Actually, Greeley argued, the concern shown for the problem of resignation is misdirected. Attention—more than that, serious re-search—is desperately needed at the other end of the manpower con-tinuum: *in 1972 there were only half the number of seminarians there had been five years earlier.* (Between 1965 and 1975 the num-ber dropped by nearly two-thirds.) Perhaps the most important, yet most overlooked, finding in the entire NORC report had to do with vocational recruiting. Sixty-four percent of America's priests in 1965 said that they actively encouraged boys to enter the seminary, but only 33 percent said they did so in 1970—a drop of over 30 percent. This decline in enthusiasm for recruiting, Greeley said, "could be the most chilling finding in our entire report."[25]

Like the majority of priests in the 1970 survey, Greeley has al-ways felt that celibacy should be a matter of personal choice for priests; yet, like the majority, he anticipates he would not marry were the choice his. He has always believed that women should have the same access to Holy Orders as men. "Why *not* ordain women?" he explains his position simply, noting in the same breath that the majority of American Catholic laity are opposed to the idea. But to him optional celibacy and the ordination of women are peripheral issues. He wrote in 1972, "If I were a bishop interested in preserving my power, I would cheerfully support birth control and marriage for the clergy, hoping that such concessions would take priests' minds off the fact that the Church is governed by a small, self-per-petuating power elite."[26]

To talk face-to-face with Andrew Greeley about the priesthood is to sense the disillusionment and the anger brought on by his dealings with the American hierarchy. One hears of seminaries that have become psychological machines, of priests' organizations that have become selfish. Of the NORC study he says, "I would never touch the project again, or anything like it, because I was caught between the militants in the priests' organizations on the one hand, rather hostile priests on the staff on the other, and the bishops on the third. The bishops figured if an objective professional study was done it would confirm what they thought was true. And then it turned out that it didn't. And so they concluded that we weren't objective after all."

Greeley's crisis was part of the larger collapse of American Catholicism—one, he insists, that was not inevitable. "The tragedy of the American Church, I would argue, is that it didn't have to be that way. There was a wealth of talent and dedication and organizational skill that got sold down the river, fundamentally by its leadership. If Cardinal Meyer had lived, it would have been a different story. If John Cody hadn't come to Chicago, it would have been a different story. If Paul VI hadn't been elected pope, it would have been a different story. If we had just a few more intellectuals, solidly trained intellectuals, who weren't trying to work out their family aggressions against the Church, against God, if there were a few more priests who could have stood for a model of priestly commitment when all the resignations were going on . . ."

His voice trailed off and he paused. "The collapse of American Catholicism was not something that was written in the cards. We were very unlucky."

Never once, though, did I hear Greeley's disillusionment affect in the slightest his feeling of commitment to the priestly life. In fact, in my very first interview with him—on a Friday evening in the summer of 1973—it took less than half an hour for him to offer, "My core identity is that of parish priest." He said it as if it were the one thing that could never be taken away from him. All the research, all the books, all his "achievements" were so much irrelevant excess created by some momentum outside himself. When we spoke the following morning about his career, I rattled off, at one point, a summary of the past several hours. We had covered the beginnings at the University of Chicago, had mentioned Ford, Rockefeller, the National Institute of Mental Health, and the National Science Foundation, had referred to Sheed and Ward, Doubleday, and the *New York Times*, had compared the reception of his work in Europe and in the United States, and had looked ahead to his then-planned move to Loyola University. We had discussed the politics of the priesthood study. I reminded him of his statement of the night before: "You still say you are just a parish priest?"

"Yes," he replied without hesitation.

"Sure," said Father Paul Asciolla, who was listening in on our conversation, "and Sam Ervin is just a country lawyer." His remark brought a grin from Greeley, but not a retraction.

Well, Sam Ervin *is* a country lawyer. He is more than that, to be sure, but the character of his roots was plainly evident to the millions of viewers watching an intricate Watergate investigation that same summer.

And Andrew Greeley *is* a parish priest. In his summer of 1973, when it appeared that he had been stripped of support from every conceivable side, when he was, in the words of his friend, "all alone," it was that identity which remained. It was that to which he returned, finding in it the meaning of *his* existence, *his* reason for being.

8   The White Ethnics

Amazement comes quickly to the face of Father Greeley when the
thought occurs that the 1961 NORC survey of college graduates—
his first involvement in survey research—did not contain a single
question concerning the ethnic identity of respondents. He was
astonished *then,* too, when he first saw the questionnaire, because
just outside the building where it was composed were clearly defined
ethnic turfs. Blacks surrounded the university; Lithuanians and
Poles lived in Marquette Park; Jews in South Shore; Irish in Englewood, South Shore, and farther out in Beverly Hills. Chinatown was
a short distance to the north. Yet the climate in the United States was
such that most social scientists thought ethnicity was no longer an
important feature of American social life—not the kind of thing,
surely, that one would bother about with a question in a national
survey.

Peter Rossi was one who thought otherwise. One of his first
questions to Greeley upon the latter's arrival at NORC was "What
are you?"

Greeley recounts the incident. "What do you mean? I'm a
Democrat."

"No, no. I didn't mean that. You're a Democrat, and a Catholic, and a priest. But like I'm Italian and Feldman's Jewish. What
are you?"

"Oh. I'm Irish."

"Oh, OK."

Greeley was surely Irish, but before his arrival at the university
he was not self-consciously Irish. He had always lived in Irish
Catholic environments—in St. Angela's parish, in the seminary, in
Christ the King—and consequently had never given much thought

to his own national background. But now it was different, and, like countless immigrants who took on national identities only after their arrival in the United States, "I became an Irish Catholic ethnic at the University of Chicago."

In 1962, thanks to the efforts of Greeley and Rossi, the second NORC survey of the June 1961 college graduates did contain an ethnic question, and Greeley used the results it yielded to demonstrate a slower acculturation process in the United States among Italians and Eastern Europeans than among Irish, Germans and British. During the ensuing years, too, Greeley fought to have a question on ethnic identity included in every NORC survey, but he was successful only half the time. By 1971, however, no one at NORC could ignore ethnicity, and no one, surely, had to ask Andrew Greeley about his ethnic background.

The reasons go back to 1969 and a meeting of Protestants, Catholics, and Jews in upstate New York to reflect on growing polarization in the United States. Asked to suggest speakers for the conference, which was sponsored by the Ford Foundation, Cardinal Terrence Cooke of New York happened to name Andrew Greeley. Greeley delivered a paper, and Mitchell Sviridoff, a Ford vice-president (and, in Greeley's words, "a precinct, neighborhood kind of guy who knew what I was talking about") happened to like it. Greeley goes on. "So one day they called me and they said, 'Hey, where's your proposal?' I said, 'What proposal?' And they said, 'To set up an ethnic center.' "

In the midst of bad times, the call was manna from heaven. Ford's interest in ethnicity "fit with my disillusionment with higher education and my profound disillusionment with being a social scientist for the Church. And I figured, and it turned out to be the case, that by studying ethnicity one could study American Catholic life and say the hell with the hierarchy." Greeley added later, "I can do nothing but speak praise for McGeorge Bundy, Mike Sviridoff, Basil Whiting, and the whole Ford bureaucracy. They have been very good to us. I'd hell of a lot sooner work for them than for John Krol."

With "megabucks" from Ford, then, the Center for the Study of American Pluralism—Andrew M. Greeley, Director—was launched as a unit within NORC in January 1971. Greeley's output on ethnicity accelerated sharply. First was an article for the *Antioch Review*—a few days to produce 10,000 words on request—that analyzed and championed "The Rediscovery of Diversity" in the United States. The article began where the secularization debate left off, with a discussion of the return of *Gemeinschaft* to overthrow rational, scientific, anonymous *Gesellschaft*. "Men were promised affluence and dignity if they yielded their old primordial ties. They now suspect that the promise was an empty one and are returning to those primordial ties with a vengeance."[1]

In 1971, America heard of pluralism once again because of blacks:

> The mainline American society may have endorsed pluralism in theory, but in fact its basic tendencies were always assimilationist. It has now, however, become official: it is all right for blacks to have their own heritage, their own tradition, their own culture. If it is all right for the blacks, then it ought to be all right for everyone else.[2]

For those who still thought ethnicity to be of little moment, Greeley assembled a grim collage. Men do not often become violent, he said, over rational differences in ideology—such as that between capitalism and socialism—but over primitive, tribal differences of "color, language, religious faith, height, food habits, and facial configuration." Millions may have died over purported ideological struggles in Korea and Vietnam, but many more—perhaps as many as twenty million—have died in conflicts having nothing to do with ideology:

> One need only think of the Hindus and Moslems at the time of the partition of India, of Sudanese blacks and Arabs, of Tutsi and Hutu in Burundi, of Kurds in Iraq, of Nagas in India, of Karens and Kachins in Burma, of Chinese in Indonesia and Malaysia, of Khambas in Tibet, of Somalis in Kenya and Ethiopia, of Arabs in Zanzibar, of Berbers in Morocco and Algeria, of East Indians and blacks in Guiana, of Ibos in Nigeria, and, more recently of Bengalis in East Pakistan to realize how pervasive is what might be broadly called "ethnic" conflict and how incredible the numbers of people who have died in such "irrational" battles. Two million died in India, five hundred thousand have perished in the "unknown war" in the Sudan, and two hundred thousand more in

the equally unknown war in Burundi. The numbers may have been over a million in Biafra and over a half million in Malaysia and Indonesia, and as high as one hundred thousand in Burma and Iraq.

The ethnic conflicts have not been so bloody in other parts of the world, but tens of thousands have died in the seemingly endless battle between those two very Semitic people, the Jews and the Arabs. The English and the French glare hostilely at each other in Quebec; Christian and Moslem have renewed their ancient conflicts on the island of Mindanao; Turk and Greek nervously grip their guns in Cyprus; and Celt and Saxon in Ulster have begun imprisoning and killing one another with all the cumulative passion of a thousand years' hostility.[3]

Ties of blood were strong, all right, demanding often that blood be shed. And perhaps such ties were deeper and more pervasive than the ties of urbanized *Gesellschaft* man. But was not the diversity they created a prelude to destruction—not at all something to be celebrated? Even if Cox overestimated the dispersal of *Gesellschaft* man, was he at least correct to take hope from his arrival? More bluntly, was not ethnic diversification evil?

One might think so until he considers the alternative— "rational, liberal, scientific, democratic homogenization"—which has failed all over the world and in fact set the stage for the resurgence of interest in tribe and clan. We simply have to face the fact that, like it or not, diversification is structured into human experience. As Noam Chomsky and Claude Levi-Strauss have suggested, "man has no other way to cope with the reality in which he finds himself, including the reality of his own relationship network, than by differentiating it. . . . Diversity may lead to hellish miseries in the world, but without the power to diversify—and to locate himself somewhere in the midst of the diversity—man may not be able to cope with the world at all."[4] Besides, there are many indications (even in grubby NORC data) that diversification leads just as often to integration—indeed, is an unavoidable precondition for integration.

America has waxed and waned on the subject of diversity, Greeley went on to say in the *Antioch Review*. Individuals are torn between pride and the sense of belonging they derive from their own ethnic groups and a feeling of resentment at being trapped by that group. "We praise the melting pot out of one side of our mouths and honor cultural pluralism out of the other."[5] It is precisely this ambivalence that explains the lack of serious research in the past quarter century on the topic of ethnicity. And what an oversight this was. Englishmen, Scotsmen, Welshmen, Irishmen, Germans, Italians, Poles, Africans, Indians (from both Asia and America), Frenchmen, Spaniards, Finns, Swedes, Lebanese, Danes, Armenians, Croations, Slovenians, Greeks, Luxembourgers, Chinese, Japanese, Filipinos, and Puerto Ricans come together and form a nation that not only survives, but works, and works reasonably well—only for years no one bothers to notice.

In *Why Can't They Be Like Us?* (1971) Greeley charged that the white ethnics in particular had been systematically ignored. Some Americans said that to speak of *differences* was destructive and immoral (though they "granted" blacks, Chicanos, and American Indians the right to their own ethnic consciousness). Others went further. *Harper's* magazine, for example, printed a cover with the stereotype of Stanley Kowalski slumping, half naked, over a bar in Gary, Indiana. It was prejudice that Greeley was talking about—and prejudice among the nation's elites. "The intellectual who 'loves' blacks and the 'poor' but has contempt for the Irish or the Italians or the 'middle class' is in the final analysis every bit as much a bigot as the blue-collar worker who 'hates niggers,' for both are asking, 'Why Can't They Be Like Us?' "[6]

So the enemy was not just a liberal elite within Catholicism but its corresponding coterie outside the Church. Intellectuals, said Greeley, constitute an ethnic group as parochial and full of hate as the white ethnics they love to parody. When he dropped that charge in the *New York Times Magazine* in the summer of 1970, he was not simply being facetious or striking an analogy. To be sure, the analogy was there. Like an ethnic group intellectuals had (1) presumed consciousness of kind, (2) territorial concentration (enclaves in New York, Washington, Boston, San Francisco, and Chicago's Hyde Park), (3) shared ideals and values, (4) strong moralistic fervor and a sense of persecution, (5) distrust of outsiders, and (6) a tendency to see themselves as the whole of reality. But Greeley's analogy was only a means to an end. Ultimately it herded a diffuse enemy together so as to make them a better target. *They*—the intellectuals—were absolutely convinced of the superiority of mind (which is to say, of their own superiority), felt that those who could articulate ideas ought to run society, and conjured up dark, sinister forces bent on the destruction of the programs of social reform they had devised (which is to say, bent on *their* destruction).[7]

The intellectual ethnic group was not paranoid, really, said Greeley. Their fears were simply the logical outcome of arrogant assumptions. They were moralistic, too, their moralism rooted in a Protestant Puritan or a Jewish messianic past and reinforced by the threat posed by the rest of society. And their behavior was full of contradictions. Theodore Roszak railed against the "technological establishment" and rhapsodized about a "nontechnological counterculture" in a book mass-produced by a very technological printing press and mass-marketed by a very establishment publishing house. And Noam Chomsky denounced American society as imperialistic and demoralized while continuing to pocket an income from an institution as much a part of the American establishment as any institution could be. Oh, they were compassionate, all right, the assault continued, but how sincere was compassion "for the poor and the black," "for drug addicts, terrorists, arsonists, rioters, Russians, Chinese, Arabs, and the Vietcong"[5] if it stopped short of the middle-class and working-class citizen, especially if he were white and over thirty? No, the white ethnic existed in the subconscious of the intelligentsia only as the hard-hat draped over the bar in Gary, Indiana—droll, quaint, boorish, and fascist. He did not even feel guilty when intellectuals thought he ought to feel guilty. Every ethnic group had a scapegoat; the white ethnic was that of the intelligentsia, and they had made him into an object worthy of condescension.

Well, what could one say about white ethnic groups— particularly from the inside? First, one could say that, to them, people like Rennie Davis, Irving Howe, Arthur Schlesinger, and Joseph Alsop were practically look-alikes. They had more in common with each other than with anyone else who was not a member of the intellectual ethnic group. And if that seemed astonishing to intellectuals, what did intellectuals know about the differences between the Polish National Alliance and the Polish Roman Catholic Union? More important than the white ethnics' lumping together—and distrusting—intellectuals was the basic fact of their existence: They were still very close to the immigrant experience and even now insecure about their acceptance. (In the 1960s half the adult Catholics in the country were either immigrants or the children of immigrants.) Scar tissue from the depression was still evident in their thinking. Well fed and well housed, they nevertheless resented the amount of their tax dollars (which were considerable) that was earmarked for welfare programs to subsidize other social groups. After all, they argued, no such subsidies ever were offered them. And they were afraid—afraid of violence, of higher taxes, of black militants and student protesters, of experts and professors, of liberal do-gooders and planners, of religious and moral corruption. They were profoundly committed to family, home, and neighborhood and feared that these were under attack, especially by black in-migration. For all their fears, however, ethnics were fundamentally hopeful. "The assumption prevalent among the elites that the ethnics are 'alienated' is not confirmed by the available data."[9]

Ethnics believed in the freedom and dignity of the individual person, were offended by social injustice, and carried a profound respect for America's tolerance of diversity.

> There is one last component that must be mentioned, and that may be offensive to some. The ethnics *like* the United States of America. The flag, the Star Spangled Banner, the Constitution, the Declaration of Independence, the Capitol, the office of the Presidency—all these are admired symbols which together sum up the gratitude the ethnic feels for what the United States has made possible for him: freedom, dignity, comfort, security—things which his ancestors in the countries from which they fled or were driven would not have dreamt possible. The ethnic is a patriot because he is grateful for what the United States has done for him. He is not, at least not anymore, a superpatriot. He was less likely than his fellow Americans to favor the Vietnam war, and his opposition to communism did not lead him to object to rapprochement with China or the Soviet Union. It was not an ethnic who said, "My country, right or wrong."[10]

Why, Greeley asked, don't we *listen* to the ethnics instead of dismissing their views as "racist" or "fascist"? As matters stand now, they are left out, isolated even from their own political leadership.

They need tax relief, alternatives in education, safe neighborhoods—why should law-and-order be a cry solely of the political
right? And they need to be *known,* known through the medium of
careful, systematic research. There was simply no demographic,
socioeconomic, or sociopsychological data on the later stages of the
acculturation process of American ethnic groups. "The ethnics are
not angels or saints, folk heroes or a new messianic people. They are
human beings like the rest of us, and they deserve to be understood
in their full complexity of good and bad, positive and negative, open
and closed just as much as anyone else."[11]

Greeley expressed all these feelings in a variety of circumstances. Asked by the American Jewish Committee in 1969 to present a paper at Fordham University, he responded with the few data
he had. His talk appeared as a small volume, *Why Can't They Be
Like Us?,* which Greeley later substantially enlarged for publication
by E. P. Dutton and Company in 1971. In the fall of 1970, just after
his piece in the *New York Times Magazine,* the higher education
journal *Change* published "Malice in Wonderland: Misperceptions
of the Academic Elite," another attack on myopic academics and
intellectuals bent on remaking the rest of the world (whether it
wanted to be remade or not), unaware of what motivated the human
beings who were to be the objects of their missionary zeal.[12] Renascent interest in the neighborhood was acknowledged in "The Urban
Church," a chapter in Daniel Patrick Moynihan's *Urban America*
(1970). And a speech at Southeastern Baptist Seminary on the
ethnic's "civil religion" was later published in the February 1973
edition of *Worldview.*

All the while Greeley's Center staff was sifting existing data for
whatever they contained in the way of ethnic information. The 1963
survey of adult American Catholics (published as *The Education of
Catholic Americans*), for example, contained an ethnic question,
and there were enough subjects in five of the response categories—
Irish, German, Italian, Polish, and French—to allow analysis. A
dozen dependent variables were chosen, and one of Greeley's first
inventories of ethnic traits was begun. It showed that the Irish, first
of the five groups to arrive in America, were the most successful of
the Catholic immigrant groups (and the most similar to Jews) in
terms of amount of education, income, and job prestige. They also

were the most pious (but the least given to religious extremism), the happiest (or at least they said they were), the most open-minded, the least racist, and the least anti-Semitic.

German Catholics were almost as successful as Irish Catholics in occupational status, only slightly less devout (and slightly more given to religious extremism), somewhat less happy, and somewhat less open-minded. Italians and Poles, more recent Catholic immigrants, were not nearly as well off educationally, occupationally, or financially as the Irish and Germans. They scored lower than these groups on happiness and open-mindedness and higher on racism. Italians were the least pious of the five groups, the most likely to live in the same neighborhood as their parents, the least likely to belong to the Democratic party. Poles were nearly as devout as the Irish and had the highest percentage of Democrats in their midst. The French—which meant, for the most part, French-Canadians in New England—were distinguished by low scores on the index of piety and high scores on religious extremism and anti-Semitism. Based on their self-reports, the French were also among the happier of the immigrant groups.

Then there was the class of 1961, interviewed for the fifth time in 1968. They provided more recent data on ethnicity, data not limited to Catholic groups, and data containing a built-in control for level of education. Would ethnic differences be apparent among young Americans "melted down" seven years before by the common experience of a college education? The answer was yes. While college education did have a leveling effect—softening Polish attitudes toward blacks, for example—differences of 20 and 30 percentage points between ethnic groups were not uncommon on many measures of attitude and behavior. To name one: 84 percent of the blacks in the class of 1961 agreed in 1968 with the Kerner Commission that "white racism is the cause of Negro riots in the city." Among white groups, 54 percent of the German Jews and 51 percent of the Irish Catholics agreed—but only 34 percent of the German Catholics and 28 percent of the Irish and German Protestants did likewise.

More comprehensive than these initial sketches was "Making it in America: Ethnic Groups and Social Status," published in the September–October 1973 issue of *Social Policy*. How were the various religious-ethnic groups dispersed in the structure of American society? What were their typical occupations and levels of education and income? U.S. Census materials and data from *Current Population Surveys* were solid on black and Spanish-speaking groups, but they were of little use in estimating the demographic distribution of other religious-ethnic groups, simply because census-takers were not allowed to ask questions about religion—and, for some, religion was an essential part of ethnic self-definition. The best source of demographic and socioeconomic information was a composite of seven surveys done by NORC between 1963 and 1972 and a composite of 20 undertaken by the University of Michigan's Survey Research Center in the 1950s and 1960s. Even these data had to be described as "shaky" and the conclusions drawn from them "tentative and speculative" because subsamples of some groups, even in a survey of ten to fifteen thousand respondents, were quite small. Nevertheless, data that allowed comparisons did check out against *Current Population Surveys,* and they left certain overriding impressions. "American society had bestowed economic, occupational, and educational success on its Jewish, British-Protestant, and Irish-Catholic populations. German and Scandinavian groups have done moderately well. The southern and eastern European Catholic groups have done less well, and the Blacks and the Spanish-speaking, quite badly." The relative positions of Irish Protestants and "Other" Protestants—groups that had been in America from the beginning, but ones that lacked a self-conscious ethnic identity—had declined over the past two decades. "Precisely because they do not identify themselves as a group and are not so identified by others, their deteriorating position is not obvious to the rest of society and perhaps not even obvious to many of them."[13]

Through all the analyses one impression became clear. When viewed from the perspective of ethnic and religious background, America was alive with diversity. Americans had not washed together into a dull grey but remained a patchwork of color. "Even when social class is held constant there are differences among ethnic groups in personal orientations, occupational values, expectations toward spouse and children, and quantity and quality of intimacy in family relationships."[14] Ethnicity *was* predictive of differences. And as for the conflict this country was experiencing, it seemed to fall into intelligible patterns when one did not shy away from mini-categories such as German Jew, Polish Catholic, Italian Catholic, English Protestant, first-arrival, second-arrival, and so on.

Journals as diverse as the *Public Opinion Quarterly, Dissent, Scientific American, Sociology of Education,* the *New Republic, Worldview, Social Studies: Irish Journal of Sociology, Eire— Ireland,* and *International Migration Review,* as well as Lee Rainwater's book *Social Problems and Public Policy,* passed these findings on to the public. *Ethnicity in the United States: A Preliminary Reconnaissance* (1974), a volume authored by Greeley and published by Wiley-Interscience, brought much of the data together and contained a statement of the theoretical outlook guiding the Center's research.

The theory began with a definition of "ethnic group," one Greeley borrowed from Richard Schermerhorn: "a collectivity within a larger society having real or putative common ancestry, memories of a shared historical past, and a cultural focus on one or more symbolic elements defined as the epitome of their peoplehood."[15] The critical observation, Greeley said, is one that Nathan Glazer made in 1954. When immigrants come to a new country, said Glazer, they do not already constitute a group or a community; rather, ethnic groups *come into existence* after immigrants arrive in a new land. When Eastern European peoples, speaking the various dialects of their villages, came together in the cities of America, they had to create a common language—and so the first newspaper in the Lithuanian language was published, not in Lithuania, but in America. Similarly, noted Glazer, the Erse revival began in Boston, and the nation of Czechoslovakia was launched at a meeting in Pittsburgh.

And recently, Greeley added, we have witnessed attempts as deliberate and self-conscious as these earlier ones to create ethnic groups. The black power movement may be seen in this light, as can the emergence of American Indian groups. Spanish-speaking persons are attempting to create an ethnic group in the Northeast, as are Appalachian whites in Chicago. Ethnic symbols, too, change in a fashion that the acculturation model of ethnicity can in no way accommodate. "One of our colleagues observed that when she was growing up in Florida she thought of herself as an American; when she went to Washington, D.C., she discovered that she was Cuban;

and when she came to Chicago, she was told that she was 'Spanish-speaking.' " The tricolor bumper stickers now proudly displayed on the cars of Americans from southern Italy and Sicily were once, in Italy, the hated symbol of the "foreign" domination of the Piedmontese. "The Sicilians came to the United States and discovered that they were Italian-Americans. Now they have discovered that they are Italian, a process exactly the reverse of that suggested by using only the acculturation picture."[16]

Something, then, about the nature of American society (or any society) brings about a need for *ethnogenesis,* the creation of an ethnic identity, among immigrants—even second, third, and fourth generation immigrants. Greeley's perspective had two major consequences. First, the American experience—not the European—came to be seen as the principal contributor to an immigrant culture. "America's ethnic groups," Greeley wrote, "are rooted only very partially in the European preimmigrant experience, and have been shaped to a very great extent, however differentially for different groups, by the American experience."[17] As a result, American Italians are very different from Italian Italians, American Irish from Irish Irish, American Poles from Polish Poles, and so on.

Second, if it is *America* that is the source of the creation and manipulation of ethnic symbols, then ethnic differentiation can be expected to continue—albeit alongside ethnic homogenization—as long as America continues. We are not headed for a melting pot, as the very powerful assimilationist mythology would have us believe. Yes, American Italians will continue to be different from Italian Italians, but this does not mean that they will become indistinguishable from American Poles or American Irishmen. Put another way, "The Kennedy administration was, one supposes, quite different from the administration of Prime Minister Sean Lynch in Dublin, but it was also very different from a WASP administration in this country, or the kind of administration we will have when finally Americans get around to electing a Jewish president."[18]

New models invariably produce new questions, and in the case of the ethnogenesis paradigm, the basic question became *why?* Why did ethnic collectivities come into being, and why, after that, were they transformed and transmuted? Greeley's answer: because the benefits of ethnogenesis outweighed the costs. Soon after their arrival in the United States, immigrants discovered that they had already been placed by the rest of society in a category based on their national origin. They also found that to succeed at the American political game one had to be part of a collectivity—why not their national collectivity? The raising of ethnic consciousness provided a number of advantages:

> The ethnic group became one of the avenues to political power for immigrants. It provided a special market in which the emerging business and professional class within the immigrant community could build its own economic base. It offered a social mobility pyramid which the more ambitious immigrants could ascend; and if the social pyramid of the host culture was inaccessible, they could at least move to the social apex within their own collectivity. And psychologically, it provided continuity between the Old World and the New and made possible the preservation of a minimum of family values that were thought to be essential.[19]

Ethnic identity was a way of stepping *into* American society, not a symptom of withdrawal from it. It was "a way for the immigrant population to look at its present and future in America rather than its past in the Old World." Polish-Americans and Czech-Americans supported nationalist movements in their own countries only *after* the United States entered World War I—a sign that their support was more an exercise in American patriotism than in Polish or Czech nationalism. And the nineteenth- and early twentieth-century Irish-Americans who favored freedom for Ireland argued that only when Ireland was a free and independent nation would Irish-Americans be accepted by native Americans as full-fledged citizens. "The hyphen in the hyphenate American was a symbol of equality, not of inequality. In an urban environment where virtually everyone—including the native American—was something else besides 'American,' one had to be an ethnic to find one's place on the map."[20]

As part of the process of ethnogenesis, personality traits were selectively reinforced as being part of one's ethnic identity, and they were therefore transmitted from one generation to the next—provided the trait proved useful:

> Did hard work and intellectual ambition prove extremely helpful in American society? Such work and ambition could be reinforced by telling children that it was an especially Jewish trait, and to be good Jews they must develop it. Did a certain kind of informal

political skill open up avenues to power and prestige? Then such
political skills could be legitimated and reinforced on the grounds
that they were Irish.[21]

Immigrants stood to gain enormously, then, from the officially
sanctioned structure of differentiation in America. There were costs,
to be sure. Jews were excluded from certain clubs and buildings and
companies, and there were similar, if more subtle, biases against
Catholics, especially those from southern and eastern Europe. And
differentiation did lead to conflict, but somehow the conflict rarely
became violent. "The immigrants never saw their claim to be
hyphenated Americans as involving any danger of tearing apart the
new society, which on the whole was relatively benign to them."[22]
By and large—if you were white—creating and maintaining an
ethnic identity provided benefits that far outweighed the costs.

Furthermore, it was required by the political and social structure in America that membership in an ethnic collectivity be
optional. One was an ethnic in America only if he wanted to be—
there was no coercion. And ethnic boundaries were permeable,
especially if one were making a good deal of money. Thus, ethnic
identification became a "limited liability"; one could call upon it
when it was useful and dispose of it when it became a burden. All of
this, at least, was the way it was *supposed* to be. It was not the way it
was for blacks (Greeley admitted that his theory "becomes a
dilemma on the subject of non-white groups"[23]), and it certainly was
not always true for whites. But the structure of permeability was at
least officially sanctioned, and that is why ethnic differentiation in
the United States has been, on the whole, rather successful. The
interesting question, of course—and one that research had yet to
answer—was: Who used an ethnic map of the world, and when, and
to what advantage? And who still does?

The emerging perspective of Greeley's Center, then, conceived
as an extension of the many forms of assimilation and acculturation theory, was on the origin and natural history of ethnic
groups—groups that were formed from amorphous collections of
European immigrants. In *Ethnicity in the United States* Greeley
listed the questions raised by such a perspective. What was the interplay between ethnic *origin* (one's actual ancestry), ethnic *identification* (whether or not—and where—one placed oneself on an ethnic

chart), ethnic *heritage* (the conscious recollection one had of his ethnic history), and ethnic *culture* (attitudes, personality styles, and behaviors associated with particular ethnic groups)? For example, the American Irish (that denotes ethnic origin) apparently had a rather weak ethnic identification and almost no consciousness of an ethnic heritage but displayed a good deal of distinctively ethnic culture—overchoosing law as a profession, for example. What of other groups? And what happened to one's ethnic identification when one's ethnic origins were mixed? Did he *choose* an identification, as one of Greeley's colleagues did between his French, Dutch, Scotch, Irish, and Sioux Indian ancestry? (He chose—what else?—to be Irish.) And did the choice affect behavior—making Greeley's colleague more politically active, for example, because it was the Irish thing to do? Finally was it true (and Greeley thought it was) that the most durable part of an ethnic culture was the expectations one had of the behavior of intimate others, of brothers and sisters, of spouses, of children, of parents?

In January 1973 the Ford Foundation extended for two and one-half years its support of the Center for the Study of American Pluralism, and it has continued its sponsorship down to the present. During the Center's life, the Henry Luce Foundation, the National Institute of Mental Health, the Markle Foundation, the Twentieth Century Fund, the National Institutes for Alcohol Abuse and Alcoholism, and the National Endowment for the Humanities have financed projects on the political socialization of children, the transmission of religious and achievement values across generational lines, the political activities of ethnic women and their attitudes toward feminism, the activities of ethnic journalists, the political participation of ethnics, and the correlation between ethnicity and drinking behavior. Sage Press published a series of monographs on religion and ethnicity, and in April 1974 Academic Press initiated an interdisciplinary quarterly entitled *Ethnicity* and edited by Greeley.

In one of his reports to the Ford Foundation, Greeley noted an improving climate for research on ethnicity. "It is now moving toward the top of the list of priorities of many Idea Merchants and Idea Consumers," he wrote.[24] So fashionable had the idea become, in fact, that in 1974 Greeley tried to put together a consortium of grants totaling five or six million dollars for a mammoth investigation of the country's diversity on the occasion of its bicentennial. Greeley's "megastudy" would have used instruments powerful enough to bring into focus smaller groups that appeared only as blurs in the typical national sample—Serbs, Slovaks, Greeks, Armenians, Orientals, Czechs, even Sephardic Jews, Kalmulks, Crimean Tartars, and Russian Germans. The project met the approval of Ford's trustees, but it was killed when the foundation suffered severe setbacks in the stock market.

Though he lost his megastudy, Greeley was at least able to use data from NORC's 1974 survey of American Catholics to update the social and economic position of Catholic immigrant groups. In *Ethnicity, Denomination, Inequality* (1976) and *The American Catholic: A Social Portrait* (1977), he published results that astonished even him. Though Catholic ethnics *felt* insecure economically (immigration and the depression were still that close), they were nevertheless making a great deal of money. By the mid-seventies Irish Catholics had progressed to the point where they were the richest and best educated white gentile group in the country. At the same time, German Catholics (early immigrants like the Irish) stood at the national average in educational attainment but far above it in family income. Southern and Eastern European Catholics, objects of bigoted immigration laws a half century before, were climbing beyond anyone's expectations. Italians and Poles far surpassed the national norm financially and were rising rapidly in their level of education (though they were still below average); Slavs had passed the norm financially but remained below it educationally. French Catholics, low in educational attainment, were only a bit above average in income. On the whole, Catholic ethnic groups (not counting the Spanish-speaking) were dead center educationally and dead center in occupational prestige. But they were second only to Jews—and moving faster than Jews—in the amount of money they made.

There was an interesting pattern in these, the most recent of the Center's data. Save for the Irish, Catholic ethnics had jobs that were financially rewarding but not prestigious. Either income was more important than prestige to those with the immigrant memory or—Greeley was becoming adamant about this—there was discrimination that excluded Catholics from the upper levels of professional and corporate success.

In the midst of it all there was time for fun, for a whole volume of honesty-compels-me-to-say's (when you hear that phrase, duck) directed at the American Irish. Parts of *That Most Distressful Nation: The Taming of the American Irish* (1972) had previously amused, perplexed, and irritated readers of the *New York Times Mazazine* (St. Patrick's Day week, 1971), the *Critic,* the *New Republic,* and *Dissent.* The book itself was a compendium of Andrew Greeley in all his personal pluralism—opinion, conjecture, advice, NORC data, secondary source history and anthropology, poetry (by Nancy McCready), autobiography. It covered safe, noncontroversial topics like religion, sex, politics, race, alcohol, and raising children. Parts were lucid and witty; parts were disjointed and hard to follow. There was haste and repetition (Greeley must have relished an anecdote about an Irish monk proving his virtue by sleeping between two maidens with pointed breasts—he told it twice within twenty-five pages). But it was all there—that is, *he* was all there, every part of him, "stubborn, perverse, wrongheaded, and paradoxical"[25]; and he spoke not from the computer terminal but from the pub.

The theme of *That Most Distressful Nation* was captured by Daniel Patrick Moynihan's opener in the foreword: "Would it be fair to say of American Irish history, as Oscar Wilde said of Niagara Falls, that it would be more impressive if it flowed the other way?" The past was one of heroic struggle—sheer stubbornness, at least— in the face of unspeakable oppression. Greeley's people endured "the most savage, the most repressive legislation that the modern world has ever seen." The penal laws reached their peak in the early 1700s. All priests in Ireland were required by the British to register their names, and those who failed to do so were to be castrated; bishops were banished under penalty of being hanged, drawn, and quartered; Catholics were forbidden to marry Protestants, with death the penalty for any priest performing such a marriage; Catholics were excluded from the legal profession; they could not acquire land from Protestants, own a horse worth more than five pounds, manufacture or sell books or newspapers, or grant mortgages; Catholic orphans were to be brought up as Protestants; their homes, in the words of an observer of the times, were "the most miserable hovels that can well be conceived."[26]

Add to that the horror, a century later, of the potato famine, "one of the great disasters of modern Western Europe," in which 1 to 1.5 million Irish Catholics died in the space of three years, "while the British Government barely lifted a finger to save them." Indeed, the head of the British Treasury saw the famine as the solution of an "all-wise Providence" to the Irish problem of overpopulation, and the London *Times* rejoiced that the Irishman would soon be "as rare on the banks of the Liffey as a red man on the banks of Manhattan."[27]

The only escape was emigration, much of it to the New World. They came, abysmally poor, unskilled, on "coffin ships" like the *Elizabeth and Sarah*. It completed the crossing in eight weeks; 42 of the original 276 passengers died en route. Similarly, the *Agnes* arrived near Detroit with 427 passengers, but only 150 remained after the fifteen-day quarantine. Of 100,000 emigrants who left for Canada, 17,000 died on the way and another 50,000 upon arrival. "Was England guilty of genocide in the 1840s?" Greeley asked. Not the way Adolf Hitler was, he said, but at least those who lived through Hitler's extermination camps "were hailed as heroes and encouraged by a world that acknowledged the inhumanity of what had happened to them."[28] No such solace met the Irish survivors who came to this country unwelcome, unwanted, and despised.

Through it all they never caved in. From the time of the Celts to the Easter Rising of 1916, the Irish never stopped rebelling. They paid for the millenium of revolt, strife, and depression with the emptiness of their cultural, scientific, and intellectual development; but the wonder was not that they failed to produce an impressive intellectual community, but that they were able to produce anything at all. A political style emerged to insure their survival. It was not unlike the *modus operandi* of the Chicago Irish politician. "Personal loyalty, informal arrangements, tight family structures, ridicule, boycott, and great love of legal learning combined frequently with little concern for the enforcement of the letter of the law, a fondness for legal contention and argument, suspicion of formal governmental regulations, indirect and circuitous ways of accomplishing one's purposes."[29]

And the Celtic poets developed characteristics not unlike those of Andrew Greeley. They were proud, sensitive, religious, bitter, and witty men; their comics were savage—no fate was worse than being a victim of the poets. "The poets loved to play with words, to deliver neat and witty epigrams, to engage in wild flights of fantasy; but they were testy, easily angered men, and when they turned their fury on you, you were in great trouble indeed."[30]

When it came to the Irish family, there were few positive things that Greeley could say about it. Drawing on the anthropological literature that existed, adding hearsay and impression, Greeley concluded that the Irish were cold, repressed, inflexible, and incapable of intimacy or tenderness. A County Mayo psychiatrist named David Dunne described the problems of his patients: "greed, envy, bitterness, frustration, sexual and otherwise, guilt, hatred, anger, a general feeling of a lack of love, often associated with a fear of love, a fear of loss, indeed a very high expectancy of and apparent resignation to loss, with consequent fear and avoidance of tenderness and intimacy." Added Greeley, "I had the uncanny feeling in reading Dunne's article that he knew my family all too well."[31]

In the countryside of Ireland the father was the unquestioned ruler of the house, but his power waned in the city; and the mother's role, already of great importance, became all powerful. In the United States Irish mothers tended to be like their counterparts in the cities of Ireland. There were even subspecies of the Irish matriarch. The Woman of Property bought and sold two-flats, moving her family from one to the next if it appeared she could clear $1,000 in the deal. Her husband was not very ambitious (which was probably why she married him), and her family looked happy (though the Irish were remarkable at concealing pain). The more common Pious Woman was usually in bad health but nevertheless worked tirelessly for her husband and children, engaged in a multitude of religious devotions, and was frequently heard to utter "I really can't complain" (though in fact she complained as much as she prayed.) Her children were devoted to her and to her Church, and many of them received "vocations" to the religious life. The Respectable Woman, by far the most common of the matriarchs, was the one who produced most of the hardworking, achievement-oriented American Irish. Her entire life, and necessarily that of her family, was governed by the simple question, "What will people say?" Her children went to college, got married, and became professionals—so they could tell themselves people were saying nice things about them.

Sex in Ireland was never discussed in the home. Girls were rarely given advice at all ("after marriage nature would take its course"), and boys learned what they had to learn from older boys and men and from watching animals. It was hard to say what sex in marriage was like, because so few would talk about it. It appeared, nevertheless, that the husband usually initiated sexual activity, employed the male superior position (without removing his or his wife's underclothing), achieved orgasm rapidly, and then fell asleep. The woman was assumed to be uninterested in sexual pleasure. Nudity was abhorred as something sexual (as was physiological evacuation), and sex itself was considered dangerous, a cause of insanity.

What about Irish sex in America? Save for the fact that children were conceived, there wasn't any. The Irish male was awkward, tongue-tied, clumsy, and rough in his attempts at intimacy. His wife's most positive contribution was to "do her duty" and never refuse her husband.

But things were changing—or were they? Actually very few data existed to substantiate or prove Greeley's "hunches, impressions, and stereotypes" of the American Irish. Indeed, survey data on Irish-American males only added to the confusion. Irish males were, in Chesterton's phrase, "the men that God made mad"; their psyches showed more contradictions than appeared in any other ethnic groups studied. Were the Irish inner-directed? Very much so—but also very outer-directed. Fatalistic? To be sure—but also very trusting. Was their heritage one of rigid, inflexible, harsh, cold family relationships? It seemed so—but in the 1960s Irish males provided their children with more physical affection than any other white ethnic group. One had to throw his hands up at the data and wait for more to come in.

There was ample data, however, to show that the Irish made it big in America. The descendants of those Celtic heroes hit it just right—the economy was expanding rapidly when they arrived, and they were a large pool of laborers who knew the language—and now, even though their progress had been slowed by the Great Depression, they were second only to Jews in economic prosperity. One hundred and ten years after the potato famine John Kennedy was president of the United States—and the immigrant era was over. Yes, the Irish were successful, but at what price? Suburban Irish communities were "terribly insecure and threatened places." And the past, save for "the creature" and memories of the crash in 1929, was lost.

Indeed, Irish propensity for drink—for "the creature"—said it all. In Ireland, 11 percent of personal income in a recent year was spent on alcohol, and the American Irish were just as addicted to drinking as their European counterparts. In the 1940s the Irish rate of admission to New York hospitals for alcoholism was three times that of any other ethnic group, and NORC data collected in the middle sixties testified that the American Irish were still number one in their fondness for "the jar." Part of the Irish heritage survived— regrettably—after all. " 'The Creature' is at first a help in the struggle for success, then an excuse for not making it, and finally a solace for failure."[32]

As for the next generation, they were Studs Lonigan all over again—a different veneer, maybe, but the same self-loathing, the same capacity for self-destruction:

> Dubious about his masculinity, harassed by his mother, nagged by his sisters, lacking a confident father to imitate, and paralyzed by guilt, Studs was already bent on self-destruction when he graduated from St. Anselm's in 1916. His deep prejudices against "smokes" and "kikes," his noisy bravado, his violence with women, and, above all, his passion for John Barleycorn all served to protect a small and insecure sense of self. Studs Lonigan loathed himself, and his whole life was a systematic effort to punish himself for his own worthlessness. . . .

> None of this has changed. The site has moved from Fifty-eighth and Indiana to Beverly, but the self-loathing and self-destruction continues. South Side Irish—a marvelously gifted and creative

people—have been bent on destroying themselves for three-quarters of a century. It looks as though they are beginning to succeed.[33]

And yet, there were some—one, at least—who had broken through, who were no longer tentative in the face of life, who had the nerve to put their despair, their hope (their Irish selves) on paper. Greeley concluded with poetry written by Nancy McCready for a toddler named Liam:

> *I shall not give to you, my son, a heritage of*
> *   splintered dreams*
> *that slushed down the sink with stale beer and*
> *   squeezed out tears of pain*
> *for all the years that might have been if I had*
> *   lived*
> *instead of killing dead my heart and ours, bit by*
> *   bit,*
> *with breaking rage and chunks of sorrow,*
> *passion which guilt turned sour and then, misunderstanding*
> *took my soul and crashed it in the night.*
> *I shall not go desperate dying into life.*
> *The enemy that dare to take the sea's surge from our eyes*
> *I shall defy and drag to hell and back and shake the*
> *   skull of suicide*
> *which says the gift will be ungiven and the hope denied.*
> *No, for we shall sing, my son, and eat the sweets of*
> *   victory.*
> *Lie peaceful down your head*
> *This hunger will not be quieted, nor ever fully fed*
> *Not before we hold the stars and until then,*
> *we'll go a'brawling and wooing life*
> *There're fights to be fought and battles won*
> *But never in the name of life direct our own undoing*
> *Nor allow while we breathe that Life should be undone!*[34]

When I first approached Father Greeley about writing this book in March 1973, he was in the midst of an intense struggle at the University of Chicago, fighting with every political instinct he possessed for a tenured position in its School of Social Service Administration. It was the eighth time he was being considered for full faculty status in one of the schools or departments of the university—all of them distinct from NORC. As he saw it then, his chances for a favorable decision were "about 50.1 to 49.9." In view of his secure position at NORC, I wondered what was the attraction of the university itself. "Why do you want in?" I asked.

He said he was tired of living by his wits—meaning, I took it, that he was tired of the demands of hustling grants to keep his Center afloat, even though he was very successful at grantsmanship. A joint appointment with tenure would relieve some of the financial drain on his NORC projects. But his *first* reaction to my question was less calculating. It was sheer instinct. "Because they want me out."

"Why do they want you out?"

He reached immediately into a desk drawer, pulled out a Roman collar, and held it up.

A short time later, despite a recommendation for his appointment from Social Service Administration, Greeley was once again turned down by the University of Chicago.

According to Andrew Segal and Don Rose of the *Hyde Park-Kenwood Voices,* several members of the Department of Sociology had not only vetoed Greeley's appointment in their own department but had also, through the years, blocked proposals for his tenure at other schools and departments in the university—and had even intervened to smother a recent offer from Northwestern University's Center for Urban Affairs. Despite a list of scholarly publications as long as, if not longer than, that of any tenured member in the department, despite the respect with which his skills were regarded by funding agencies (wrote Segal and Rose), Greeley's opposition, led by Edward Shils and Morris Janowitz, considered him "undistinguished" and "lacking in depth."[35] Some even questioned his ethnic studies as a rationalization for racial hostilities. Supporters of Greeley attributed his rejection to the traditional friction between survey researchers and academic sociologists, to NORC's marginality vis-a-vis the university proper, to Greeley's propensity for stepping on toes, to jealousy—and to sheer anticlerical prejudice. He was a victim of exposure, said others; he had published too much; he had said too many things too loudly. Greeley later opined that some of his trouble stemmed from his article on intellectuals in the *New York Times Magazine.* But he remained convinced that the basic reason for eight successive rejections by the university was his Irish Catholic priesthood. Peter Rossi, who had tried to secure an appointment in sociology for Greeley when he first came to NORC, agreed. "Everyone will admit anticlericalism is going on," said Rossi, "but nobody wants to go on the record. One high-ranking member of the Sociology Department told me years ago, 'I am opposed to the appointment of a Catholic priest just as I would be opposed to a Communist; both are so in the thralls of their party lines that they couldn't be objective.' "[36]

A year after the incident a bitter Greeley told me of a conversation with Rossi. "I remember saying to Pete Rossi a year or two ago, 'Pete, you know all these guys that now hate my guts were friendly when I came.' And I said, 'How come?' And he said, 'Well, they thought you were going to be a convert.' And I said, 'You mean leave the priesthood and the Church?' He said, 'Well, maybe that. They would have liked to have had that, but even short of that, they thought you'd start seeing the world through their viewpoint; and what they discovered is that you didn't and wouldn't, that you'd insist on being your own obnoxious Irish self.' "

Nothing will erase the scars of Greeley's dealings with the university. Though he did not come to Chicago seeking an academic career, though he has never needed the financial security that tenure brings, his anger was aroused in 1967 when the unanimous recommendation of the Department of Education for his appointment as professor was killed at upper levels of the university's administration. Wrote Greeley to the *Hyde Park-Kenwood Voices:*

> It was only after that appointment was denied me—after five months of being assured that there would be no problem—that I began to want what had been offered and then snatched away. Similarly, I had settled down once again to the NORC role two and a half years ago when the new dean, Robert Adams, summoned me to his office, read a memo from his secret file (which he implied Mr. Shils had written) calling me a stereotypical New Leftist, told me an injustice had been done, and that he would see that the wrong was righted.[37]

The wrong was never righted, and now, having battled the forces across the Midway for the last time, a pervasive motivation of Greeley's is "showing those S.O.B.'s, getting even with them." An offer from a prestigious university would show them (though Greeley would probably refuse it—as he did one from Duke University—because he "belongs" in Chicago). The largest grant ever conferred to a sociologist would surely show them. (Greeley was after it when he proposed his bicentennial megastudy to the Ford Foundation.) Greeley's voice toughens as he reflects on the entire affair. "I have learned about evil—implacable enemies who make me an inkblot, friends you cannot count on."

Because NORC did not give him the support he felt he deserved in the crisis, because, too, he had been passed over for the NORC directorship in 1971 (Greeley attributes this to anticlericalism on the part of NORC trustees and university officials), Greeley prepared in the spring of 1973 to pull up stakes and move his Center for the Study of American Pluralism to Loyola University. In July, Richard Matre, vice-president and dean of the faculties at Loyola, announced that Father Greeley would become a professor there and that Greeley's Center would be housed on Loyola's Lewis Towers campus. But in the middle of August a letter reached Greeley at Grand Beach indicating that Loyola could not implement the agreement they had negotiated—Greeley's research efforts would have to take a back seat to his teaching duties. Greeley went out to water ski, returned, and then called NORC director Jim Davis. "Jim, I think I know where I can sell you a full-fledged research program, if you're interested in buying."

Davis was very interested. "I can't criticize someone for changing his mind," he told Greeley. By 3:30 that same day Greeley had driven to Chicago and was in Davis's office proposing a deal. The two came to terms quickly. Greeley would get a ten-year contract at the same salary offered by Duke University, promotions and raises for his colleagues, and an agreement to take two months of his salary from NORC overhead rather than from his projects. Greeley walked down to Bill McCready's office and said, "Bill, unpack. We're staying."

The wounds from NORC's lack of support healed quickly (Greeley has never considered NORC part of the "university"). But not so Greeley's outrage at the University of Chicago. Of late, he has been quick to cry prejudice—against Catholics, against priests, against the Irish—wherever he sees it. In February 1973, *School*

Review published his charge that state aid was not going to Catholic schools—the only system capable of breaking up the soft, inept monopoly that is public education—because of powerful elements of anti-Catholic nativism. In March, on the occasion of another demonstration in the *American Journal of Sociology* that Catholic intellectuals from the class of 1961 were on schedule in the development of their academic careers, he proposed a study of anti-Catholic feelings at elite schools, pointing out that social scientists argue (as some did at a conference in 1971) "that the Catholic absence from academia in the past was the result of intellectual inferiority but that the absence of women and blacks was a result of discrimination."[38] A year later he charged in the *Critic* that "the sign 'No Irish Need Apply' . . . still hangs at the entrance to most intellectual literary circles and at the backs of most senior chairs in the country's major universities."[39] He said more in *The Communal Catholic* (1976) and *An Ugly Little Secret* (1977):

> ITEM: The stereotypical white ethnic—meaning racist, hard hat, ignorant, hawk, slob—is a euphemism for Catholic. You can denounce white ethnics and still feel virtuous that you are not anti-Catholic, even though all white ethnics seem to be Catholic. And of course you need not be deterred by the data that show that ethnic Catholics are less likely to be racist and more likely to have been against the Vietnam war from the beginning. . . . Catholics are conservative and that is that . . .

> ITEM: The Institute of Urban Life in Chicago finds that Poles and Italians are almost totally absent from the boards of large corporations. The various keepers of the nation's conscience, like the National Council of Churches, would have worked themselves into paroxysms of guilt if the finding concerned blacks; yet they remained completely silent . . .

> ITEM: The anti-abortion issue, led by four pathetic cardinals presenting their views before Congress, is described as a Catholic ploy to impose its moral views on Society. . . . Actually, . . . while the overwhelming majority of Catholics and Protestants support abortion if the mother's life is in danger or if there is risk of delivering a defective child, the majority of both groups are against abortion if the woman simply does not want any more children. Thus, by opposing abortion on demand, the Catholic hierarchy is speaking for the conscience of the majority—however crude and inept it may be as a spokesman. Don't hold your breath to read that in *The New York Times.*

ITEM: A Jewish leader chided me because Catholics were not vigorous enough in their support of Israel. It was not, he told me, high enough on our agenda. I asked him how high Ulster was on his. He told me that was different. How different? Well, the killing in Ulster was senseless violence, and the Irish had never been victims of genocide. I asked him if he had ever heard of Cromwell, and he asked me what that had to do with it.[40]

He was angry in the aftermath of his final defeat by the Department of Sociology, but there were other feelings too. A man who had set out in 1960 as a commuter between Christ the King and the University of Chicago, who had begun to bridge the worlds these institutions represented, now found himself an outsider to both. "I have been disowned by both my parish and my university. I have been blacklisted in both my diocese and my profession," he wrote in "Confessions of a Loud-Mouthed Irish Priest." "What's more, I have managed to achieve all these things in less than a dozen years and, to tell the truth, without even seriously trying."[41]

He had been forced to leave Christ the King a decade ago, but it had never been clearer that the parish was where he belonged—spiritually if in no other way. "I don't live in the neighborhood just now, and when I show up there some of the inhabitants reach for their squirrel rifles, but just the same, I am at ease in the neighborhood, understand its people from the inside, and can be both critical of them and sympathetic toward them without having to fall back on bathos or nostalgia." Yes, for all its faults, Christ the King had it all over the University of Chicago, *Gemeinschaft* over *Gesellschaft*, the neighborhood of the ethnics over the Big World of the intellectuals. A priest he was, but a *parish'* priest, a neighborhood priest. An ethnic too, unalienated, his roots still intact; in view of the Big World, "that's about as bad as you can be."[42]

He explained: in the neighborhood, friends come first, ideas second, but in the university it is ideas first and friends second—if at all. The neighborhood is a place where trust, fidelity, counting on people are a necessity; without them, homes are overrun by terror. But loyalty is counterproductive in the Big World of the intellectuals. There, contract, short-term commitment, an intelleuctalized code of moral principles are the order of the day; the emphasis is on mobility and career success; one is committed to his friends only if it is "rational" and conducive to one's self-interest. The Big World runs on ideas, true; but, "as a young Irish lawyer in Chicago puts it, 'Someone who won't be loyal to a friend will never be loyal to an idea.' "[53]

Greeley may never make it back from the university to the parish, but he will remain convinced that the neighborhood is right about what it takes to make society work and that the Big World is wrong. And those in the Big World who make and implement social policy had better begin to believe that "the people in the neighborhood may know something about human life that we have forgotten."[44] Greeley will continue to be a scholar in the cosmopolitan world of university, foundation, and government, but only as a "spy from the neighborhood," only to convey the wisdom and strength of *his* people.

"I am, damn it, still capable of standing by my own kind, come what may, and I wouldn't trade that for anything—not even for a membership in the National Academy of Science."[45]

9

Politics:
Conscience or
Coalition

On May 17, 1968, Philip and Daniel Berrigan, two Irish Catholic priests, one of them an early friend of Andrew Greeley, invaded the offices of Local Board 33 in Catonsville, Maryland, stashed 300 draft files into wire baskets, took the baskets to the parking lot outside, and (TV cameras recording it all) burned them with home-made napalm. In August of that year, the nation's television viewers saw the Irish Catholic mayor of Chicago, Richard J. Daley, shout obscenities at a man trying to address the Democratic National Convention, and they watched his police brutalize angry demonstrators outside the convention walls. Nothing could have intensified the conflict between Andrew Greeley and the liberal intelligentsia more; nothing could have been better calculated to widen the chasm between them; and nothing, surely, could have revealed more dramatically the political soul of the neighborhood—than Greeley's denunciation of the Berrigans and their "prophetic act" and his espousal of the Chicago-style politics of Mayor Daley.

The mayor of Chicago—what else was he but a bad joke, inarticulate, lower-class, profane, a tyrant sitting on top of a machine? This man was preferable to a pair of nonviolent clerics putting themselves on the line, expressing their country's moral revulsion at the Vietnamese war? Preferable, later on, to George McGovern, who identified with the best impulses of his time, who had the courage to state in clear terms that the war was immoral and that America should "come home" to her true values?

In January 1971 the *Holy Cross Quarterly* took up the Berrigan flag and devoted an entire issue to the consequences of their raid in Cantonsville. It was appropriate that the *Quarterly* do so. Daniel

Berrigan, like the priests who teach at Holy Cross, was a Jesuit, and Philip Berrigan graduated from Holy Cross in 1950 before becoming a Josephite priest. When the *Quarterly* came out that January, both brothers were in prison for destroying draft records, and Philip was under indictment for plotting to kidnap Henry Kissinger and blow up the heating system of some federal buildings in Washington. (Daniel was named a co-conspirator in the case; both were cleared when it later came to trial.) William Van Etten Casey entitled the issue's editorial "Thank you, Dan and Phil," wrote of the Berrigan case as a "collision of conscience with the state," and added, "I believe they are the living extension of one of the roles that Christ took upon himself—a harsh, demanding, unpopular, and, at times, a necessary role."[1]

The *Quarterly* was not alone. *Commonweal* said the Berrigans were calling for a moral revolution based on the personal conversion of individuals."[2] Francine du Plessix Gray celebrated their Catholic radicalism in the *New Yorker* and later in a book entitled *Divine Disobedience,* and Gary Wills lauded their resistance for *Playboy*.[3] Others spoke of the Berrigans as a challenge, a burden, "prophetic," if not models then at least signs. Noam Chomsky argued that it was the actions of persons like Philip and Daniel Berrigan that brought the war before an otherwise apathetic and ignorant American public. Opinion polls, like those showing that antiwar demonstrations boomeranged (they increased, rather than decreased, public support for the president) were, to Chomsky, "meaningless."[4]

In the midst of all the adulation, Father Greeley, not at all of the opinion that the polls were meaningless, let fly a vicious attack. In a syndicated column reprinted in the *Quarterly,* Greeley acknowledged that Daniel Berrigan was nonviolent, all right, but beware—the logic in his thinking led inevitably to violence. "Make no mistake about it. The self-righteous moralism, displayed in the Berrigan interviews will not tolerate the immorality of those who dare to disagree with him. If Daniel Berrigan was in power, I would be in jail—and not for destroying government property either, but because I was immoral."[5]

"Turning Off the People" is how Greeley had described radical protest like that of the Berrigans in the June 27, 1970, issue of the *New Republic.* Between 60 and 90 percent of the American people, he asserted, had been alienated by such protest. Many of them were the white ethnics to whom he was close. Revisionist history notwithstanding, these people were anti-Communist; they knew from first-hand experience of Hungary, the Berlin Wall, Czechoslovakia, the "Communist menace" in Europe. And they were deeply patriotic to a country that had given them financial success and personal freedom. How could the student protesters, the children of the well-to-do, knock America? they asked. "I don't know the exact cost to the peace movement of burning the American or waving the Vietcong flag, but my impression is that these incidents have been of extraordinary symbolic importance." Indeed, to the ethnic, protesters and Wall Street bankers were cut from the same cloth:

> From the perspective of the Polish TV watcher on Milwaukee Avenue on the northwest side of Chicago, the long-haired militants are every bit as much part of the Establishment as are the presidents of corporations, Wall Street investment bankers, and other Anglo-Saxon and Jewish members of the power elite. In their frame of reference, Richard Nixon to some extent, and Spiro Agnew, to a very considerable extent, are *anti*-Establishment figures, and someone like David Dellinger with his Yale degree is an Establishment personage. They see the protesters and the militants as sons and daughters of the well-to-do, who have attended elite colleges and are supported financially by their parents through all their radical activity. A Harvard graduate is, after all, a Harvard graduate whether in a picket line or in a board room of a large corporation.[6]

If the goal of the protesters was to demonstrate the immorality of the United States in Vietnam—or simply to demonstrate the immorality of the United States—and then to use rational discussion to convert others to their point of view, they could not have been more unsuccessful. Not only was their initial premise arrogant, said Greeley, but their style often dripped with contempt for the people they wished to win over—like the Milwaukee Avenue TV viewer. Their demonstrations were to convert him to their cause? There wasn't a chance in a million, Greeley insisted, that they would succeed.

Not that it was impossible to win the white ethnic population to the cause of peace. Ethnics, and along with them the majority of Americans, were *confused* by the war; that is what Greeley heard in the neighborhoods, what he determined from the polls. People complained of American involvement in Vietnam (their sons, after all, were fighting the war and dying in it), but in the same breath they condemned the Berrigans and "all those hippies who burn the flag." They said, let's get in and get it over with or let's get out. Were they hawks or doves? Moral or immoral?

Actually, what data did exist—piecemeal indicators from Gallup, Harris, and NORC—revealed that ethnics were at least as dovish, and probably more so, than the typical American. In 1967 only Catholics from Eastern Europe—perhaps because of the proximity of their homeland to Communism—were more hawkish than native or Western European Protestant Americans. In February 1970 blue collar workers were *above* the national average in favoring withdrawal from Vietnam (and Catholics were more in favor than Protestants). Further, the more involved an ethnic was in his community (the greater his "ethnic identification"), the more likely he was to be a dove on the Vietnam war (and, incidentally, the more likely he was to be in favor of racial integration). In the face of such evidence, Greeley asked a meeting of political scientists in the fall of 1971, why does the stereotype of the racist-hawk white ethnic persist among so many liberals?[7]

Would it not be better, he went on in the *New Republic*, to avoid condescending labels and try to converse with the white ethnics, with "middle America"? If one wished to gain support from the American population for withdrawal from Vietnam, he would, first of all, separate "peace" from the "peace movement," and particularly from its radical fringes. He would also root appeals to the cause of peace in American patriotism rather than in the "hate America" rhetoric of the radicals. He would ask the ethnic why we were under obligation to defend a country that did not want to defend itself (that was a line of reasoning the ethnic understood). And, finally, he would search the ambiguities of the war for instances, no matter how vague, in which American objectives seemed to have been achieved. To describe the war as a total waste was simply counterproductive.

Counterproductive—Greeley's critics seized upon that word. What, after all, did opinion polls have to do with conscience? Did one take a moral stand only if the majority of Americans agreed with it? Noam Chomsky could only dismiss Greeley's views as "outlandish," "fantastic," and "weird," asserting that the audiences *he*, Chomsky, had spoken to were genuinely moved by witnesses like the Berrigans.[8]

So the argument penetrated to instincts deeper than philosophies. Was one to bear witness to the impulses of conscience, as the Berrigans did, even when the testimony might have unknown, and possibly detrimental, effects? Or was one to leave those impulses aside and determine, coolly and pragmatically, what it would take for the cause to succeed? And if one did bear witness, and if he paid the ·consequences for doing so, would he be at all able—psychologically—to accept the evidence (should it arise) that his action was in vain, or worse, self-defeating? And how did the pragmatist, "doing what he had to do," avoid dishonesty, avoid telling the people one thing while believing another, avoid telling one group *X* and another *Y*, all in the cause of building support for victory?

In the middle of the fury Greeley countered with his answer: Richard J. Daley. The mayor of the "despised Second City" was many things in Greeley's hands, a weapon first of all, something to brandish in the face of all those New York liberals. It was their sophistication versus Daley's malapropisms; their moral purity versus his machine's corruption; their appeals to conscience versus his political deals. All Daley did, Greeley said, was win. All he did in the last election was run against a Jewish candidate and get 65 percent of the Jewish vote. "He is neither smooth nor handsome, articulate or witty. . . . And though Daley is not nearly as pretty as John Lindsay, he just wins by almost twice as much."[9]

Why was Daley successful? The fundamental problem of urban government, Greeley argued, was not corruption (though there was corruption aplenty) but powerlessness. The federal government refused to give the cities real power; the taxation powers of the cities were meager at best, and most of their affluent citizens left for the suburbs on evenings and weekends. In addition, the mayor of

Chicago had very little statutory power, certainly less, say, than the mayor of New York. The task of a mayor, then, and especially the mayor of Chicago, was to amass enough personal power to get decisions made and implemented, to get the city to "work." The alternative to collecting power was anarchy, the sheer inability to govern at all.

How, then, did Richard Daley amass power? Dispensing jobs was one way. As head of the Cook County Central Committee, he retained the capacity to provide large numbers of people with employment. (The organization, one black radical remarked, saw to the employment of a higher proportion of blacks than any other corporate bureaucracy in the Chicago area. The reason was neither "affirmative action" nor a love of blacks. The mayor simply could not survive without the black population in his coalition.) A second way of gaining power was to offer to the loyal wards such services as prompt street repair, snow shoveling, and garbage removal (ideologues hated to bother with these "trivia"), and to delay them in the wards headed up by mavericks like Bill Singer. Especially important was the mayor's ability to dispense wealth (in the form of insurance business, for example)—or at least his willingness to let others accumulate wealth. "Dick has made a deal," one of Daley's supporters told Greeley. "He has let them get rich and they in turn have given him political power."[10]

Strong mayors of Chicago—and only Anton Cermak and Richard Daley have been strong mayors—were also masters at the art of power brokerage. Daley took it as a given that the city was composed of a diversity of national, racial, economic, and religious groups, and he saw his role in that mix as "arranging and rearranging power and resources in such a way as to prevent one group from becoming so unhappy with the balance that they will leave the system."[11] He knew that the balanced ticket was essential to victory in this power brokerage game and that to exclude a group from its place on the ticket was to insult and offend it. Any group that could deliver votes was heard from and responded to, not all the time, but at the *right* time—when the majority would not reject the response, when the leader of a constituency simply *had* to have a concession to retain his credibility with his people. As one leader put it, "The mayor doesn't give us everything we want, but he knows what we have to have, and that he gets for us."[12]

Mayor Daley also derived power from bestowing recognition on the various ethnic communities in the city. The communities called it "respecting" them. He expressed a sense of pride in the city as a whole, calling a Picasso sculpture "a great honor for the city of Chicago" even though personally he thought it horrendous, mediating a strike by the Chicago symphony orchestra so Chicago might continue to have "the world's finest orchestra—a real champion." Ludicrous as his simple-minded pride might appear to Hyde Park intellectuals, it struck others in the city as a genuine concern for their place of residence.

Clout in Springfield and Washington was the final source of the mayor's power. If he had influence with the state and federal governments (because he delivered Chicago for the winning gubernatorial or presidential candidate), he could use it to bring resources to Chicago. And that was a strength he could use to build up his own position in the government of the city.

Votes were the essential currency of the machine system. If Daley had power in Springfield and Washington, it was because he could deliver Chicago. If a ward committeeman had power with Daley, it was because the committeeman could deliver his ward. And if precinct captains had any clout with their ward committeeman, it was because they could get out the Democratic vote in their precincts. Finally, there was the citizen. He had a vote, something *they* wanted, and he found his precinct captain to be marvelously responsive to his requests when the captain knew that there were two, perhaps as many as four or five, solid Democratic votes under that citizen's roof. The citizen, in this system, had far more power than when he stood helpless before a government bureaucrat.

What, then, of the Daley organization? Too much corruption? There was no doubt about it. Was it on its last legs? It would survive as long as Richard Daley survived, but because of its inability to attract young, enthusiastic Democrats and keep them in the fold, it might not outlive him by many years. Not only that (Greeley listed the machine's faults), the "Chicago system" neglected groups in the city that were unorganized, inarticulate, and powerless; and it overlooked the presence of small but potentially explosive cadres. Nor did it know how to communicate with intellectuals, because its concrete and instinctual style was "not likely to be swayed by the moralism, the dogmatism, and the perfectionism of the academic."[13]

"Those experts," the mayor is supposed to have said, "they don't know nothin'." *That* was a loss, because the intellectual was better able to spot long-range trends and anticipate problems than was the politician whose primary concern was staying afloat in the present.

The response to Greeley's articles on Mayor Daley was hardly warm. A *New Republic* piece, in fact, was a direct hit on a hornet's nest. As Greeley explained later in the *Bulletin of the Atomic Scientists:*

> The article was not a defense of the Cook County organization; I know its weaknesses better than most Americans. But it was not the usual ritualistic condemnation of the Daley machine that is *de rigueur* for most American liberals, and I found myself being clobbered from all sides. The *Chicago Journalism Review* published a series of vitriolic articles which were personal attacks on me and the mayor without any attempt to respond to the contents of my article. Professor Harold Isaacs of the Massachusetts Institute of Technology described the article as a "love letter to Mayor Daley" (which it most assuredly was not). The editor of *The Maroon,* University of Chicago student newspaper, called me on the phone to ask whether I was in favor of "political corruption." One of the members of the sociology department denounced me as a racist, and another opined—with unintended flattery—that I was nothing but a loud-mouthed Irish priest. Studs Terkel had a nasty comment to make in his review of Mike Royko's *Boss* in *The New York Times Book Review.* . . . The word went around the Hyde Park community that I was the "house intellectual" of the Daley organization.[14]

Greeley was hardly Daley's house intellectual. "I have never met the mayor and have never spoken with him on the phone," he wrote.[15] But he had chosen Daley—not without qualification—and rejected the Fathers Berrigan—again, not without qualification. He said it was because Daley knew how to win and because the Berrigans were morally arrogant and sure to lose. But there was more to his choice than that, for it fit into the ongoing momentum of his disaffection with "those university-and-media-based liberals and intellectuals" (many of whom lived in Hyde Park) who did not know Chicago from the inside, who did not know its mayor from the inside, who did not know the Irish, the Italians, and the Poles from the inside, who did not know Andrew Greeley from the inside. Richard Daley was all that they were not and all that they despised;

he was that part of Andrew Greeley that they were not and that they despised. And so he was flung in their faces. There were important political messages in these articles, to be sure, the beginnings, in fact, of a "Catholic politics" cemented in the neighborhood experience of Catholic people; but the raw skin, the sensitivity leaning toward paranoia, the cries "I am I" and "my kind of people are to be respected" were as much a part of these articles on politics as were the analyses of a loyal liberal Democrat who, above all, wanted to win.

Greeley had some unsolicited advice for the National Democratic Party, too, but early in 1972 publishers were not interested in passing it on. So Greeley waited until the crushing defeat of George McGovern, revised the manuscript, and had it published by New Viewpoints as *Building Coalitions* (1974). His goal now (he told *Time* magazine) was to tell the party "how to put itself back together." His targets were the images of America in the minds of the liberal leadership in 1972, for it was those pictures, he argued, more than stands on specific issues or mistakes in campaign strategy, that brought about the Democratic presidential disaster.

The McGovernites, alas, were possessed of a *religious* (there was no better word for it) picture of American society. To them, said Greeley, America was sick, or worse than that, evil and corrupt. Its people were guilty of racism, either by active discrimination or passive acquiescence; they were apathetic about their country's imperialistic war of aggression; they were unconcerned about the coming environmental crisis. These same people, however, possessed profound spiritual resources, and they were capable of repentance, of reform, of "coming home" to their true values. Already there were signs of hope: oppressed blacks, Spanish-speaking persons, women, and youth were aligning themselves with enlightened members of the professoriate and with progressive strains within the Democratic Party to form a New Coalition. The coalition was *for* the forces of liberation, *for* abortion, *for* amnesty, *for* legalized marijuana, *for* the emancipation of homosexuals. The New Politicians knew that the coalition would alienate many regular Democrats, but their calculations showed that the attrition of these would be more than offset by the "great legions" of young voters—twenty-five million of them—who would be lured into the fold. One could do without the corrupt bosses of the old politics. One could, in fact, do without corruption—if people were penitent and "came home." There was an inevitability to the movement, Greeley noted; the New Politicians saw themselves on the crest of the wave of history, and one either rode it to the shores of the Promised Land or fell off and drowned in its wake.

Granted, Greeley commented, this was a lofty, noble vision. But it belonged in a church and not in the political arena. It was the *cleric* who urged his people to a maximum of generosity and moral concern. The *politician* was satisfied with whatever generosity he could get from the voter *and still win.* "Winning isn't everything perhaps, but, as Charlie Brown has observed, losing isn't anything." Winners, not losers, shaped the direction a country took. And if the Ph.D.'s weren't advising their politician employees of that basic reality, they ought to be fired. "Better they be unemployed," Greeley told the politicians, "than you."[16]

The analysis went on. One avoided being the loser by getting enough votes—an obvious truth, so obvious that only someone like the mayor of Chicago could see it. And one got enough votes by understanding the voter. The picture in the minds of the McGovernites (as well as pundits like Eric Sevareid, David Brinkley, James Reston, and TRB) was that 1972 presented the voter a "clear choice." One was either "liberal"—and bought the entire liberal package on peace, inflation, poverty, abortion, marijuana, amnesty, busing, military spending, and racial quotas—or one was "conservative" and rejected the entire package. But what, Greeley asked, was the essential connection between the "liberal" stands on all these issues?

> An Irish lawyer is against the war and against abortion, for a family assistance program and against the legalization—or even against the decriminalization—of marijuana. He thinks his positions are consistent: war and abortion are murder, family assistance and drug control are both necessary for an orderly society. Is he a "conservative" or a "liberal"?

> A Detroit housewife, who is vigorously opposed to busing even though her son is in an integrated high school and she strongly supports integrated schools, thinks of herself as consistent, be-

cause, in her judgment, both stands come from a concern over quality education. Is she a "conservative" or a "liberal"?

The black man who dislikes the militant leaders (and slightly more blacks dislike the militants than like them), is opposed to busing (as are about 45 percent of the blacks in the country), and is bitterly opposed to the legalization of marijuana (as are about 66 percent of the blacks in the country); but, nevertheless, he enthusiastically supported George McGovern as a friend of the black people. Is he inconsistent? Is he a "liberal" or a "conservative"?

The Polish physician who is against the war but also against the decrease in military spending on the grounds that both weaken America's international position—is he inconsistent? Is he a "liberal" or a "conservative"?[17]

The smart politician, Greeley contended, avoided the one-dimensional thinking that lumped all of these people into the "center." He knew that forcing "clear choices" on complex individuals meant losing elections. He understood that one man's consistency was not another's, that the logic separating "law and order" from "peace in Vietnam" in one man's thinking held them together in another's. An astute campaigner in 1972 would have separated issues of substance—like peace, race, poverty, and pollution—from issues one did not commit political suicide over—like amnesty, abortion, and marijuana. He would have realized that three-fifths of the American population was willing to support liberal postures on the former but that a majority was against amnesty, quotas, and busing. Skillful strategy would not have soured the pot by mixing the "liberal" positions on the latter with the "liberal" positions on issues of greater substance.

The reform Democrats of 1972 were aware (rightly so, Greeley advised) that the public admired a man who was firm and unswerving in his commitment to truth, who was willing to sacrifice his political future because of commitment to principle. Compromise and the manipulation of truth by a politician were seen by outsiders as signs of personal weakness and corruption. And while the New Coalition's image of the voter was correct in this regard (they nominated a man who was "right from the start"), the image was incomplete because it was not pluralistic enough. For if a political leader *did* take a firm, vigorous stand on what seemed to be truth to *one* group of the electorate, he would be rejected by countless other groups who did not see truth in the same way. "For what seems Truth to one is Big Lie to another, and what is morally imperative action to one is down the road to hell to another."[18]

Make no mistake about it; "telling the truth, the whole truth, and nothing but the truth, as seen by each person in political oratory would increase viciousness and hatred throughout society."[19] In a pluralistic society there were as few truths clear to everyone as there were choices clear to everyone. The politician, then, was in a bind from which only a few could escape (or even turn to their advantage). He had to be the honest, uncompromising leader the public wanted and still make the compromises essential to the maintenance of the political process. Like the ancient Israelites, he had to build bricks without straw:

> The political leader, then, is forced by the nature of the circumstances in which he finds himself to evade and avoid, to sugarcoat and to mislead more than the rest of us. He does so not because he is dishonest (thought he may be), not because he likes to manipulate people (though it is very possible that he does), but because his role is essentially one of "conflict management." The conflict manager must be extremely careful of what he says and how he says it.[20]

In the last fifty years, said Greeley, only Franklin Roosevelt and John Kennedy had managed conflict with skill and grace. Relying on the analysis of Andrew McFarland, Greeley categorized Taft, Wilson, Harding,. Coolidge, Hoover, and Eisenhower as having a low tolerance for conflict. Truman, he judged, was good at the political game and seemed to enjoy it, but he had occasional fits of temper. Lyndon Johnson was a skilled practitioner of conflict management in the Senate, was flexible as President in matters of domestic policy, but lost his cool and refused to accept the criticism of subordinates in the cross-pressures generated by Vietnam. The background of one president made it impossible for him to become a hot-tempered isolate: "One cannot imagine that cool and aloof Boston politician, John Kennedy, cutting himself off from dissenting opinion or losing his cool because, as a Catholic, he was an outsider."[21]

In Greeley's view, the best of the political leaders was not a mere juggler of pressure groups, trying to give each the concessions it wanted when it had to have them. He also educated the public (white America's change in racial attitudes over the past twenty years was to a large extent due to political leadership) and moved them—carefully, it was true, because he could not move too far beyond the coalition that was supporting him. A national political leader had to be particularly adept to handle the problems of the seventies:

> A national political leader in the 1970s will have to possess extraordinary skills of bargaining and coalition formation. He must liquidate much foreign military involvement and still prevent the resurgence of isolationism. He must respond to legitimate demands of the militants and at the same time persuade other Americans that the demands are indeed legitimate. He must persuade 'middle Americans that the fundamental principles on which the society rests are not being destroyed but are rather growing and developing. He must restore confidence in the integrity and honesty of public officials. He must begin to find solutions to the technical problems of pollution, waste, and conservation of resources in an exceedingly complex and advanced industrial society. Even though he probably will not be able to convince some of the young, he still must realize that he has on his hands a whole generation that has every reason to be cynical about politics and politicians. Finally, he must find some way to end the peculiar economic situation where depression and inflation coexist and reinforce one another.[22]

In a chapter entitled "Facts in Black and White," Greeley set about to alter another picture in the minds of the Democratic leadership, that of the state of race relations in America. In the 1972 strategy of the New Politicians, Greeley saw an assumption that blacks and working-class whites could not be brought together in sufficient numbers to win an election. Hence the working-class white had to be dismissed (how else, after all, was one to deal with racism, bigotry, and "backlash"?) and his absence made up for by the more tolerant legions of the young. The strategy, of course, failed.

None of those, Greeley asserted, who designed the 1972 Democratic campaign were aware of the fact that "white backlash" simply did not exist in the proportions the media led us to expect. Indeed, if

survey data (such as the data Greeley had been monitoring at
NORC) had been studied carefully, it would have been evident that
"white backlash" did not exist at all. Despite all the turbulence of
the late sixties, despite prime-time coverage of riots in Watts and
Detroit, despite newspaper accounts of blacks arming for guerilla
warfare, despite the emergence of Stokely Carmichael, H. Rap
Brown, Eldridge Cleaver, and Bobby Seale as national per-
sonalities, whites over the past ten years had continued to show
greater and greater acceptance of racial integration. Greeley had said
it before in *Scientific American* and *Public Opinion Quarterly*. In
1972, 86 percent of a probability sample of white Americans agreed
that whites and blacks should go to integrated schools—that was 23
percent more than in 1963, and 56 percent more than in 1942. A
similar increase in acceptance was evident on questionnaire items
dealing with residential, social, and marital integration, and all
indications were that the trend would continue. Even if one took the
minimal position—that these replies represented changes only in
what whites thought they *ought* to say—the shift was nevertheless
dramatic. There was no evidence at all of the white backlash "discovered" by less representative samplings of the climate in
America.[23]

But wasn't opposition to busing as intense as it appeared in the
media? To this, the NORC data said yes. In 1972 only 6 percent of
whites in the South and only 15 percent of whites outside the South
were in favor of busing black and white school children from one
district to another. (The figures for blacks in favor of busing were 52
percent in the South and 55 percent outside the South.) The
majority of whites, then, who endorsed school integration in principle were against integration as achieved by busing. Were they
hypocrites? Were they covert racists? Or were they afraid of danger?
Committed to the principle of neighborhood schools? Dubious of
the effectiveness of busing in improving the quality of education?
Whatever the case (the data were not refined enough to say), it would
have been most inaccurate to write off their feelings about busing as
so much bigotry—especially in view of the fact that a substantial
minority of blacks agreed with them. Indeed, all the other evidence
indicated that white America's attitudes toward racial integration
had been consistently moving to the left. For politicians the message was clear; a style that adapted itself to "white backlash" was re-

sponding to something that wasn't there, whereas an assumption
that persons in the center could be led even further to the left in the
matter of racial integration was in tune with the thinking of the
American population.

Responses of black Americans to survey questions were also essential to the political strategist of the seventies. Greeley fused his
own reading of black political leadership and the results of opinion
polling in the late sixties: "black political leadership is becoming
much better organized, much more sophisticated, and much more
insistent . . . blacks do not want to withdraw from American society
. . . now they want to be involved on their own terms, which is to
say they want the rest of society to accept their right to dignity and to
respect while maintaining a cultural heritage of their own."[24] To
sample the data: in 1966, 80 percent of American blacks said they
preferred to live in an integrated neighborhood; 63 percent would
choose an integrated club rather than an all-black club; 38 percent
already belonged to an integrated church. In 1968 less than 20 percent of blacks interviewed in fifteen major cities gave separatist responses to each of ten questions dealing with various aspects of integration. At the same time, however, the majority of blacks endorsed
cautious militancy (in 1966, for example, 77 percent thought the
federal government would do little about civil rights were it not for
demonstrations, but only 15 percent said in 1968 that blacks should
be ready to use violence to gain rights). Blacks also strongly supported black pride and black solidarity. In 1968, 96 percent said
"Negroes should take more pride in Negro history," and 70 percent
agreed that "Negroes should shop in Negro-owned stores whenever
possible." Data just in from a 1972 survey did not alter the basic picture. Blacks combined strong endorsements of racial integration
with equally strong feelings that one must insist on solidarity
among one's own people. An emphasis on black culture was not
equivalent to a desire for separation.

Other data showed that it was erroneous to assume that black
political objectives always conflicted with those of whites. In 1968 a
CBS survey found that blacks endorsed goals of better jobs, better
education, better housing and police protection, and more government effort to help blacks solve problems. Most American whites did
not object to such goals, which were at the top of the black agenda
(only 16 percent of whites, for example, were opposed to govern-

ment job training programs—which 89 percent of blacks wanted). Busing, forced integration of white neighborhoods, and a guaranteed family income were the three practical issues on which a consensus between black and white did *not* exist. While there were some issues dividing blacks and whites, then, there were considerable areas of agreement—areas upon which Greeley said wise political leadership ought to capitalize.

In *Building Coalitions* Greeley had few solutions to the "racial problem"—nor, incidentally, has he ever offered many. He is highly impressed by the changes in white attitudes monitored by NORC and says that they "have been so great that you could say that ours is probably the least racially prejudiced of any large multiethnic society in the world." He insists that nothing is solved by having "experts" take from the middle-class white—take in the form of unfair taxation, decreased property values, closed doors on neighborhood schools—and give to the poor black. America *wants* racial justice and peace. Survey data show that the majority would even accept a 10 percent tax surcharge to achieve them (provided the surcharge were accompanied by a removal of inequalities in the tax structure). And half the racial "problem" would disappear if "solutions" did not exact such a price from the white population. Instead of compulsory busing, for example, why not guarantee to school districts within a metropolitan area a subsidy of three times the per-pupil cost for every minority child they enrolled—up to a limit, say, of 15 percent of enrollment (or whatever the percentage of minority children in that area)? No child, white or black, would be *forced* into busing, yet high-quality suburban education (and buses to get to it) would be available to inner city students on terms the suburban districts would find financially irresistible. How much panic selling of white homes would there be in neighborhoods faced with racial integration if we had property value insurance? "I'm absolutely convinced that half of our racial problem in the city would be solved . . . if you knew that a black face showing up down the block wasn't going to plummet your investment by $20,000." Why not, in addition, grant a $1,000 income tax deduction for every immediate neighbor one had of a different race? Greeley's outlook is straightforward; you cannot change confirmed bigots, but you can take the financial loss out of racial integration—and even, in some cases, put profit into it.

In *Building Coalitions* Greeley insisted that blacks were an absolutely indispensable part of the liberal Democratic coalition—so indispensable, in fact, that in 1976 "a black vice-presidential candidate on a 'national unity' ticket could well represent one of the most brilliant political ploys of the century."[25] (Greeley had advocated the 1972 nomination of Andrew Young along with Edmund Muskie.[26]) In a tantalizing footnote the reader is informed that more Americans are now saying they would be willing to vote for a qualified black presidential candidate than were saying they would have voted for a qualified Catholic in 1960. Will the Democrats read the times correctly and be brave enough to nominate a black for the vice-presidency? "Doubtful," Greeley prognosticated. "Very doubtful."

And where did all the Catholics go in 1972? And where would they be in 1976? (The question is practically the same as "Where did all the ethnics go?") In 1972 the media were saying that Catholics were deserting the Democratic Party, and to some extent the media were correct: 48 percent of the Catholic voters chose George McGovern—more than the Protestants who voted for McGovern but fewer than the Catholics who usually voted for the Democratic presidential candidate. (Since 1928 the only Republican to garner a majority of the Catholic vote was Eisenhower in 1956.) The McGovernites said the reason for the Catholic defection was the behavior of President Nixon. He courted Cardinal Krol, promised support for parochial schools, and expressed his opposition to abortion. But Greeley argued that such an analysis was superficial. Catholic attitudes on abortion at the time of the election, for example, were nearly indistinguishable from those of Protestants. Besides, the analysis overlooked more profound sociological events: (1) Catholics were "making it" into the upper middle class and were feeling the political cross-pressures of their religious and ethnic heritage, which inclined them to be Democrats, and their new-found social class, which steered them toward the Republican Party; (2) at the same time, Catholics who remained in the working and lower classes were being hard pressed by the new black militancy and felt, as a result, that their own interests were being overlooked by the party that traditionally stood up for them. Most important, that party, for all intents and purposes, kicked them out of the coalition in 1972 when it insisted that they be ideologically pure and buy the entire platform prefabricated by the New Politicians.

When NORC surveyed America's Catholics in 1974, Greeley discovered that pressures to abandon the Democratic party had not taken a serious toll. Catholics were as Democratic in the seventies as they were in the fifties—just to the left of center—even though their religious affiliation was clearly more tenuous. What was the presidential ticket for them in 1976? Greeley's choices were Morris Udall and Jerry Brown. "Of course, it will never happen, but they'd win going away."

Throughout *Building Coalitions* Greeley argued for congruence between political style and the basic structure of the American political system. There were no analyses of the economics of political power, no tales of Big Money secretly finding its way into campaign coffers, no uncovering of power elites or an Establishment controlling American society. To the contrary, the political realities that Greeley saw were spelled out quite explicitly in James Madison's Federalist Papers and in the Constitution itself, and they were quite simple—to gain power one must gain the support of the people; one gains the support of the people by representing their interests; to increase one's power, one bargains and negotiates with other representatives, trading off support in one area for support in another. The trick, if one wishes to effect change, is not to spread power out but to concentrate it. Madison was not an eighteenth-century prophet trying to provide a structure for pluralism in some distant future; he was, rather, trying to cope with the extraordinary pluralism all about him. His political experiment has produced a structure and a culture of marvelous flexibility for absorbing new groups and for undergoing rapid social change without collapse. "I happen to think it is the most noble work of polity that human ingenuity has ever devised."[27]

On the heels of *Building Coalitions* came a syndicated column, Greeley's first in the secular press. It began in July 1974, appearing twice a week in twenty newspapers across the nation (that number has more than doubled)—among them the *Chicago Tribune*, the *Detroit News*, the *New York Daily News*, the *San Francisco Chronicle*, and the *Denver Post*. It was Greeley's chance to speak—to shout, if necessary—on behalf of Middle America.

> Most of us—God forgive us for it— are "Middle Americans." We are not poor or nonwhite. We are heterosexuals and if we are

women our consciousness has not been raised. We are not part of
the "third world."

On the other hand, we don't have Ph.D.s or live on the East Side of
Manhattan or Cambridge or Chevy Chase or Berkeley. We don't
teach at the great universities or write for the important intellectual journals or work for the "national media." Some of us are
even in the most unhappy of categories—white Protestant males
over 60: the kind of people Ms. Clare Randall, the new general
secretary of the National Council of Churches, is busy cleaning out
of that organization.

We are, in other words, the bad guys.[28]

Or *are* we—90 percent of America's population—the bad guys? *We*
wanted to get out of the war long before the government did—even
though the "peace" movement drove some of us into the government camp. *Our* racial attitudes and behavior have changed
remarkably in the past twenty years. We have been ahead of our
government on pollution and gun control. Labeled militant anti-
Communists, we accepted the detente with Russia and the rapprochement with China with amazing ease and good grace.
When meat prices go up, we stop buying meat—despite Earl Butz.
When big cars become uneconomical, we stop buying big cars. Beset
by an oil shortage, we reduce consumption by 8 percent (and we are
smart enough to blame the shortage on the government and the oil
companies—not on the Israelis or the Arabs or the Russians). "Mind
you," Greeley set the tone in his very first column, "the American
people, like all people, have faults. But from my part of the bench
they look like the most generous, most sophisticated, most resilient
population that humankind has ever known."[29]

In his ensuing columns Greeley overlooked nothing:

Nixon: "What offends me most about him is not that he is a
crook but that he is a dumb crook. Dishonesty in a President of the
United States is neither unusual nor particularly offensive, but
stupidity is intolerable."

Nixon's resignation: "Richard Nixon was driven from the
Presidency by a massive coalition representing most of the mainstream of our society. He was thrown out by the American people."

Gerald Ford: "He is exactly what he always was: a small town,
Middle Western, conservative Republican who almost never reads a

book. . . . On his record he is the enemy of the poor, the black, the workers."

Ford's pardon of Nixon: "The fix was in. I'll make you Vice President, Jerry, and you pardon me. Explicit? It didn't have to be. Ford stands revealed as the political hack he always was. . . . Nixon gets amnesty without an indictment, without a plea, without a trial, without a verdict. The young men who would not fight in Viet Nam have to work their way back."

Food: "The American food-producing system works. The socialist food-producing system that is to be found in countries like China and Russia does not work."

Oil: "The oil countries have done evil things to the rest of the world—not merely, not even mainly, to the West. Much of the suffering in South Asia this winter will have been caused by a fertilizer shortage produced by the high price of oil."

Amnesty: "It should be amnesty for everyone—the draft resisters and the little Watergate fish as well as the big ones."

The economy: "I can tell you one group that won't be called upon to sacrifice: those corporate administrators whose monopolistic control enables them to fix prices in many major industries."

The sexual revolution: "I wish these sexual revolutionaries appeared a little more joyous and happy and a little less somber and earnest when they appear on the late TV talk shows to preach their gospel of liberation. It doesn't look like they are having much fun."

Racism: "I am completely committed to eliminating not only the last vestige of racial prejudice from American society but also the residual effects of the prejudice and injustice of the past. I believe in this—as do most Americans—because no other course of action is appropriate for those who buy the vision of American democracy. Still I gotta feel guilty? Well, sorry about that, but I won't."

WASPs: "The English Protestants started this country. They set up its political structures and its political philosophy. They let the rest of us in; they were, in other words, true to their own principles, though at times it must have been against their better judgment."

The IRA: "If it were from any other country in the world, our fashionable liberals would hail its members as revolutionary heroes."

Marlon Brando: "He should give land to the Italians. He never exploited Indians, but he sure exploited Italians."

Mike Royko: "He is crude enough to fit the stereotype of the Chicago Slav and liberal enough to appeal to the contempt civilized Americans have for Chicago and 'da Mare.'"

Abortion: "I can't figure out why abortion supporters don't come right out and say it's moral to kill babies under some circumstances."

The fall of Saigon: "We 'lost' in Viet Nam not because the enemy were better fighters or better human beings, but because the American people quite properly decided that we were going to lose, and through their Congress forbade any further involvement."

Patty Hearst: "If you think you are without sin, then fire the first machine gun."

John Kennedy (once proposed as a doctor of the Church): "What a President does in the Oval Office is what counts and not what he does in bed at night—or in the afternoon, or any other time."[30]

Over the months Greeley turned out to be *for* Peter Rodino, Otto Kerner, Edward Levi, Pat Moynihan, "da mare" (as in, "da mare looks good, don't he?"), pluralistic integration, illegal aliens, New York City, clout (but not reform, thank you), the Chicago Bears, Columbus Day, Lent, haunted houses, and front porches. And he was decidedly *against* psychohistory, "Libthink," Clayton Fritchey, clerical black, *Nashville*, socialism, the *Christian Century*, the Minnesota Vikings, the Detroit Lions, the Green Bay Packers— and the end of summer. Once he reflected on himself as a liberal:

> I am a liberal [without quotation marks] and always have been and confidently expect to be so always. There was a time when American liberalism was flexible, pragmatic, experimental, when it could make common cause with working men and women, with "ethnics," with those who did not go to graduate school.
>
> There are many liberals of this variety still in the country, but unfortunately, the name "liberal" has been appropriated by a narrow, doctrinaire clique that is about as tolerant of dissent as the Congregation of the Inquisition used to be. I don't know how this clique ever came to monopolize the word "liberal"; maybe the rest of us are to blame for letting them do it.[31]

"John Cogley first pointed out to me that Greeley has, probably, the greatest natural vein of journalistic talent of any American

Catholic; he is a natural-born pamphleteer, a polemicist who writes quickly, crisply, colorfully. Francis X. Murphy recently likened him to Belloc and Chesterton."[32] Michael Novak wrote these words in *Commonweal,* but not everyone shares Novak's opinion. To Mike Royko, formerly of the now defunct *Chicago Daily News,* Greeley is "an intellectual priest who dabbles in journalism," who preaches how lucky we are to have "lardy little pocket-stuffers guiding our city."[33] And Greeley's reaction to readers who are put off by his columns? "If you're going to write a column," he told me, "it has to be a column that challenges people to think. Otherwise they are not going to read it. People will say (oh, it strikes me as the most mindless thing anybody could say), I don't always agree with your column. Well, of course, you stupid so-and-so, you don't always agree. If you did you wouldn't read it."

Still, there is the matter raised by the Berrigan brothers. I asked Father Greeley what had been his position on Vietnam, and he replied, "I was against it from the beginning on the purely pragmatic grounds (and I'd still be against it on pragmatic grounds) that the United States has no business getting involved in a land war in Asia—just no business. Now if there is a local administration capable of maintaining itself, then I can see us sustaining them. We learned in Korea that over the long haul (and the long haul is reasonably short) the American people will not support a massive military involvement not on our continent. The same thing could be said, I think, of the First and Second World Wars.

"I remember saying in 1965, when the secret escalation was going on, that Lyndon Johnson was the smartest politician in the United States and that he was not going to have a major army in Vietnam when the 1966 congressional elections came along. It was just unthinkable that he would. But he did."

"And weren't the radical protesters the first to cry out against the war?" I noted.

No, he replied, David Riesman was, and he later turned against the radicals. "It is surely the case that the perennial dissidents in the society were the first ones to *militantly* cry out against it. They would have cried out against anything in the United States, just on principle. They happened to be right on that one."

Then I went after the nub. "Where does morality enter into politics?"

"Oh boy, that's a tough one." Greeley was silent. "First of all, I don't believe you can derive a political program from a moral code. That is to say, there is no such thing as a moral environmental policy that one can induce *a priori* from one's moral convictions. There is no such thing as a single policy to deal with any problem that has a monopoly on morality." Another pause, and he continued. "Morality in politics involves the exercise of the classic virtue of prudence. He who is imprudent in politics is immoral. Now, what's imprudence? Well, in American society, imprudence, first of all, is doing anything that drives a major component out of the coalition which is the society or the coalition which is your party. Immorality is excluding any American from the rights that all Americans have by law or by Constitution. Is busing moral or immoral? I don't know, and I don't know how anybody else does. Stealing from the public fisc is immoral. Lying to the public is immoral. Tolerating injustice about which you can do something is immoral."

"Is Watergate—what Nixon did—moral or immoral?"

"Well, it's terribly dumb. Yeah, sure it's immoral. It's immoral to deprive people of their rights to privacy and enter somebody's office. That's wrong. Obstructing justice is immoral. Violating an oath of office to uphold the Constitution is immoral."

"Is the corruption in Chicago politics immoral?"

"You better believe it is."

"And Daley letting the men around him get rich—is that immoral?"

Greeley was more hesitant. "Hard to tell. Hard to tell."

"You don't know the facts."

"Oh no, I know the facts. What I don't know is how accurate his judgment is that much of that has to be tolerated if you're going to govern the city. I just don't know. I mean, I guess any political system has to tolerate a certain amount of corruption. Does he have to tolerate as much as he does? I don't know."

"Do you distinguish between politicians who are more and less moral?"

"Well, the first thing I look for is competency. I mean, is the man capable of putting together a coalition that can win an election and govern a country? If he's not competent, he can be a saint, and I don't care. . . . Well, ok, suppose he's competent and he's a crook. Well, if he's a competent crook running against an incompetent saint, I think I'd probably take the competent crook."

Greeley has always insisted on the complexity, the amorphousness of human life. "There's more to reality than moral dicta," he will say, speaking of Catholicism in the same breath with politics. Or "I am opposed to preprogramed moral systems." Or "I don't know of any problem that faces the United States today for which there is a clear moral solution." We need moral codes, ethical systems, to be sure, he says, but "you can't fit everything that happens in human life into the neat categories of an ethical system." Moral principles are clear and unambiguous, but moral practice is chancy and uncertain and obscure. "When you make a moral decision, when you apply your principles to the circumstances in which you find yourself, the best you can hope for is that you haven't made too much of a mess of things. You have tried to act sincerely and honestly, to do what is best, to live your principles in the crazy, foggy, confusing world of daily life." Reflecting on Vietnam in a column, he added, "It took moral courage to resist the war, but it also took moral courage to fight in it. . . . I am outraged by the rigidity of those who think their moral decision is the only decision that men and women of good faith and intelligence could possibly make."[34]

So Andrew Greeley, in his own words, is nonideological, pragmatic, flexible, "a religious believer but a political agnostic." He cites Geno Baroni: ideology doesn't get the sidewalks fixed. Most things don't work, and so you keep trying new things. If you are bound to a policy because it's morally correct, you lack the capacity to change should it fail. Who is the ideal politician? Greeley feels that David Martin, writing in *Dissent*, came closest to identifying him:

> Consider the following proposition: that the highest moral responsibility could conceivably reside in a civil servant or a politician at the ministry of defense, who uses the coolest rational calculation to tread that narrow edge which is marginally closer to survival than all the alternatives. . . .

His highest achievement will be a tiny victory, his normal achievement just to survive. This he will never be able just to explain, and may have to accept the mortification of having to claim that a tiny victory was a great one. He may even acquire a reputation among the cognoscenti for naive reasoning and dishonest appeals, simply because the public neither wishes to know his actual reasons nor would be willing to face the stark alternative involved in that reasoning. It may even be that he is a man of the highest intelligence who must accept the contempt of an intelligentsia which has never tried to understand why he must appear stupid in public and appear ignorant of what he may know better than anyone. Perhaps such a man has some claim to his humanity and ours.[35]

"Are you a politician?" I asked Andrew Greeley.

"No."

"An adviser to politicians?"

"No." He did tell me, however, that since his articles on Chicago politics, he has made one good "organization" contact and that since *Building Coalitions* he has been talking to several well-known political figures.

If not a politician, then, or an adviser to politicians, Greeley identifies with certain types of political social scientists—his close friend Pat Moynihan, for example. Greeley met Moynihan in 1962, just after he received his Ph.D:

Pete Rossi dragged me off at the ASA meetings in Washington to a Trotskyite reunion in a room in the Shoreham hotel. The whole crowd that went to Townshend Harris High School, CCNY, and then Columbia after the war were assembled there—Bell, Glazer, Lipset, etc. There was one face that clearly didn't belong. The face looked at my collar and said, "What are you doing here?" I looked at the face and said, "I might ask the same of you." The then Assistant Secretary and now Ambassador Moynihan and I knew we had each encountered one of our own kind.[36]

Greeley later wrote of Moynihan, for whom he has immense respect: "To say that he is Irish is to say that he is a realist in an age of romantics, a pragmatist in an age of ideologues, and a sentimentalist in an age of sophisticated cynics. There was too much pressure in the history of Ireland for the mick to afford romanticism. Those who survived were too shrewd to be caught in the trap of ideology, and they suffered too much to remain cynical for very long." Moynihan was formed "in the world beyond the university where the dogmas, the rituals, and the conventions of academia do not carry much weight."[37]

Greeley hinted there about the source of his own political instincts: an Ireland that needed to survive, immigrants from Ireland who had to adapt to a new country. Greeley's father was a nonideological, liberal Democrat, a loyal member of the Cook County Organization, "an uncompromising believer in all the principles of the New Deal." So subtly are these instincts passed from one generation to the next. When young Andy was four years old, he stood by a railroad station, holding his mother's hand, looking at a poster of Franklin Roosevelt. It was 1932. He asked his mother who the man in the picture was. She said, "That's Roosevelt; he's running for president." "I remember," Greeley says of the incident, "her absolute confidence that he would win." In 1932, it hadn't been so clear that he would.

10   Intimacy

Intimacy is a game.

When Greeley says this, when he introduces his books on interpersonal contact with such titles as *The Friendship Game* (1970) and *Love and Play* (1975), he is not expressing his despair at the sham and the phoniness of human relationships, not trying to expose the myriad ways in which we subtly manipulate each other, not thinking of people who are, as we say, "just playing games." His views are not a reaction to Eric Berne's *Games People Play* (New York: Grove, 1964), even though they stand in stark contrast to Berne's. To Berne, the best of social intercourse is game-free; autonomy, spontaneity, awareness, and especially intimacy begin where game-playing leaves off. To Greeley, the problem in interpersonal relationships is not that people *play* but that they have lost the capacity to play *well*. With fun and enjoyment gone, "playing games" comes to mean deceit and mutual exploitation.

The difference between Berne and Greeley, of course, has to do with an interpretation of play. "The 'play' crowd has long since forgotten what a game is," says Greeley.[1] In a game, in the very best game, the players artfully combine rigorous discipline with grace, ease, and spontaneity. Indeed, it is the long hours of arduous practice, the work of getting to know the playmate's moves (and the playmate may be a spouse, a dancing partner, or a wide receiver), that enable two people to abandon themselves to play. True play—play as children play with their best friends, with their favorite toys—involves respect for the playmate and respect for the toy. It brings on a change in consciousness; one is transported from the profane world of work into a world whose moods are so trusting, whose sounds are so gentle, that one hears in them the rumors of an

201

202   *The Best of Times, The Worst of Times*

Absolute. *Paradisos*, after all, is the Greek word, not for "heaven," but for "park."

Play is a word about which we are profoundly ambivalent. It rings pure, clear, and innocent; but there are murky undertones—as when one is said to "play around" or to have a little "plaything." We praise the play of children but feel guilty if we play ourselves. Play, too, is an experience about which Father Greeley admits a personal ambivalence. "I enjoy it," he told me. "I like nothing more than goofing off, but I have a very strong work ethic, and it has taken some effort to play." His father lost his leprechaun after the Great Depression, and Andrew was "trained in nice Protestant virtues: diligence, responsibility, honesty." Andrew nearly lost his leprechaun, too, in his personal "crashes" of the late sixties and early seventies; but he has, he thinks, coaxed him back to life—and none too soon. "I have strong playful strains in my personality, but it takes effort to let those strains out."

The paradox of *working* at play: I saw it in action during a break in our interviewing when Father Greeley, with grim, almost compulsive determination, took his guests water-skiing. Hardly a smile crossed his face—reviewing one's life is no easy task—as he piloted his boat up and down the Indiana-Michigan shoreline and then took his turn plunging into the icy waters of the lake, rising up on his skis, and skittering back and forth across the wake we left. Later he told me that Grand Beach was a place to *work*—at least it was that way in the beginning. Only slowly, laboriously, has it become a place to play as well.

In the late 1960s, out of experience, out of need, out of curiosity, Father Greeley began to write about the cycle of work and play. A new "theology of play" was appearing on the heels of the "death of God" (Harvey Cox's *The Feast of Fools* was the unlikely sequel to *The Secular City*), and its tenets spoke to Greeley's growing realization that he, like many of Beverly Hills's upper-middle-class Irish, was simply working too hard. Robert Neale's *In Praise of Play* helped him articulate his position. "The worker is a mundane man, a man so tied to the monotony of everyday life that he cannot pull himself out of his worldly concerns to engage in the sacred play that is religion. The worker must use the world, manipulate it, bend it to his will. The player accepts the world and delights in it."[2]

A Future to Hope In, following the Dutch scholar Johan
Huizinga, saw play as the basis of ritual, poetry, music, dancing,
philosophy, even the rules of warfare. "Civilization is, in its earliest
phases, play. It does not come *from* play, like a baby catching itself
from the womb. It arises *in and as* play and never leaves it."[3] Mankind has used technology to master the world, said Greeley, but in
the process has lost touch with the world and corrupted it. If he were
not so serious, if he thought of the world as a playground, if he
treated his playground the way children treat their favorite corner of
the park, he might recover his respect for nature and his sense of
unity with it, might recapture what is at the core of his civilization.

Besides, work has become so sophisticated—much of it is no
longer "servile" but "liberal"—that unless man is playful he will
not be very good at it. Persons who overcommit themselves to work,
who pride themselves on seventy- and eighty-hour work weeks, are
actually counterproductive. "The professional (man or woman)
who has confidence in himself, stable friendships, skills in the art of
playfulness, and a happy marriage will be able to do more in a
twenty-four-hour work week than his opposite member would be
able to do in a seventy-two-hour week."[4] The person who over-
works cannot permit himself to "let up" for fear that if he does his
basic lack of talent will become manifest. He has swallowed the
assumption of modern industrial capitalism that what we *do* is
synonymous with what we *are*. But try to tell Professional Man—
Greeley was pointing the finger at himself too—that he can afford to
relax. He'll only say you're kidding. Tell him his career will profit
more from reading a sonnet or painting with water colors, and he'll
reply that you don't know how hard things are at the office. "Tell
him that the key positions in society must be manned by playful,
speculative men who understand that wisdom comes only with the
ability to be detached and relaxed, and he says that maybe when the
kids get to college he will have time to visit museums."[5]

It is not easy to play.

The sheer fun of play was hardly the motif of Greeley's first
complete volume on intimacy, *The Friendship Game.* That book,
written in the aftermath of the collapse of his New Community,
emphasized the difficulty, the terror, the pain, the convolutions and

distortions of close relationships. It began, "Man is essentially a lonely creature" who would like to be free of others and, like Alan Ladd in *Shane*, "ride off toward the mountains leaving human intimacy behind." And it ended with nothing more than, "like it or not, all of us have to learn to love one another."[6] Between beginning and end there was little in the way of fun.

What did Andrew Greeley, "trained to believe that friendship was something that he was not to be permitted,"[7] then realizing that friendship was at the core of the Christian message—what did he learn about this most difficult, demanding, exhausting of games?

He learned, first of all, about the experience of fear, of terror as primordial, and of the same type, as the infant's fear of falling. If we leave ourselves open to others, they may kill us, mutilate us, either physically or emotionally. We know the trepidation others instill in us, but we are shocked to discover that *we* terrify *them*. "Frequently, the terror flashes through the eyes of someone whom we would have thought immune from fear, and surely from fear of us." One sees "in his eyes the look of the haunted animal awaiting death." He is afraid of us and we of him, said Greeley; the mutual terror forms a bond that makes demands of its own. It is only through an invitation to friendship, a call to put aside the terror, that the chains of fear can be broken. The invitation says, "I will actually let you see me be afraid of you if you will let me see you being afraid of me."[8] The words contain a foretaste of pleasure and joy, but they demand just as surely a risky leap into an abyss.

And friendships fail, and people fall into the abyss. Why does it happen? Again we sense Greeley's understanding of the young of Beverly Hills. Friendship fails because of shame, because of the feeling that one is inadequate. To offer friendship, one must believe that he has something worth revealing to a friend, that he has intrinsic value that others will find attractive. The dancer, in other words, must have some initial confidence in his ability to dance. When someone engages in the slow, steady process of self-display (not crude, indiscriminate exhibitionism, which is actually a cover), he must assume that he is attractive. And the truth is that we are all attractive, though we *choose* inadequacy and shame because they excuse us from breaking out of the barriers that surround us. "Shame justifies our frigidity; frigidity in turn reinforces our shame. We are not good enough to be friends; we will not try to be a friend to anyone; we will strongly resist attempts at friendship from anyone else. Furthermore, as we become more practiced in our frigidity, we develop methods of blaming it on others. We offer ourselves to others in such a way as to guarantee that they will reject us."[9]

People lose at friendship, then, because they want to lose. They are psychologically frigid because, in the final analysis, they choose to be. Why is it so important to be a loser? What are the payoffs in self-defeat? For one thing, said Greeley, the loser has the power to punish all those who have invested in him and expect something from him. His failure hurts them—and he wants to hurt them. For another, he is able to maintain a solid defense against anxiety. If success is not really possible, then there is nothing to be anxious about. And his attitude can be veneered with the pride and self-respect of a perfectionist. "If he only had more time he would have done it perfectly but, as it is, the unfair time limitation imposed by a hostile world forces him to produce something that is so far beneath his own high standards that he can disavow all responsibilities for it."[10]

Greeley had often seen self-defeaters and self-haters in his life. That is how he described the Catholic left, Catholic educators, the Berrigan brothers, the reform Democrats, the New Breed turned New Community. Of the latter he said, "Sometimes, as a matter of fact, I am convinced that I have dealt with a whole generation of losers. Most of the young people with whom I have worked in my life are not risk-takers. They differ only in the degree to which they seem committed to imposing defeat after defeat upon themselves."[11]

Greeley had said it elsewhere: People become losers because of their familial past; and if one invites a loser to friendship, he can count on that crippling past's coming to the surface. In a sentence that might have been taken from Berne, Greeley commented, "we can expend all the energies of the relationship on fighting with surrogate parents and really ignore each other."[12] Psychoanalysts call the phenomenon transference (and, unlike Greeley, they see it as an instrument of cure). Because of transference we selectively perceive the other, seeking out the weak links in his personality; we distort; we construct a tightly interlocking network of hurts, injuries, and angers. We force each other to respond with the neurotic in him, not with the healthy; with the worst, not with the best. Gradually there builds an unconscious emotional investment in maintaining the inauthenticity that has stolen into the relationship.

The way out—the way beyond the terror and into the delight—is to admit what is happening and to refuse to enter the quagmire. One must be his best, most integral self in a relationship. He must remain true to his most authentic insights and instincts. If a friend demands that we abandon our privacy, our freedom, our selfhood, if he insists that we belong so totally to him that we become less than human, we must adamantly refuse. It is extremely difficult, it requires a vigorous sense of self, to reject the neurotic demand without rejecting the friend, but it must be done.

If we must offer the other, our most confident self, we must also elicit the best in him. "A man, for example, may be terribly insecure about his masculinity, and yet with the slightest show of encouragement from his wife rapidly grow in confidence about his maleness; his wife, in her turn, may be deeply troubled about her adequacy as a woman, and yet be on the verge of breaking out of those troubles with the slightest reinforcement from her husband."[13] Friends are firm, yet warm. They confront, yet support. They make demands, yet offer tenderness. They *challenge* the other—do so relentlessly—insisting that they be who and what they really are *without ever implying in the challenge a withdrawal of affection*. Demands are not to be a condition of love, but something that flows from love that is sure of itself.

There is, in other words, commitment in friendship. Friends recognize freedom, said Greeley, including the radical freedom to withdraw from the relationship, but there seems to be a turning point in a select number of relationships beyond which commitment to the relationship is no longer optional. That turning point (and most friends think they have reached it before they really have) is a trap, "a trap that we have freely chosen, a trap that oddly enough liberates us more and more."[14] Freedom is admirable, but it is most admirable when it is focused and disciplined. Radical commitment to each other enables friends to explore each other freely, without fear; it enables them to make demands—with skill, of course, and with patience and sensitivity and an appropriate sense of timing. It also allows them to accept, for the moment at least, the incompleteness and imperfection of their relationship.

The wonderful thing about the friendship game, said Greeley, is that, if both sides play well, both sides win. And we must win some of the time, for there is no other way to be a human being. "Friendship is the only way that we can come to see the riches of our own possibilities, when the admiration for those possibilities is so powerfully reflected in the face of our friend that we can no more escape it than we can the glare of the rising sun." With friends we are more relaxed, more sensitive, more creative; we are more excited and at the same time more serene; more energetic, yet more casual; more confident, but also more vulnerable. With friends we breathe purer air, hear sharper sounds, see more dramatic colors. "Friendship, indeed, seduces us into being ourself."[15]

And writing about friendship seduced Greeley into revealing himself, "perhaps more than I would want." He tells us that it is hard for him to resist irrational demands without losing his temper; that he is an expert at sulking; that he should get out of frustrating relationships sooner than he does. He speaks of an inability to combine tenderness with firmness. "Curiously enough, or perhaps not so curiously considering the chemistry of sexuality, I am much better at challenging women than men, for with women I can be gentle and tender and supportive while at the same time being insistent and demanding, but I have no idea how to be gentle and tender with other men."[16]

He has been torn by doubts as to whether the challenges he makes to friends are valid ones. And he has learned of the special problems of the person with talent:

> The gifted person does not have to have friends as gifted as he. What he needs, rather, are friends who are strong enough to enjoy his gifts without being threatened by them. Strong enough to have loved him for what he is without having to try to cut him down to size, gentle enough to heal his wounds when his enemies yap at his heels, tender enough to caress him out of his moods when he is depressed and discouraged by the animosity of others which, try as he might, he simply cannot understand, and resourceful enough to persuade him that he is indeed lovable, not merely despite his gifts but, in fact, because of them. The giant on the mountaintop looks so mighty and powerful that one would conclude that he does not need friends. In fact, he needs them more than others, or the mountaintop will turn into a wall and he will become humpty-

dumpty, and the king's horses with the king's men will arrive to
support him just a little bit too late.[17]

In an interview he reiterated that point. "I can have really close
relationships only with people who aren't threatened. Otherwise,
just forget it." He has learned, he says, that he is most effective and
most attractive when he is vigorous and forceful, that no purpose is
ever served in human relationships by being less than one's most
direct and authentic self.

The style of *The Friendship Game* is that of the "spirituality"
columns Father Greeley was writing at this time for the *National
Catholic Reporter*. The words are *spoken*, some of them actually
dictated, others verbalized as they are typed. "When I type, I talk
aloud. This sounds corny, or odd, but I *hear* it. I write what I hear. I
know what I am going to say, and it flows," he told me. "When I
have a clear and powerful insight, and I am writing with attention
to it, the words fairly dance on the page before me. I say things I am
not conscious of ever having thought before, in ways that surprise
me."[18]

Greeley says he writes as a social scientist, but in books of this
type the social scientific content varies. In *The Friendship Game*,
there is no empirical research on friendship or self-disclosure,
though there is ample, and sometimes indiscriminate, use of psychoanalysis. To borrow terms from cognitive psychology, Greeley
writes as a *sharpener*, not a *leveler*. He accentuates detail, highlights
differences in opinion, does not plow hills into valleys to even the
horizon. Or, to use a dichotomy I have developed elsewhere (*Fantasy as Mirror*, New York: Jason Aronson, in press), he is a *projector*
rather than a *reflector*. Concerned with the vigorous expression of
himself, he necessarily fails to mirror empathically the ideas of
others. Sharpening ideas and projecting oneself, it seems to me,
clarify issues; they also heighten the emotional content in communication, move the focus from *what* is said to *who* is saying it, and
increase the potential both for warm, enthusiastic support and
bitter, hateful denunciation. The stakes are high when a sharpener,
a projector, writes.

There is another pair of words, too, that helps depict this man
when he writes about intimacy. In *The Duality of Human Existence*
(Boston: Beacon, 1966), David Bakan used the word *agency* to

subsume those human motives whose goal is self-protection, self-assertion, conquest, mastery—motives that create separation. Its opposite is *communion*, a word that summarizes desires for openness, for contact, for being at one with other organisms. Greeley's approach to intimacy—communion—is, paradoxically, agentic. Union is not the given; separation is. And separation is not overcome by *being with* the other; rather, one *builds* an edifice, a bridge—slowly, painfully, skillfully—and hopes it will support him as he dares the odds and crosses the chasm to reach the other. Friendship is a "challenging and demanding game"; with "practice," the right "tactics," the right "strategy," one can win at it, master it. Friendship is not letting the other, or the self, *be*; it is making extraordinary demands on both partners in the relationship. The self is not water, but rock. The relationship does not grow on its own terms; one controls and directs it. Friendship is not trusting and adapting to whatever emerges; it is "choice, . . . a long series of decisions, . . . a determination to push on in the face of obstacles that strongly suggest we should not push on."[19]

Even Greeley's way of knowing is agentic. He approaches the dynamics of interpersonal relationships with the rational, mechanistic descriptions of psychoanalysis. He attempts to order what is disordered, find logic in the illogical, control what is uncontrolled, bring intellect to the depths of emotion. Mystery is not allowed to *be*. The human psyche is a cave, and Greeley explores it with a searchlight that reveals the formation of stalagmites and stalactites, that shows where a stream turns a corner or disappears under a wall, that lights up the twisting, deceptive routes of tunnels wide and narrow. He learns of the depths—agentically—by mastering them. He does not know the cavern—and the human person—communally, dousing the light, experiencing the essential blackness of the place, feeling the coolness in the air, sensing the current of the stream around his legs. He does something to the cave rather than, mystic-like, allowing the cave to do something to him.

Why is friendship so *hard*? Why is play something to *master*? I think of Father Greeley's upbringing in a nondemonstrative Irish family where intimacy was avoided—and of his seminary training, which taught that intimacy was to be shunned. I recall the experiences of a precocious child, whose talent set him apart from his grade-school chums, made friendship with them difficult; and I remind myself that this pattern repeated itself in Greeley's priest-hood years. He is a celibate, too; he has never *felt* sexual union, which he says is the prototype of all human friendship. But these experiences and these freely chosen circumstances, in Greeley's view, were not crucial in shaping his thoughts on friendship. "Intimacy is hard for everybody. It's not any harder for me than for most people." *The Friendship Game* was written amidst the pain of a broken community, and that explains some of the emphasis on the difficulties of interpersonal relationships. But Greeley also wished to counter the preaching of "pop psychology," which said one could attain intimacy in a weekend; and he knew of couples in their middle years who had given up on their relationship because intimacy just wasn't supposed to be *that* hard.

There is more, too. My thoughts go back to Andrew's father, a man of "immense integrity," who lived, psychologically, at some distance from his son. Not only was he a model of hard work, striving, and loyalty; not only did his fate in the depression make his son anxious to guard against a crash; but the very fact of his distance made him something to reach for, in his son's words, "a figure to stir up all kinds of ambitions." Father Greeley is the kind of man who strives, reaches, places strenuous demands—upon himself, upon others, upon relationships. Intimacy is another arena in which to achieve—not collect trophies, but simply do extraordinarily well. Greeley does not expect to have a lot of friendships in his life, but "Do I have high expectations of it when it exists? Yes, it turns out I do. I wouldn't have thought I did, but people tell me I do."

When I asked Father Greeley, a celibate, what his sources were for books like *Sexual Intimacy* (1973) and *Love and Play* (1975), he quipped, "That's my affair." He never did answer the question directly, saying only that anyone who is a parish priest and has eyes and is sensitive to human relationships knows what he knows. "I can walk into a situation where there is a man and a woman present and in a very brief period of time intuit what is going on between them. It's not hard. It's a burden, because maybe you wouldn't want to know."

Whatever their sources (Greeley occasionally named a research report but always shielded the identities of friends with whom he had conversed), these books were destined to arouse, and in many cases shock, their intended readership. For the Catholic Organization Man and his wife whose life together had grown drab, routine, and lifeless, Greeley fused religion and sexuality, not so the former oppressed the latter, acting as a superego to an id, but so the two met, liberating and reinforcing each other. The books were not how-to-do-it sex manuals, though the practical Greeley could not avoid chapters like "How to Be Sexy"; nor, on the other hand, were they codes of morality. They were, rather, theological reflections, exercises in interpretation, direct outgrowths of *Unsecular Man.* Men and women understand their mating experience in terms of the symbols their cultures provide. It was Greeley's hope that such symbols, especially the ones of the Judeo-Christian religious tradition, would underwrite—not frustrate, as they have in the past—the quest for genital intimacy.

Why *this* effort at this point in time? Because someone asked him to write a pamphlet, Greeley offers. But there is more—a statement made at the More Lectures at Yale in 1970: "Sex is certainly the most corrosive issue facing Roman Catholicism at the present time, an issue that, for the Catholic Church, is something analogous to what the Vietnam war is for the American republic. It is . . . the only subject on which the mass of the population is as disaffected as the elites."[20]

A Catholic writing about sex in the early 1970s ought to touch upon birth control, abortion, homosexuality, premarital and extra-marital intercourse, divorce, celibacy—any topic that invites moral comment. But Greeley argued that religion is not a moral code and that religious interpretation of human behavior has little to do with specific prohibitions or permissions. Issues of indissolubility, reproduction, the importance of human life, respect for the body are *secondary* considerations for a theology of sexuality. Before looking at these, one should ask, simply and bluntly, what resources do religious symbols (in this case, those of the Judeo-Christian system) make available to facilitate and promote intimacy, to heighten the ecstasy of lovers writhing in genital union?

A chapter of another Greeley book, *The New Agenda* (1973), recalled the sexual doctrine of "apologetic" Catholicism. One could not enjoy "voluntary" sexual pleasure outside of marital intercourse, and "involuntary" sexual feelings outside that context were not "seriously" sinful if one did not take pleasure in them. Of course, no "artificial impediment" was to stand in the way of conception. Greeley found nothing in the New Testament to justify such an approach and identified other forces in the West—Platonism, chronic underpopulation, Puritanism, eighteenth-century casuistry—as sources of the rigid, juridical, sin-obsessed approach to sex that led ultimately to the disastrous *Humanae Vitae*. New Testament symbols have nothing of that. On the contrary, "It is surely no misinterpretation of the intent of the twenty-fifth chapter of St. Matthew to say that the Christian believes what Jesus has told him, 'Whatever you do to your spouse, you do to me.'" The New Testament forces us to ask, "When a man patiently, gently but demandingly, brings his prudish and frightened woman to orgasm and teaches her how to be an enchantress, is he doing something to God? And when a woman pursues her husband so effectively that he simply cannot avoid her sexual entanglements and is persuaded that she wants him even more than he wants her, is she doing something to God?"[21]

Not only does the New Testament ask these questions, Greeley asserted, it answers them clearly in the affirmative. That affirmation has to be placed in the context of enormous changes in sexuality in the past century and a half. "In our era the problem is not underpopulation but overpopulation; marriage is no longer an important institution for the transmission of property; infant mortality rates are low, life expectancies are long, and the amount of time a child is dependent on his parent has trebled over even a century ago."[22] With changes in the role of women, with the virtual perfection of methods of contraception, sexuality has evolved into a means of finding personal fulfillment and happiness.

Contemporary sexual standards allow anything. "Pre-marital, extra-marital (or in the slick euphemism of Eugene Fontinell, 'co-marital') intercourse, homosexuality, necking and petting, masturbation, and everything else short of bestiality (and in some cases I suspect even that is not excluded) become legitimate forms of human behavior, so long as they are 'growth-producing.'" Shallow, glib, prone to self-deception, the New Sexuality nevertheless has hit upon a central insight: sex is between persons and not between organs. "It is embarrassing to observe that Carl Rogers certainly perceives that and Paul VI apparently does not."[23]

What the New Sexuality misses, however, and what the story of Yahweh and his people, of Christ and his Church, celebrate, is that "the psychodynamics of intimacy are such that there is a strain toward permanency in any important intimate relationship," that "the kind of consideration, self-discipline, trust, tenderness, patience, strength, and affection that are necessary for genital intimacy to be growth-producing are much less likely to exist if one can obtain orgasms elsewhere whenever one feels like it or whenever one is able to persuade oneself that such orgasms are self-fulfilling."[24] Permanency and exclusiveness, however, cannot be *legislated* into a relationship. They are not a wall that the conscience builds out of a sense of ought. They are, rather, desires that arise instinctually if a relationship is maturing in intimacy.

In such an atmosphere of growing commitment, one wishes to be "sexy" for his or her partner. Being "sexy"—a chapter from *Sexual Intimacy* on this topic appeared in *Redbook* magazine—means creating an erotic atmosphere around oneself, inviting potential sexual partners, enjoying playfulness and variety in a genital relationship. "The sexy person says in effect, 'I am not merely a woman or a man. I am a playmate, a lover with whom you can have all kinds of fun. With me, even some of your wildest fantasies can be enjoyed in reality. I am not just an outlet like everyone else of my sex. I am a challenge and an opportunity.'"[25]

Father Greeley continued. We often are not sexy because we feel inadequate. "One is afraid to reveal one's sexual organs because they may not be good enough. Physical shame is intimately connected with human shame; fear to reveal sexual organs results from feelings of human inadequacy." Shame—over our bodies, over our selves—inhibits openness and playfulness, blocks the communication of sexual hunger, grays the revelation of sexual fantasies. Were we aware of our bodies as instruments of playfulness and delight—"the nerves and muscles of the human body, and particularly of the human sex organs, were made to be played with by a member of the opposite sex"[26]—were we struck forcibly by the attractiveness of that figure in the mirror, were we to work at and learn the skills of erotic self-display and seduction, we would be a mystery, a challenge, an opportunity to our spouse. We would be "sexy."

At the heart of sexiness is the element of *surprise*. Two lovers know at the beginning of the day that they will make love in the evening. Is their routine predictable, devoid of variety and wonder? Or are there questions on the margins of awareness that tease and puzzle each of them throughout the day?

> The husband, for example, may be asking, how will she respond? Will she be hungry and passionate, perhaps even more aggressive than I? Will she be shy and passive? Will she want me to take her directly and forcefully—perhaps even on the living room floor after the children are asleep, or shall I make it a long and involved seduction scene? Will I wait until we get into bed, or will I begin to undress her? What will she look like? What will she be wearing? Will she have on that transparent lingerie in which she looks so delicious? Will she let me take off her bra?

> And the woman will be semiconsciously dwelling on similar questions. When will he start? Will it begin even before supper or will he wait? Where will his hands and his mouth go first? Will he be in one of those moods when he wants to strip me leisurely? Shall I turn the tables on him tonight and strip him first, or will I surprise him with my plan to trap him at his work in the library when I approach him wearing only panties and a martini pitcher—or maybe only the martini pitcher? Will I kneel on top of him, forcing my body down on his?[27]

If surprise is at the heart of erotic invitation, it is also at the heart of God's invitation to his people. "God's intervention in our lives was a total and complete surprise. Yahweh on Sinai caught Israel flat-footed, and the resurrection of Jesus caught the apostles equally flat-footed. Yahweh proclaimed on Sinai, and Jesus renewed the proclamation, that life is wonderful and filled with surprises, the greatest of which is God's incredible love for us." The realities spoken of by the Judeo-Christian symbol system insure that the wife who catches her husband flat-footed in the library is acting in accordance with *the way things are,* for it ". . . is strict theological truth to say that the capacity to cause surprise and delight in others by erotic self-display is a continuation of Yahweh's work."[28] Religious symbols exist not to crush sexual intimacy but to facilitate it.

Sexual Intimacy went on to discuss the "insatiable female" and the "uncertain male." Research indicates that a woman can experience orgasmic satisfaction indefinitely, that "uninhibited by cultural and psychological barriers, a woman's sexuality appears to be both more intense and more demanding than that of a man."

Powerful cultural restraints that have long controlled female sexuality are currently being lifted, and that presents a dilemma for most women: orgasm has become obligatory. "Intense sexual pleasure is now all right, but how does one go about experiencing it?" Greeley's answer is that her lover must understand what it takes, physiologically, to arouse her ("he has his hands, his mouth, his penis—what does he think they are for?"[29]), and she must guide him, bluntly and explicitly, to the kind of refined knowledge he needs. It is not easy to begin communication. One does not break out of well-established patterns of shame, reticence, timidity, and fear without a good deal of pain. But there is no other way to grow.

The male, on the other hand, is afraid of failure and rejection—and his sexual failure is more obvious than that of the woman. He also finds it difficult to combine strength and tenderness, agency and communion, the instrumental with the expressive. Expected to be hard-driving, ruthless, and ambitious in the world of his career, he is supposed to be compassionate, tender, and sympathetic at home. The dilemma extends to his lovemaking. "The net result is a male who, in the genital encounter, is neither agentic enough nor communal enough. He does not know either when to be strong or when to be weak, or how to take, or how to permit himself to be taken, and you really cannot be virile unless you can combine the expressive with the instrumental. The 'stud' may 'ball' a woman but that's all he can do. The virile man, on the other hand, knows how to make love, knows how to combine aggressiveness with tenderness, demand with surrender." Further, though he may be reluctant to admit it, a man needs to be mothered. "To be 'mothered' means to be smothered with affection, to be covered with sensuous attention, to have every part of one's being, body, and spirit gently and passionately caressed, to experience a relationship which furnishes the psychological equivalent of a hot bath and a warm, dry robe after coming in out of a cold, damp rainstorm."[30] There is no limit to the amount of caressing—direct, physical, sensuous, "obscene" caressing—that a man can absorb. It may be easy for him to become aroused physiologically (and to get "laid"), but if arousal means more than the stimulation of erectile tissues, if it means the development of confidence in one's ability to combine strength and tenderness, agency and communion, then arousal is extremely difficult. Courage is needed for the man to admit and communicate a need to surrender, for the woman to break through his defenses and offer what he desperately needs.

And such courage can be underwritten only by an act of faith in oneself, in the other, and in reality. One has to believe that reality (and one can spell it with a small *r* or a capital *R*) is ultimately gracious, that things will be all right in the end. It is precisely such a conviction that Yahweh communicated to his people, that Jesus ratified with his death and resurrection. These religious symbols ought to persuade Christian lovers to take the risk of self-exposure. "If Yahweh can admit he 'needs' the affection of his beloved, then why should any man be afraid to admit the same thing?"[31] And if Jesus rose from the dead, why should husband and wife doubt that risk and pain and death in their relationship now will mean joy and resurrection later on?

Indeed, the most striking characteristic of the entire Judeo-Christian symbol system is the *fidelity* of God to his beloved people. In the book of Exodus Yahweh made it clear that no matter what we did as his people, he would remain our God. In the sexual imagery of Osee, Jeremiah, and Ezekiel, he emphasized that, though we whore with false gods, he will never turn his back on us and seek another people. So, too, should husband and wife be faithful to each other.

But Greeley's understanding of faithfulness in marriage was not the traditional one. "I am suggesting that marital fidelity ought to mean a commitment to improving without limitation the quality of one's total relationship with one's spouse, especially and particularly the quality of lovemaking. The unfaithful person, then, is not so much the one who has a playmate somewhere else, but rather, one who does not by seduction and facilitation keep his wife a playmate. Similarly, the unfaithful woman is not so much one who goes after another man as one who has stopped (or in fact never began) going after her husband."[32] One is either having more and more fun in bed or less and less. Fidelity is a commitment to seek more. Infidelity is giving up.

Fidelity provides lovers a safe arena in which to fight. "Lovers must fight. They can only love if they fight; it enhances the quality of their love. Love without conflict is tame, passionless, dull." Fighting says that lovers care about their relationship, that they are not afraid to reveal their anger, to show the raw edges of their personality. In a genital relationship one must demand from the other—as Yahweh demanded from his people—the best that he or she is capable of giving.

> The young man whose passive wife closes her eyes when he is doing to her the things a man should be doing to a woman ought to be possessed by outraged fury. He ought to shake her angrily until her eyes open wide and shout, "Damn you! Look at me when I play with you!" . . . Similarly, the young woman whose husband is a timid and disappointing lover is scarcely being very effective when she buys him a book. She should face him with withering scorn and demand, "Don't you know anything about how to seduce a woman?"[33]

Sexual Intimacy emphasized the need for practice, skill, determination, and work in a genital relationship. One of Greeley's favorite analogies, used already in *The Friendship Game*, was the tough but sophisticated professional quarterback—a Tittle, a Jurgensen, a Unitas, a Tarkenton—who had the guts, the instincts, the savvy to read the defense of the opposition, to call the right audible, to deliver the ball under pressure—to win the game. Critics, when they did not scoff at the idea of a priest writing about sex, said Greeley "romanticized" or "idealized" the marital relationship; but he was in fact setting high, almost impossible levels of performance, just as he had done in *The Friendship Game*. Greeley's Christians had to be the best at everything, and that included lovemaking. "The God of the Testaments, New and Old, is not a 'nice' God at all but a lover consumed with *eros*. It is disgraceful for his followers to mate with each other in any but the most fervent, erotic way."[34]

Greeley's sequel to *Sexual Intimacy*, a small volume entitled *Love and Play*, retained the agentic, striving motifs of its predecessor—lovers had to be strong, competitive, and demanding—but its mood was more authentically playful. Greeley wrote of suspense in play, of lovers who remained mysteries to each other—teasing, surprising, seducing enigmas—not only in their bed but in their entire life together. If you know all there is to know about your spouse, he said simply, the game is over. The truth of the matter is that human beings are extraordinarily complex; the mystery of the other is never exhausted; the more we discover, the more we realize there are heights and depths and breadths yet unknown. It all depends on how the relationship is defined. "Another human being is either a closed and uninteresting book or a constant and endless source of fascination. Whether he be interesting or not depends as much on our definition of and response to him as on any intrinsic quality of his own nature."[35]

To explore the mystery of another is extremely erotic—is, in fact, the most erotic thing a human being can do. "When that exploration is reinforced and facilitated by sexual lovemaking, the lovemaking becomes an episode in a grand adventure, taking on an intensity of pleasure that it would otherwise not have." The trouble is that exploration takes time and skill and patience; and being explored, well, it permits another to have a frightening amount of knowledge and power over one. All in all, "it is much, much easier to buy a copy of *Playboy* or advertise in one of the spouse-swapping journals."[36]

If play is suspenseful, said Greeley, it is also fantastic. It delivers itself to the ingenious, creative, energetic impulses of the imagination. The fantasy world of lovers is raw, primal, infantile, perverse. Incest and rape, homosexuality and sadomasochistic orgies exist in the same chaotic preconscious that is the source of our most beautiful religious symbols. Shall this uncontrollable wellspring of "dirty thoughts" be capped? Or shall lovers allow it to burst forth, even delight in its force and vigor? There is only one answer for the Christian who plays: Let the imp out of the bottle and listen to what he has to say. Couples will vary in the extent to which they share sexual fantasies, and Greeley advised that communication along these lines remain optional; but, by and large, the "slow, gradual, tasteful, witty sharing of daydreams is probably a sign of healthy development." A woman yearns in fantasy to caress and kiss the penis of a young lifeguard on the beach; indeed, if the truth be told, there are many, many penises she would like to kiss. She never will—but there are always her husband's organs to be kissed whenever she wishes. And her husband daydreams over a scotch in the golf course bar that tall, athletic women with large breasts take off all his clothes and tie him to a bench. They pinch him, tickle him, play with him, kiss him, make him suck on their breasts, then drag him off to the shower to cover him with soapsuds and embrace his wet, slippery body. "Chances are that his fantasy will not come true, but a warm, soapy, stimulating shower with his wife is another matter altogether. She may resist at first, but if he is afraid to ask, afraid to try, afraid to insist (as many men are), then an opportunity for playfulness that would creatively release some of his fantasy energy has been passed by."[37]

Play is suspenseful, fantastic—and festive. The ancients *celebrated* when a young animal was born, when the seeds were planted in the fields, when the first fruits were harvested—when life won a victory over death. In like manner should sexual play celebrate life, rejoicing in all the goodness and dignity and strength and growth that one has experienced. The organs of the other may simply be sensitive glands that one enjoys touching; or they may be revelations of grace, love, and elegance at the core of the universe. Christian lovers know—or at least they should know—that breasts, vaginas, and penises are more than organs. When they unite there is "a revelation, a sacrament, the Eucharist, a participation in the basic life forces of the universe."[38] Their union should bring to mind the festivals of the ancients, celebrations that fused religion and sex in sheer exuberance over the fact of life.

Sex and play, finally, are humorous. The naked human body (even a beautiful one) is funny, if only because we spend most of our time wearing clothes. And sexual arousal is even funnier; men and women of reason, sobriety, and control, aristocrats and paupers alike, are reduced to the same common denominator, thrashing about, uncontrolled, like the animals they are. Parents find children precious, important, beautiful— but also funny. The laughter of lovers at each other, expressed in a similar context of mutual affirmation, adds immeasurably to their relationship. It hints, too, at other things: all laughter is a laughing at death, according to Peter Berger's *A Rumor of Angels* (New York: Doubleday, 1968), a response of confidence to those fears and anxieties ultimately rooted in death. The private jokes of lovers are rumors of "a great Cosmic Joke in which life successfully puts down death."[39]

Suspense, fantasy, festivity, and laughter. They are woven into the fabric of a relationship strengthened by long years of discipline and practice. You have to work at play, said Andrew Greeley, until you get good enough at it to relax and rejoice in it. In discussing the dynamics of games, *Love and Play* was actually pressing for fidelity in a sexual relationship; its basic position was that true playfulness can only occur in an environment created by permanent commitment. Children do not play with strangers or casual acquaintances—they play with friends. How can lovers do otherwise? In the words of D. H. Lawrence, "Where there is real sex there is the underlying passion for fidelity."[40]

And so, Christian lovers, said Greeley, play with each other in defiance of death. Tease, surprise, seduce, sing, dance, clap your hands. Believe in the import of Scripture: "life, for all its tragedy, is still ultimately a comedy, indeed, a comic, playful dance with a passionately loving God."[41]

We have come to the heart of Andrew Greeley.

11   The Yahwistic Myths

And so we seek to understand the man. Enough of the survey research entrepreneur, the lay psychologist, the giver of advice, the caustic journalist. Enough, too, of selves closer to the core: Chicagoan, Irish-American, Democrat, man of the neighborhood, even Catholic priest. I have chosen in this book—and it is a choice—to see a man, to define his core, by listening to how he interprets reality, by asking what meaning he ascribes to the events of his life—to the victories and defeats, to the coming and going of friends and foes, to the fundamental births and deaths that these are. I am looking at a man's ego rather than his id, "explaining" him by describing his belief system rather than by speculating about the vicissitudes of his libidinal development, capturing his adult years rather than reacting to his first psychological steps. May I leave Father Greeley with some of the mystery that any human being possesses.

As far back as 1961—and, really, as far back as an unpublished master's thesis—Andrew Greeley was writing about the religious myth. To him, myth did not mean fable or fairy tale, but "a universal category of belief." To speak of "the soteriological myth," for example, did "not imply that redemption is a self-deception, but merely that there seems to be a universal tendency for man to believe in redemption and a redeemer."[1] A decade later, articles in *America* and *Concilium*[2] and books like *Come Blow Your Mind with Me* and *Unsecular Man* argued against the urgings of theologian Rudolph Bultmann and Bishop John A. T. Robinson that religious symbols be "demythologized." Greeley contended that the 1960s had witnessed a decline of confidence in rational enlightenment and a resurgence of interest in the intuitive, the mystical, the psychedelic. It was hardly the time to evict the mythological from religious traditions; on the contrary, one ought to make it feel more at home, understand it on its own terms, and, if necessary, translate it into propositional language. One had to ask what the *imagery* of the Judeo-Christian tradition provided in the way of answers to humankind's fundamental religious needs.

Clifford Geertz had written of religion that it presented a conviction about the inherent structure of reality and told man how to come in contact and be in harmony with that reality. That is what the Judeo-Christian—the Yahwistic—myths were all about: explaining, speaking to the whole person (the poetic as well as the cerebral sensitivities), communicating a conviction, and—a favorite word of Father Greeley—*underwriting*. To underwrite is to reassure, to back up, to guarantee safety in the face of risk, and so to say, go ahead and take a chance. In the face of the complexities, the pain, the signs of death in human life, Greeley believes that this—underwriting—is the function of the Yahwistic symbols. What, then, are the convictions they generate about human living and human dying? Divested of thousands of years of accretion, what are they saying about the structure of reality?

To hear Father Greeley answer these questions is to hear *him*.

Jesus.

Who was he? What does the Jesus symbol—stripped of the piety, the theological controversy, the ecclesiastical triumphalism that has encrusted it—what does it convey about the inner meaning of human life, about the structure of the universe? If the deposits of later centuries are scraped away, the "historical" Jesus stands forth "unique, original, and startling. It is small wonder that he frightened and shocked his contemporaries and that they would not accept what he said. It is also small wonder that we have done our best to obscure the shocking nature of the symbolism of Jesus ever since."[3] So Greeley wrote in *The Jesus Myth* (1971), a book that brought the approach of Clifford Geertz to the latest in New Testament scholarship.

It is—and was—hard to categorize Jesus. He dominated the crowds, was master of his band of disciples, yet always insisted he was the servant. He was familiar with publicans and sinners, yet the quality of his friendship was determined by him, not by the publicans and sinners. He was not a political revolutionary (and many Jews were estranged from him because he was not), yet he wept over the impending fate of Jerusalem and was executed as a political agitator. "In other words, Jesus went about providing answers to questions that no one was asking and refusing to answer the questions everyone thought important." The establishment Sadducees, corrupt heirs of the ancient church, would have nothing to do with him. The Pharisees, "liberal reformers filled with self-righteousness and zeal," were horrified by his disregard of the law and his condemnation of their moral arrogance. The Zealots, hoping for a drastic political reorganization that would right the injustices all around them, were disillusioned by his refusal to act as a political messiah. And the Essenes, who had withdrawn from a corrupt society to build a perfect world of their own, were no doubt appalled by his proclamation of a kingdom for all men. "One can imagine that a frequent question people asked about him was, 'But where does he really stand?' "[4]

To those who would ask such a question, Greeley continued, Jesus said simply: the kingdom of God is at hand. His words were not a threat (though many have turned them into precisely that) but a proclamation of incredibly good news and an invitation to a banquet. A new reign was about to begin and that was cause for celebration. Rejoice, Jesus said, because at the core of the universe is an incredibly generous and loving God. God is like the father of a son who has frittered away his inheritance. When the son crawls home to beg forgiveness, the father rushes out to embrace him, silences his carefully rehearsed statement of sorrow, clothes him in the finest of garments, and throws a party, complete with music and dancing, good food and good drink. God is a shepherd crazy enough to track down one lost sheep when ninety-nine are safely in the herd, an employer lunatic enough to give workers a full day's pay for only a single hour's work. "What is the universe all about?" Greeley asked. "The reality with which Jesus felt so intimate was passionate love, so passionate as to appear by human standards to be insane."[5]

If we listen to the parables of Jesus, said Greeley, we then discover that God is throwing a party and that we are all invited. It is up to us to accept the invitation, to say firmly and decisively that we will come. How foolish it would be to act like the invited guests in the parable of the Great Feast and say, I just bought a field and have to look after it; or, I must try out five new pairs of oxen; or, I just got married, please excuse me. If we pass up this invitation we will not get another. The host will go out to the streets and alleys, if necessary, and ask others to come, saying to us, you will never again taste of my dinners.

The invitation of Jesus was good news—fantastic news. "The message responds to the most basic and agonizing question that faces all who are part of the human condition: Is everything going to be all right in the end? Jesus' response was quite literally to say, 'You bet your life it is.' "⁶ Human beings hope against hope that life is not capricious, that there is purpose behind it all, that death is not the final answer. They do, as Freud said, *wish* for a God who assures order and meaning and immortality. What Jesus said, in effect, was that our wildest dreams, our loftiest hopes, our maddest fantasies, our deepest wishes are true. And more: the heart of reality is even more gracious and more beneficent than we could possibly imagine.

The good news was not cheap consolation, not "pie in the sky when you die," said Greeley. Jesus did not deny the terrible realities of injustice and suffering and death; he said merely that love will triumph in the end. His message is not opium for the masses; on the contrary, it will not tolerate the discouragement that causes so many social movements to burn themselves out in a few years. It conveys a fundamentally optimistic view of reality, a view that gives (or at least ought to give) hope and confidence, qualities that underwrite sustained commitment no matter how completely the sky clouds over.

The challenge laid down by Jesus was ethical, but not primarily so. The principal responsibility of the invited guest was to accept the news of the kingdom and enter the feast *now*—without delay, without hedging, without looking back. This "basic existential leap" in which we "decisively commit ourselves to the notion that the Really Real is in fact insanely generous love"⁷ produces a *metanoia* (or total transformation of the person), and the ethics of the kingdom *follow from* the *metanoia*. If one goes all the way in his acceptance of the great assurance offered by Jesus, he will experience the love of God and naturally (though still not without pain and difficulty) extend that love to others. He will feel the forgiveness of God and thus have the wherewithal to forgive others. The Good Samaritan was not paying the price of admission to the kingdom when he stopped to help a man who should have been his natural enemy; no, he had already entered the kingdom and could not do otherwise. Nor is the Sermon on the Mount strict moral imperative; it is nothing more than a description of the style of life of those feasting at the banquet given by the Lord.

As for the resurrection of Jesus, said Greeley, it is something that can never be confirmed by historical fact (the only fact of which we can be certain is that the early Christians had a profound experience of Jesus immediately after his death). What the Easter symbol *means* is far more important than the details of the resurrection. It means that the Really Real is love so powerful that even sin and death cannot contain it; it is love so resourceful that we too (in what manner we do not know) shall live. So the issue is not our belief in the way in which Jesus lives but our acceptance of the kingdom that his resurrection validates and our confidence in the belief that victory is ultimately assured, that everything will be all right in the end.

Why, then, do so many refuse to accept this incredibly good news? Not because what Jesus said was burdensome or threatening, Greeley answered, but because it was hopeful, spectacularly hopeful, *too* hopeful. Men have rejected this message not out of greed or ambition or fear, but out of cynicism, not because events in Jesus' life (and the existence of God) are impossible to verify, but because men "believe that evil triumphs over good, that life is absurd and is a tale told by an idiot, that the Really Real is malign, and that only a blind fool would believe that things will be all right in the end."[8]

Then too, accepting the invitation to the kingdom is not easy. It was not easy, Greeley wrote, for his New Community. Having discovered the possibility of leading a life of confidence, hope, love, and joy, they suddenly realized that these make demands. They understood "how much they would have to give up, how many of their foolish fears and defenses they would have to put away, how open their lives would be to ridicule and laughter, the many risks they would have to take."[9] It became clear—though no one would admit it—that the joys of the banquet were simply not worth the demands it made.

So, strangely enough, the Jesus symbol—the most important religious symbol in the West—stands for gaiety, not fear, for self-confidence, not self-deprecation, for invitation, not condemnation. And, even more strangely, it has been rejected (and distorted by

"Christians") precisely because of this, precisely because it is good news, not bad.

Greeley wrote more about Jesus—a collection of meditations entitled *Jesus Now* (1972), a piece in the *New York Times* that was reprinted later in a number of other papers including the *Chicago Daily News* (where it drew the ire of readers as a "contumelious attack on the Divine Founder of Christianity"[10]). *The Jesus Myth*, itself one of the few books written on Greeley's own initiative, was his most popular work and is now available in five languages. "Why was it so popular?" I asked. "Because it's about Jesus," he said—and no more than that.

The Father, Yahweh.

The facts seem to be these. A group of Semitic slaves, a grab-bag collection of tribes, really, escape from Egypt. Some of their number have an experience near a sacred mountain in the desert; then all of them come together and form a unity around a belief in one common God.

Many questions of fact surround this remarkable social and political event. What really happened on Mount Sinai? Was Moses an actual historical personage? Did God personally engrave letters on stone tablets? But these questions, failing to take the mythmaker on his own terms, miss the point. What matters is that Israel chose the symbol of the covenant (*berith*) to describe for itself the nature of the Holy it encountered in the desert, and the question we should ask, the *religious* question, is "What kind of relationship between man and God does the covenant symbol describe?"

Greeley's development of an answer appeared in *Youth Asks, Does God Still Speak?* (1970) and *What a Modern Catholic Believes about God* (1971), but its most complete articulation was *The Sinai Myth* (1972). The latter pushed his interpretation of the Judeo-Christian symbol system back, beyond the Jesus myth, to its very origins.

We err, Greeley said, if we think the Sinai experience recorded in the book of Exodus was primarily ethical. Sinai was a religious event, an encounter of man with God, and "the ethical code which emerged from that encounter was simple, not especially original, and rather of secondary importance."[11] The Ten Commandments are part of a larger religious revelation; they do not enumerate the conditions for earning Yahweh's favor but the consequences and evidences of accepting it.

At the center of the religious experience of the Israelites was the feeling that God had offered a covenant—a promise, a treaty, a pact, an agreement—and that they had accepted it. The covenant, freely entered into by both sides, established a permanent relationship with responsibility for *Chesed*—love, loyalty, ready action—on both sides. The idea seems commonplace now, but at the time it was radical, perhaps "the most dramatic change in the whole history of human religions." In other religions God was identified either with nature or with society, "but for Israel the relationship with God was the result of positive action on the part of Yahweh himself. It was an action that demanded a positive response from Israel."[12] This Holy encountered in the desert was at the same time more powerful *and* more benign than that encountered in any religious experience before or since.

The fundamental insight contained in the symbol of God the Covenanter is that he is involved with his people, he is committed to them, he cares for them. At the time of the Sinai revelation it was an unbelievable perception, too good to be true. "Yahweh is not merely a God, not merely a Jewish God: he is a pushy Jewish God who refuses to leave his people alone."[13] The history of Israel subsequent to Sinai, said Greeley, is a record of a "jealous old peasant warrior sitting up on the top of Sinai and growing wrathful over the infidelity of his people."[14] He is angry not because the rules are broken time and again, but because he is jealous. And his jealousy is based on love.

We learn of the love in Osee and in parts of Jeremiah and Ezekiel. Here Yahweh is symbolized as husband and lover, indeed a "cuckolded husband who will not give up on his love."[15] Israel has been a harlot, a bride unfaithful to Yahweh, but still his passion for her cannot be cooled. Though sexual imagery pervades human religion, this image of God "hung up" on his people through all their whoring is so revolutionary as to be blasphemous. "Not only is the Really Real a Thou who cares for us and pursues us, it is now even a Thou of whom it can be said that he is sexually aroused in our presence: an idea which was shocking to the Jews, profoundly

scandalous to their neighbors, and difficult enough for the Jan-
senists and the Puritans in modern Christianity to give much cre-
dence to."[16]

At the core of the universe there beats passionate love; that is
what Old Testament myths *qua* myths mean to Andrew Greeley. It
is the same meaning he found in the New Testament symbols of
Jesus. Indeed, all that Jesus did was renew the theophany of Sinai.
"It is not a new Yahweh that we encounter in Jesus but rather a
more highly developed, more explicitly stated and more richly
symbolized Yahweh."[17]

"God in your work gets more and more insanely generous," I
commented to Father Greeley.

"Yep. Right. That's what he's like."

"Why?" A psychologist, I was thinking of "compensation" for
the losses of the past few years, of "projecting" goodness *out there* to
balance the evil he had seen. But no.

"Because I understand the Scriptures better. I think that's in the
sources."

I pursued. "Is it that life is getting more vicious?"

"No, I don't think so. I've thought about that, but I don't think
that's the case, because he operates at a totally different level of being
than that. I think it's a cop-out to say, well I don't mind the bastards because God loves me. I do mind the bastards."

Whatever the origin of Greeley's position—and I am one to
believe in congruence between the experiences of a man, like loss
and loneliness, and what he seeks and finds (often because it's there)
in Scripture—Greeley's Yahweh is indeed that pushy, demanding
old warrior sitting on top of Sinai. He cares for you (so much that
sometimes you wish he'd leave you alone), but you don't exactly
mess with him, and you'd better tip your old sailor's cap when you
mention his name—or else he might send some more big waves and
remove the last smidgen of sand from under your house. You can, as
"one of his creatures," write a book of *Complaints Against God*
(1971) and gripe about the 747, April snowstorms, the necessity of
sleep, and, well, that whole silly notion of his that he *wants* us. And,
you know, you can even call him "The Boss" or its Irish equivalent,
the "Ole Fella."

As a matter of fact, who ever had a conversation with the

Absolute, the Infinite, the Ground of Being, the Prime Mover, or
Ens a Se? And who's interested (so Greeley wrote in his column) in
"a punctilious, persnickety, tough deity who insists on being
referred to piously as 'Almighty God. . . The only God worthy of
believing in is one you can call 'The Boss.' " Blasphemy, maybe, but
the Ole Fella himself told us to do it:

> On Sinai he announced that he had entered into an intimate,
> personal relationship with his people—uninvited and frequently
> not wanted. "I am Yahweh your God." Period, paragraph, end of
> revelation. All else since has been explication.
>
> Then someone came along and referred to God as "Abba,
> Father"—a term of familiar affection even more daring than
> "Boss." He added something about not calling us servants but
> friends. He also said that the Kingdom of Heaven was like a great
> banquet.
>
> Only a whimsical, crazy God could get so involved with his crea-
> tures. The creeps and squares have never been able to buy that and
> have tried to deceive the rest of us ever since.
>
> [Really told 'em off, didn't I, Boss? Let's have another party.][18]

The Spirit.

Scripture says little about this, the most ethereal of the Christian images of God. It refers to the Spirit as advocate, comforter,
source of strength, wind, fire, and light. We are told that we are to be
born again of the Spirit, that the Spirit will be with us until Jesus
returns. There is little else.

If the Spirit makes only the briefest of appearances in the Bible,
he is just as evasive in the works of Father Greeley. But he is there,
darting up for acknowledgment in the titles of tiny volumes of reprinted columns like *The Life of the Spirit* (1970) and *The Touch of
the Spirit* (1971), flitting into a paragraph or a chapter of a book
about God. He is in Father Greeley, too, who will tell you quite
seriously that he listens hard to what the Spirit—even though he is a
mischievous prankster—is trying to tell him. "The Holy Spirit," he
relates, "is that power in the cosmos which speaks to that which is
most unique and most creative and most special in all of us."

The Spirit speaks to our spirit, St. Paul says, unlocking the fear
and timidity that close us in, activating what is most visionary, most

playful, most hopeful, most open within us. The Spirit is *wind*: "at times He whirls down the corridor of our house like a tornado; at other times He barely touches us as does a spring breeze."[19] The Spirit is *fire*, melting our frigidity, stirring us to passionate enthusiasm. The Spirit is *light*; it shines on our talents and refuses to let us cover with a bushel whatever makes us different from others. Do we know if the impulse we feel comes from the Spirit? If it leads us to risk ourselves and grow, if it elicits the best we are capable of (as it did the apostles on Pentecost), we should have no doubt as to its source.

The Spirit, blowing where he will, stands for improvisation, surprise, playing it by ear. "The Spirit simply will not be tied down, and when someone announces here the Spirit is, we have Him here, please come and see Him, they find that by the time they get us to the room where they claim to have Him, the nimble, agile Spirit will have flown the coop and will be somewhere else, perhaps laughing at our foolish notion that we could capture Him."[20] Never, never does He provide the simple, magical answer, says Greeley. God's appearance on Sinai was a surprise; the Good News of Jesus was a surprise; what the Spirit has in store for us will likewise be a surprise. Life for the Christian, in fact, should mean developing the capacity for surprise, the capacity to cope with the greatest uncertainty of all—death and what comes after.

Activating the unique in all of us, teaching us to relish the unique in others, surprising us, refusing to be captured, the leprechaun-like Spirit is the principle of diversity in the Judeo-Christian symbol system. Yahweh the Father stands for unity; without him there would be the chaos of the scattered tribes of Israel. Jesus the Son does too; he came, after all, to make us one. But the Spirit symbolizes and underwrites differentiation; without him we would have a religion of dullness. It is the Spirit who inspires us to experiment with alternatives in education, in Church structure, in priestly ministries; it is the Spirit who had dabbed the American landscape with ethnic variegation (and who zips in and out of the offices of the Center for the Study of American Pluralism); it is the Spirit who rejoices over a political structure that respects diversity; it is the Spirit who says Christian spouses must tease, surprise, and seduce each other and love with polymorphous perversity.

In another paper, Greeley continued. One could, he said, create a "theology of pluralism," a theology consonant with the stops and starts, the whirls and twirls, of this poltergeist Holy Spirit. Such a theology would be rooted in the American experience of unity amidst diversity and would resonate with the ancient philosophical and theological mystery of the One and the Many.

Why did God will that the Many be *so* diverse? Greeley asked. Wouldn't one language, one religion, one race have been enough— especially when one realizes that evil is deeply involved in diversity, that it is precisely over *differences*, differences as important or unimportant as skin color and facial configuration, that men fight and die? Perhaps the Scholastic theologians in the Middle Ages were right. They concluded from the tower of Babel myth that it was sin that introduced diversity into the world. On the other hand, were it not for the particularities of space and time that produced Shakespeare, Dante, Mozart, and Jesus—and Thai silks and Jewish humor and American black music and Irish whiskey—humankind would remain deprived of its storehouse of creative riches. Why would God tolerate such a paradox, good and evil stemming from the same fact of our differentiation?

There must have been a party, Greeley (now a mythmaker himself) mused, a splendid party where God got drunk and decided to show off for the angels. So he spewed out creation in reckless abandon, in senseless superabundance—all those galaxies, all those stars and planets, and on this earth such a mosaic of birds and reptiles, fishes and mammals and peoples in all those sizes and shapes and colors—and said, "There. Look at that! What a marvelous joke!" But, alas, we humans lacked a sense of humor and instead of delighting in the differences we thought it better to fight over them—thus Jesus was necessary to make us one again.

A homemade parable, explaining nothing but articulating completely Greeley's conviction, thought as well as felt, that human diversity is "a manifestation of the overwhelming, overflowing goodness and power of the divine love."[21] It is human sinfulness that refuses to revel in the diversity, that leads us to be frightened of those who are different from us, to strike out at them before they come to destroy us.

The Devil.
Satan, Lucifer, Prince of Darkness, call him what you will. To

the Buddhists, he was Mara; to the Assyrians, Pazuzu; to the
Babylonians, Tiamat; to the Egyptians, Set. Among Algonquin
Indians, he is Gluskap; in Siberia, Ngaa; among Teutons, Loki;
among Celts and Slavs (one of the few things upon which they
agree), Dis. He takes many forms. You may encounter him (or her,
or it) as a snake, a crocodile, a pig, a billy goat, a coyote, or a crow.
Or you may see a humanoid, male or female, with a hundred
thousand serpents coiled about it, or a huge hook on its head, or a
belt of skulls around its waist; you may even meet a strong, attractive young man—the fallen angel that Christians think of him as
being. Father Greeley really wasn't very interested in this character
until the *New York Times,* on the heels of *Rosemary's Baby* and *The
Exorcist,* asked him for an article. It was then that "I began to reflect
on why the devil myth had the powerful appeal it had, and . . . of
course: because you can subsume under it a lot of data—the data of
the evil that exists, and the struggle between good and evil, the
struggle between life and death." Greeley gave the *Times* what they
wanted and didn't stop until he had produced an entire book on the
topic, *The Devil, You Say!* (1974).

What is the significance of the devil myth, one so pervasive that
it unites in belief such diverse persons as Pope Paul VI and Charles
Manson? Quite simply, it speaks to the mystery of evil (not the
"problem" of evil, which is something college sophomores argue
about). It is concerned with the nagging questions humans have
always asked: Why does evil always seem to be overwhelming good?
Why do we experience in ourselves the constant battle between love
and hate, life and death, being and nonbeing? Why do we find ourselves doing the evil we wish to avoid and omitting the good we had
hoped to accomplish? The story of the devil does not provide a solution to these problems, nor does it create syllogisms to explain them;
rather, it expresses the response of the entire person toward a
mystery for which he has the greatest respect.

Greeley's book on evil cast in the form of demons all those
forces that had attacked *him.* He spoke of the Devil of Ressenti-
ment, Envy Himself, as the most powerful of the spirits that tor-
ment human life (and, at the same time, as the one we are most secre-
tive about). Envy says, in the words of social philosopher Max
Scheler, "I can forgive everything, but not that you *are*—that you are

what you are—that I am not what you are—indeed that I am not *you*."²² This devil operates as assassin, muckraker, second-rate scholar, inadequate athlete. These, like most of us, are fascinated by greatness but resent the fact that greatness is not theirs. So they must cut others down to their size. If the other is a gifted child, peers, teachers, and even parents ridicule him and remind him of his place—so he won't get a big head, they say. With adults the devil is more sophisticated, bringing into line talented novices in whatever profession—or, if they won't conform, condemning them to lives of lonely eminence. Greeley had seen it all and felt it, almost from the beginning of his life.

Envy is so utterly debilitating that its object may feel he is losing his mind. He attempts to be friendly and generous toward others, yet they are vicious to him. He does not understand—how can he, when he himself has never felt the emotion that is directed his way?

Envy's enemy is the Angel of Nobility, that force which gives us a sense of self-worth *prior to* comparisons, which eliminates the need for comparisons. Nobility—one need not be a public figure to feel it—comes from naive self-confidence, the self-confidence that belongs to one who believes, truly believes, that at the heart of things is graciousness and love more powerful than he can imagine.

A second source of evil, Greeley wrote, is Alienation, the devil who whispers in our ear that we can be free, fully human, and fully ourselves if only we break with our past. "Get out or they will destroy you just like they destroy everyone else." Alienation demands our liberation from the biases of neighborhood, ethnic community, town, and church. "Graduate schools, professional schools, and the institutions that train artists, musicians, and actors, as well as the colleges that feed their graduates into the elite universities, all assume that it is necessary to deracinate the young person as a prelude to making him an intellectual."²³ Alienation was hard at work in the sixties, insisting in the exuberance of Vatican II that immigrant Catholicism be *totally* destroyed, making it fashionable for Americans to hate their native land as they protested its policy in Vietnam.

The Demon of Alienation is, of course, a liar. You think you can leave home, but home comes with you, whether you admit it or not. The Angel of Loyalty is honest about the matter: "Take a good hard look at home. . . . Let there be no doubt in your mind that it may be narrow, inflexible, repressive, but also be clear that it offered goodness, richness, warmth, and support."[24] Loyalty, like that of Yahweh toward his people, is not blind. For all its devotion, it remains critical and demanding.

And there is the Gnostic Demon, agile on his feet, coaxing his victims to be "with it," tantalizing them with the Real Secret that will make them superior to everyone else. People with education are the targets; they are the ones in contact with the journals—like *The New York Review of Books,* the *Partisan Review,* the *New Yorker,* and *Commonweal*—which disseminate the latest fads and fashions. The Gnostic Demon is abetted by the Demon of Righteousness, who persuades us that we are right, "so right that our righteousness unites us with the basic cosmic forces,"[25] and his cousin the Ideological Demon, who preys on intellectuals looking for system, order, neatness, and precision as a way of coping with the messy complexities of life. "Label it," he says, "and you will understand it." The Do-Good Devil is another close relative, perhaps the craftiest of the clan. He poses as an exemplary Christian, as the Angel of Generosity, and tempts us to force virtue on others (and therefore to control them) whether they want our virtue or not. These demons are out in full force these days and having the best of it with their opposite forces, the Angels of Wisdom, Humility, Pragmatism, and Freedom.

What *evil* has Andrew Greeley seen in his life? Envy, alienation, gnosticism, self-righteousness, ideologism, do-goodism are the names he chose for the forces responsible for his losses, for his present isolation somewhere between church and university. And how strong are these forces? Strong enough for him to say, "I do not expect to see much of what I stand for vindicated in my own lifetime."

So the devil, that symbol for evil more cunning and more powerful than we can imagine, has prevented him and will continue to prevent him from the victories he seeks. But not—and this is how he locates evil in the Judeo-Christian symbol system—from Ultimate Victory. At the core of the universe, far deeper than evil can penetrate, is relentless, passionate love. Jesus assured us that we were already on the winning side, on the side of graciousness, that life for all its tragedy is ultimately a comedy. One must, therefore, out of religious conviction if not out of temperament, trust the Eros in himself, not the Thanatos, listen to the hopeful impulses, not those that urge despair, risk love rather than hide in hatred. The myths of the tradition that began with Yahweh have it that such an attitude is in strict accord with the way things are.

Greeley, then, like the Irish whose religion has always enabled them to bounce back, will never quit. As he told me, "I believe in the triumph of good over evil in the long run, of light over darkness, of love over hate, of life over death. Since I believe that, I keep working." And when evil stalks him down again—as it surely will—not as a pig, a crocodile, or a billy goat, surely, but maybe as Fear or Pride or Privatism, he is likely to take the attitude of St. Dunstan, Abbot of Glastonbury. One day that venerable man was busy making a chalice when the devil appeared to him. Without batting an eye, Dunstan removed his pliers from the hot fire and clamped them on the nose of Satan, who ran off with a howl and was never seen around those parts again.

Mary.
How is it that one whose description in the New Testament is so limited has called forth so much in the West? All the great Gothic cathedrals, all the paintings, all the poetry, all the sculpture—what is the power of *The Mary Myth* (1977)?

Now that the immigrant Church has collapsed, of course, the lady of Bethlehem sleeps in deep oblivion among the Catholic elite who write books. (Indeed, when the *New York Times* asked Greeley for an article on Mary—even after he had begun his book on her—Greeley's first response was, "Mary who?") In immigrant Catholicism Mary stood for defense of the faith, stern moral obligation, and, above all, purity. She meant that necklines were not to be too low or hemlines too high. To that end, Catholics engaged in processions, novenas, and May crownings; and everyone carried a rosary even though it was often broken into several discrete pieces. Small wonder that the elites today have nothing at all to do with her.

But if one views the Christian symbol of Mary against the history of world religions, Greeley wrote, he will begin to glimpse the source of its power and he will know that it cannot remain dormant for long. *Mary speaks to the universal intuition of God as androgynous, as feminine as well as masculine.* The fertility and vegetation deities of premodern humans were hermaphrodites, or at least female one year and male the next. From these androgynous deities developed a panoply of gods and goddesses, differentiated males and females—not a denial of the notion that the Ultimate was bisexual but a result of the difficulty humans experienced in dealing with a deity that was masculine and feminine at the same time. We moderns have chosen out of convenience to address God as male, though there is no reason why we could not do exactly the opposite. "We have gods and goddesses, and underlying the vast systems of ritual and cult we build to those deities there is still the notion that in whatever is *really* Ultimate, the two are combined."[26]

When Yahweh elbowed his way into the history of Israel, he warned his followers against the fertility cults—and the pagan goddesses that were part of their rituals. *He,* Yahweh, was the one God; any other deities, male or female, were inferior to him and not to be taken seriously. From now on *he* would be responsible for fertility. And so it happened that goddesses vanished from the scene, though sexual differentiation remained part of the religious imagery of Israel: Yahweh became the spouse, the passionate, jealous, sexually aroused lover, in pursuit of Israel his bride.

A female deity did not return to the Judeo-Christian tradition until the second century A.D. when Mary emerged (it is not clear how) as an object of devotion. As a symbol of the feminine aspects of God, she was to become a rich source of inspiration—painted, carved, written to, sung about, labored for. Of the many themes contained in the mythology surrounding Mary, Greeley chose to analyze four: Madonna, Virgo, Sponsa, and Pietà. Each speaks to a basic human dilemma, each carries a conviction about reality that underwrites a particular response to that dilemma.

Motherhood is the most elemental dimension of sexual differentiation, said Greeley, the one from which all other dimensions are derived. Women bear children and nurse them; men do not. So women have appeared in religions as the bearers and nourishers of life, as the Great Mother, as the rich, primal, undisciplined Chaos brought into order by the masculine principle. Isis, Demeter, Juno,

Ishtar, Artemis, Artargatis, Rati—the list is endless. As Madonna, Mother of God, Mary is like these, but different. She is not chaotic like the raw primal mass, nor is the life she offers potentially destructive. She is not identified with fertility but is the servant of Yahweh and the channel of his fertility. As such she reveals the life-bestowing, life-protecting (and sometimes fiercely protecting) aspect of whatever is at the center of the universe.

The Madonna, then, the tender, proud, and strong woman of Michelangelo's *Holy Family,* speaks to our anxiety and fear and despair. These are the portents of defeat and death. But encountering motherhood as a sacrament, "we become aware of the overwhelming power of life. . . . We perceive it as a gift, a given, as something wildly, madly, exuberantly gratuitous."[27] We restructure our perception; behind it all there is a Giver, utterly beneficent, of whom even the lovely-eyed Madonna is but a pale reflection. Despair? Hardly. One is reborn in hope.

As Virgo, the second theme analyzed by Greeley, Mary is *not* a symbol of repression and frigidity, *not* a negative sex goddess, though for all practical purposes today that is the meaning of her virginity. Greeley left untouched the debate over the physical virginity of Mary and pursued the meaning of *virgin* in its origins and in its most sublime traditions. Here "fresh," "renewed," "restored" are the connotations of the word. Mary, Semper Virgo, symbolizes how one can be transformed spiritually by woman (a hard saying in a *Playboy* culture that worships orgasm as the only meaningful sexual interchange). As Madonna she gives life, and as Virgo, she restores life to the freshness of its first moment, taking the role of goddesses like Sophia, Kwan-yin, Shakti, and Tara, assuming the power of the moon, the lotus, and the lily.

Our weariness in dying relationships, our despair of becoming anything but the routine, destructive selves we are, are rooted in the belief that "things" simply do not change for the better. To this existential fatigue the Mary of ·El Greco's *Assumption,* bathing the whole world beneath her in new light, says, "You are wrong." It *is* possible to be inspired, to be renewed, to begin again. The virgin stands for a second chance. Her flowing blue and red robes serve to protect us, to underwrite the risk that opting for newness brings with it. One can trust, be loyal, restore his commitments.

Sponsa is an image of Mary that deals with death. As seductress, Sponsa "deprives us of the individuality and the rationality of life in the frenzy of orgasmic release." She is like the fertility goddesses, like Lillith and Astarte and Aphrodite and Venus, but she is not a goddess of orgies. She is, rather, the counterpart of Yahweh, and he was far from those "lusty, roustabout, horny gods of antiquity." Yahweh lusted not after our bodies but after our whole selves, body and soul, and he did so in the context of sustained commitment. "God as the pursuing male is an image that is open and explicit in the Christian religion; but God as the woman, attractive, charming, fascinating, is also strongly pictured in the Christian heritage through the Mary myth. Mary reveals to us God as alluring, tempting, charming, arousing, attracting."[28]

It is the experience of loneliness, constriction, and alienation to which Mary responds as Sponsa, said Greeley. In the midst of our isolation there are times when we encounter something or somebody that invades our personality, demands our interest, arouses us. We need to abandon ourselves to it, to him, to her, and to do so passionately. The ability to say, with the strength and passion of Botticelli's *Daughter of Zion*, "Be it done unto me according to Thy word" frees us, removes our inhibitions, eliminates the separation. We die to ourselves, we give ourselves over to the passionate goodness of the universe. And we are able to celebrate.

The final abandonment of ourselves to the universe is, of course, death. We return to that from which we came, and the Mother who once gave us life now receives us back. How will she greet us? Like the Indian goddess Kali, sitting amidst flames, adorned with our hacked-off hands and heads, consuming the entrails from our open bellies? Like the Aztec Ilamatecuhtli, who castrated her son and ripped out his heart? Or like the *Pietà* of Michelangelo, who received the dead body of Jesus in loving arms and pressed his head against her soft breasts? How do we reunite with the raw, elementary forces that produced us?

We humans are ambivalent about life and death. The goddesses who bring one also bear the other. What is the attitude of whatever is "out there" to our return? The answer of the Christian symbol system is captured in the expression of Mary the Pietà. She is sad, deeply sorrowful, yet resigned and serene, anticipating somehow the resurrection of her son. She reassures us that our return to the great cosmic processes from which we sprang will be serene and blissful, and she holds out the promise of life after that. In response, we give up our panic and defensiveness in the face of death. We accept it and experience, paradoxically, the phenomenon of rebirth. Giving life, freshening it, attracting it back, receiving it tenderly. Madonna, Virgo, Sponsa, Pietà. In the Ultimate there is both male and female, pursuit and seduction, fatherhood and motherhood. As a result, we can, with the greatest assurance, give ourselves over to the rhythms of androgyny in each of us. Even more, we can face life and death with hope, trust, abandonment, and serenity.

The power of the Mary myth needs no further explanation.

Greeley summed it all up in his book *The New Agenda:* "It is not merely that the Yahwistic symbol system is hopeful, not merely even that it is the most hopeful symbol system the world has ever known. It is an absurdly hopeful symbol system; it represents hopefulness beyond which man simply can't go"[29]—Jesus inviting us to a party; Yahweh pursuing us relentlessly; the Spirit calling forth our diversity; Evil, for all its power, overcome; Mary nourishing us in life and holding us in death. The promise of these myths is very real to Greeley, explaining, I am sure, his persistence in the face of defeat and isolation.

Make no mistake about it. Greeley was devastated by the past and is pessimistic about the future. "American Catholicism is going through a period of emotional exhaustion," he wrote in *The New Agenda*. "Powerful currents of excitement, hope, disappointment, anger, frustration, and bitterness have swept the Church. Now our energies are spent. . . . We say to hell with it and try to forget the last decade like it was a bad dream." Immigrant Catholicism died a tragic, unnecessary death, but that is over, so "let the dead bury their dead."[30] The trouble is that the future is no less bleak than the past. American Catholicism will continue to erode until it becomes indistinguishable from any other American denomination.

But still he *hoped*. It was only a flicker, but it was nevertheless hope. "During the pause that we are in now—and it is likely to be a fairly long pause—some people in the Church will be engaged in

forming the New Agenda; indeed, I have the impression that this
New Agenda is already beginning to emerge, though very slowly
and hesitantly."[31]

The fashioners of the New Agenda are young and few in
number. (Our thoughts return to his baptism of the New Breed.) But
they are sober, realistic Catholic intellectuals, disciplined, nuanced,
sophisticated, willing to develop in their own good time. They have
none of the headstrong—and potentially destructive—enthusiasm of
the New Breed. They are not asking the old questions or, like the
majority of their peers, trying to provide new answers to the old
questions. They are, rather, formulating a new set of questions and
with them a new set of goals for American Catholicism in the
seventies and eighties.

In his book Greeley outlined their (really *his*) agenda for the
future. The first task was to abandon the question of old apologetic
Catholicism, "Can you prove the existence of God?" and ask
instead, "Can you tell me, by revealing your religious myths, who
your God is?" The next was to eliminate "Is the soul immortal?" in
favor of "Is life absurd if man does not survive?" Instead of waiting
for the end of the world—as one did in the old Church—or for the
New Age of the secular ideologies—as many did in the new
Church—the architects of the New Agenda advocated confidence in
graciousness and work *now* to renew the social order. In the old
Church it was "What does it take to be a practicing Catholic?" but
on the New Agenda it was "How can a human find ecstasy of the
spirit?"

Finally Greeley tackled the issue of the uniqueness of Catholicism. The old question was "How was the Church different from the
world?" and the old answer was "Radically different"; the Church
had the truth and the world did not. The new answer was that
nothing in the Church should differentiate it from the world. But
the fashioners of the New Agenda were on an altogether different
tack. They asked, "What *unique contribution* can the Church make
to the world?"

The answer Greeley offered was that the Church can provide
confidence. For in one sense Christianity has added nothing new to
the human condition. "Many of the writers of the early Church
refused to think of Christianity as a new religion but saw it rather as
an integration of everything that was good and true and virtuous

already existing in the world." "Catholic" meant precisely that—universal, pluralistic, comprehensive. The novel element in Christianity, if there is one, "is not the human aspirations that it responds to but the confidence of the response." What Christianity does is confirm and validate "the most powerful and most hopeful insights that constitute the very structure of human existence."[32] It says what man has always hoped for can be—no, *is*—true.

Greeley's work in theology—he speaks of *The New Agenda* and his books on the Judeo-Christian myths as "theological reflections"—has been influenced by young men such as John Hotchkin, John Shea, and David Tracy. Greeley is also a close friend of Hans Küng (whom he describes as a "conservative") and was, from 1969 to 1977, the American sociologist on the editorial board of the international theological journal *Concilium*. Gregory Baum, a fellow editor of *Concilium*, has described Greeley's theology as "popular" and "pastoral." Baum wrote, "Because he deals with difficult and often ticklish theological issues in a manner not customary in professional theology, his thought has not been given adequate attention." It is regrettable, said Baum; Greeley's orientation as a social scientist and his emphasis on the experimental aspects of religion represents "the most fruitful trend in American theology today."[33]

Whatever the judgments of professional theologians upon his work, I find that *The New Agenda*—and later books like *May the Wind Be at Your Back* (1975), *Death and Beyond* (1976), *The Great Mysteries: An Essential Catechism* (1976)—speaks to one of the central mysteries of Greeley's person: the stark contrast between despair and hope. I have heard close friends say he is a pessimistic man, and I have seen utter dejection on his face. I have read, too, in *The Sinai Myth*, a book about hope, quite an admission:

Whether my life is pervaded by trust, joy, hopefulness, and a "radiation of graciousness" is a question about whose answer I must remain extremely skeptical. I am one of those who spent his earliest years in the midst of the Great Depression, a time filled with both the general tragedy of those years and the special ones in my own family. When I see movies of the little boy I was before the disaster of the Depression, I am astonished at what a joyous, spontaneous little child he was. I have to go to the very depths of my own consciousness to find even a trace of that joy remaining.

Seriousness, diligence, responsibility (why else would someone write so many books?), a sober, at times grim dedication to work—these are the realities that have filled my life as long as I can remember. What else does one do, after all, when one has unconsciously accepted responsibility for the Great Depression?[34]

Greeley's intellect, he said, tells him to hope but his "primal, semi- and unconscious emotions say something quite different." He added, "As long as I live, I will need to make a constant effort against the morose and melancholy proclivities of my personality."[35]

But I have also asked Father Greeley to describe the Spirit and I have watched him think back to the summers, before the depression, when his family trundled off to Twin Lakes, and I have seen him become a new man, one as bright and witty and hard to capture as the impish ghost that brought him forth—counterpoint to the somber worker that is his father's son. The sudden change brings to mind an expression of Freud's, "Mental life consists of contradictions and pairs of contraries." And one of Chesterton's, a favorite of Greeley's, "Hope is only a virtue when the situation is hopeless." Extend the melancholy in this man; you also stretch the joy. Deepen the despair; you raise the level of the hope. Make him more alone; the core of the universe becomes more intimate.

If the Yahwistic myths reveal Greeley as a man of hope despite a fear of losing all, they also speak to his experience with American Catholicism in the sixties and early seventies. The immigrant Church fell apart, he said, because of a lack of confidence, a failure in nerve, a sense of worthlessness—because of self-hate. Self-hate is what he saw when Catholic liberals refused the news of a coming Catholic intelligentsia and when they read *The Education of Catholic Americans* as a confirmation of failure. Self-hate is what he saw in the American Irish, in the talented young of Beverly Hills who could not bring themselves to write. Self-hate is what he saw when priests attacked their priesthood, Catholics attacked their Church, and Americans attacked their country. Self-hate is what he saw preventing friendship and foreclosing sexual intimacy. Self-hate says, I am no good, that to which I belong is no good, I am utterly worthless.

From his wrestling with Old and New Testament scholarship Greeley isolated the core of the Judeo-Christian symbol system. One could not imagine a God or a world view more suited to the spiritual and existential needs of the American Catholics of his experience. Incredible, but there it was in Scripture—at the center of everything, pursuing you relentlessly, believing in your worth, is infinitely gracious love. Jesus' message was not so much a command to love as an allaying of fear: "It's all right to love." *That*—the Great Assurance—is the ultimate meaning of things, *that* is what you hit at rock bottom, *that* is "what it's all about," and *that* is what Andrew Greeley hopes will carry American Catholicism on its New Agenda through the seventies and eighties.

Epilogue:
Grand Beach, Michigan,
1973-1977

Home to Father Greeley is a big white house atop a sand dune on the eastern shore of Lake Michigan. "Anyone who is interested in the atmosphere in which a writer works must, I think, know about Grand Beach if he is to know about me," he says. His sister says the place is Twin Lakes—and all that Twin Lakes stood for—reincarnate. I'm glad I visited him there in the summers of 1973, 1974, and 1977.

My first impulse as a guest in Greeley's home is to stand on the edge of the bluff and simply *be* in the vast presence of lake and sky. Straight ahead, where the two merge, is the source of things—of wind, of weather, of waves, of good and bad fortune for Grand Beach. On the horizon to the left, barely visible, are three tiny pegs, all that remain here of Chicago's largest skyscrapers, and, farther on, smoke from Gary's industry. In the course of a day at Grand Beach guests come and go, doing what they please in this great open house. The phone, carried out to the edge of the cliff, rings and is answered. Cabin cruisers move slowly down the shore; speedboats pull skiers; and sailboats nearly capsize. Inside is a huge banner quoting Hillaire Belloc:

> Where're the Catholic sun does shine
> There's music and laughter and good red wine
> At least I've always found it so
> Benedicamus Domino

In the evening the sun has moved to the west and faces you directly, the bright glare of daytime now a peaceful gold. As darkness threatens from the rear, the color intensifies and promises more. Then a path appears on the stilled waters, straight from the setting sun to you. You may move, or even turn your back and walk away, but the shimmering trail follows. Even before you face the lake again, you know it is there. You know as well that each of those who are with you, diverse though they be, sees a path, his or her own, across the same Endless Waters to the same Eternal Fire.

When I first spoke with Father Greeley in July 1973, it was the coldest day of summer. Chill winds sent breakers headlong into the sandy cliff on which we sat and talked (and sometimes shouted above the wind and waves). The level of the lake was high, and Greeley's home was in trouble. Two doors down, the house of a neighbor was halfway over the edge of the eroding dune. Beneath us, lining Greeley's part of the beach, was a thick concrete wall, brand new; beyond it huge gray bags of cement, looking like the backs of small whales, blunted the force of waves before they struck the wall. All day trucks dumped sand over the cliff to replace what the lake had washed away. Sometimes it was blown right back.

Andrew Greeley at that moment was at the nadir of his career. Of his past achievements he said, "That and fifty cents will get you a ride on the CTA. The things that really mattered to me, the things in which I invested a good deal of my selfhood, have all failed." The University of Chicago had made its final refusal of a tenured position. The Archdiocese of Chicago would have no part of his wish for occasional parish work. His home, all he had left, gave every promise of succumbing to the lake. The waves of his dream were quite literally after him.

"When someone writes *The Catholic Experience* in the year 2000," I asked him at that time, "how would you like to be remembered?"

"As one of the theorists of the new Church," he said, "as one who bridged the gap between immigrant Catholicism and Vatican III." Then, constructing a wall of his own, he added: as one who wouldn't "buy shit" or "repeat cliches," as a stubborn, independent, troublemaker who challenged people. Later he said, "The older I get, the more I see in myself the 'old fellow' (his father) when he told off Anton Cermak (mayor of Chicago)."

"Did your father often tell people off?"

"Yes. Oh, yes. Telling people off—perhaps a more gentle word for it is integrity, a more flattering word. Refusing to knuckle under to Cody is just the same thing as his refusing to knuckle under to Cermak. And, in both cases, at considerable cost."

Through the remainder of 1973 Greeley's wall held. When I returned in 1974, his reconstituted cliff still stood, impressive but far from beautiful. His home was safe at last, but it was still a house built on sand. One needed great conviction and hard work to keep it, to keep oneself, together. A little clout with the Ole Fella wouldn't hurt either.

So Greeley's conviction smothered his despair, and he worked on. In the *National Catholic Reporter* he staked out another alternative within the American Church, that of "communal Catholicism."[1] The term described a collectivity committed to Catholicism as a world view and as a community, unembittered by its parochial roots (even proud to be Catholic), self-conscious in its attempt to grasp the human and religious meaning of being a Catholic in the United States. Communal Catholics were *not* organized and were supremely indifferent to the institutional Church. They could not care less about what bishops did or failed to do (save with regard to parochial schools, of which they were staunch supporters). In the midst of charismatic renewal and Marriage Encounter and liberation theology—all of which Greeley continued to dismiss—an amorphous collection of ex-New Breeders caught his eye and captured his hope. His critics said Greeley's portrait was no more than a "sociology of his friends," that communal Catholics were irresponsible vis-a-vis the Church, that their children would never remain Catholic. Greeley, of course, thought them more powerful, though he conceded that their influence would be felt only in the long run.

Greeley extended his ideas in a book bearing the name *The Communal Catholic* and hinted there at a "Catholic alternative to capitalism and socialism." Between agribusiness and the collective farm there is another option, he said: the peasant and his family on their own plot of land—or, in another context, the experiments by Volvo in Sweden. The Catholic alternative begins with the recognition that *Gemeinschaft* has not caved in to *Gesellschaft*. Thus it values family, neighborhood, the local, the "particularistic"; it is upset by the way both capitalism and socialism have damaged these. It stresses loyalty—as diffuse, informal, and communal a virtue as one can find. It is optimistic about human nature and is willing to trust it; large bureaucracies, therefore, whatever their ideological trappings, are not needed to manipulate it. In the words of British economist E. F. Schumacher, "Small is beautiful." Greeley's alternative was not uniquely Catholic (Gandhi, for one, expressed similar views), but it did represent a perspective to which Catholicism had been historically committed, both in the high tradition of papal encyclicals and in the low tradition of parish and precinct. It is to these historical roots of a Catholic social ethic that Greeley has devoted *No Bigger Than Necessary* (1977).

In the summer of 1977 Greeley's makeshift levee was stronger than ever, and his sand dune had been terraced, landscaped, lined with stairs, and outfitted with an attractive wooden deck. His personal wall was holding, too, and his despair was likewise landscaped with hope. Suddenly the Spirit was back, sowing playfulness, joy, and unprecedented diversity: children's stories, novels, short stories, science fiction, screenplays, poetry, and photography—all to be published by Father Greeley in the years ahead.

Greeley's attraction to fiction began on a Saturday morning when he wrote a children's story, *Nora Maeva and Sebi* (1976), at the request of a publisher. He enjoyed himself so much that a trilogy of novels is now in the works. First to appear will be *The Magic Cup*, a sixth-century Irish version of the quest for the Holy Grail. In it the Irish Lancelot, one Cormac MacDermot, ends up with the cup and the girl, both of which stand for God. Greeley contends that a happy ending to the quest is truer to the original Celtic myth than the Arthurian saga, which was heavily influenced by French Manichaeism. *The Magic Cup* will be followed by *The Final Planet*, a story of the Irish of the future. A creaky old spaceship of monks and nuns presided over by an Irish mother, the Abbess Deirdre Cardinal Fitzgerald, seeks a resting place among the galaxies. It comes across Zylong and the Abbess sends poor Seamus O'Neill to explore it—just as its communitarian culture is about to blow up. Greeley's plans for a third novel on the Irish of the present are still vague because, he says, they are harder to face. In the meantime he is finishing another children's story, *Liam and the New Dog*.

Parts of Greeley's novels and nearly all his short stories deal with women. A few of the stories may turn up in *Ellery Queen Mystery Magazine*, but most will appear in a book of songs and tales to be called *Women I've Met* (or, depending on his nerve, *Women*

I've Known). Greeley's heroines are strong, beautiful, and troubled. His heroes do not possess them physically, but, rather, penetrate them spiritually, examining their deepest feelings, seeing their distress, and healing them. In the process the men are transformed by the power of the women and give themselves over to intuition, compassion, and play.

As late as 1974 Greeley had ruled out the possibility of poetry because he had "no ear for it." But in 1977 his first poems were published in *The Mary Myth*, and more were scheduled for *Faces of Ireland* and *Women I've Met*. The transition came suddenly. "I was flying home from Ireland after a fantastic period and was reading a book on Mary. I just began to hear music and words. I pulled out a pencil and wrote a poem." Most of Greeley's poetry, like most of his fiction, is about women—about Madonnas and bitches, tomboys and nymphs, wives and nuns, little girls and grandmothers. Why women now? An editor's idea, he says, admitting however that "maybe at the present age in my life I have some need to articulate more clearly my relation as a celibate with women."

Greeley is also taking pictures these days, another sign that his mood is on the upswing. A set of Irish landscapes appeared in a book of meditations, *May the Wind Be at Your Back*, a volume of which he is "inordinately proud." A portfolio of brightly painted homes was published in the *Chicago Tribune*, and shots of kids, grownups, stores, houses, and ethnic festivals will be scattered throughout *Neighborhood* and *Faces of Ireland*. Greeley is experimenting with television, too. For several months he was a guest critic on Chicago's educational channel, and he has just completed his first television script. It is about a beautiful space commander named Cassie, whose inner pain is reached and healed by an Irishman straight out of *Star Wars*.

Some of the new genres have come easily to Greeley, but others, the fiction in particular, have been difficult to master. Greeley's new outburst has not dampened his interest in survey research, thanks to the timely arrival of another muse, the conversational computer. "It releases the flair and creativity of the researcher in a way it's never been released before." But Greeley is through with what he calls "Catholic writing." "With *The Great Mysteries* and *The Mary Myth* I just exhausted myself. My stomach knots up every time I think of writing for the Catholic marketplace. Most of the people in the Catholic marketplace are priests and nuns, and priests and nuns bother the hell out of me." The only Catholic book left in the hopper is *The Making of the Pope, 19—*, "one-third sociology, one-third journalism, and one-third espionage." Its final chapters await the actual election of a successor to Paul VI.

Other signs of rebirth have lit up Greeley's world: the doubling between 1963 and 1974 in the percentage of American Catholics who receive Communion weekly, the desire in 1977 of some in his devastated underground parish to meet again. These signs of life bring me back to my first interview with Father Greeley, the one that found him so depressed. I recall asking him what season of life he was in, expecting something around September. But my question was wide of the mark. He said his life was not as grand as the huge cycle of a single year, but rather a succession of springs following autumns, of births following deaths.

When my questions were done that day, Paul Asciolla and I slid down the steep sandpile to the lake and surveyed the damage along the shore. Then we climbed back up to the house for a sauna and shower. In the meantime Father Greeley straightened up a bit and did some dictating. After the six o'clock news he made his favorite Caesar salad and served us dinner. A young couple arrived—the niece of Cardinal Meyer and her husband (the night before I had learned their nationalities long before their names). We chatted briefly over a dessert of Michigan blueberries, in season now, and cream. Then I said good-bye to Paul and to the young couple. Father Greeley walked me to my car, invited me back to Grand Beach, and wished me a safe trip. I looked to the west as the sun slipped into the water, sure to rise on the next day.

Notes

In the following notes all books and articles are by Andrew Greeley unless otherwise indicated. For bibliographical data on books, see the following section, "Books by Andrew M. Greeley."

Preface

1. *Priests in the United States*, p. 178.
2. *Sexual Intimacy*, pp. 99–100.
3. *Complaints Against God*, p. 65.
4. *Building Coalitions*, p. 13.
5. *Come Blow Your Mind with Me*, p. 226.
6. Peter Steinfels, "Andrew Greeley, Divine Sociologist," *Commonweal*, June 12, 1970, p. 286.

Chapter 2

1. *What a Modern Catholic Believes about the Church*, p. 18.
2. Ibid., p. 19.
3. *The Church and the Suburbs*, p. 9.
4. Ibid., p. 188.
5. Ibid., pp. 122–123.
6. "The Vanishing Hero," *America*, December 12, 1959, p. 350.
7. "No More Radicals?" *America*, March 19, 1960, p. 733.
8. *Strangers in the House* (rev. ed.), pp. 37 and 52.
9. Ibid., pp. 155–156 and 167.
10. *And Young Men Shall See Visions*, pp. 3–14, passim.
11. Ibid., pp. 32–58, passim.
12. Ibid., pp. 9–10.
13. Ibid., pp. 96 and 153.
14. Ibid., pp. 175–176.
15. *Letters to Nancy*, passim.
16. Ibid., pp. 35–36.
17. Ibid., pp. 45–53, passim.

18. Ibid., pp. 84–106, passim.
19. Ibid., p. 182.
20. *And Young Men Shall See Visions,* p. viii.
21. *The Church and the Suburbs,* p. 84.
22. "Quadrigesimo Anno and 'New' Problems," *America,* December 13, 1958, p. 340.
23. "Sociology of Religion," *The Critic,* August–September 1962, p. 12.
24. *Letters to Nancy,* p. 8.
25. "A Farewell to the New Breed," *America,* May 4, 1966, p. 801.
26. "A New Breed," *America,* May 23, 1964, p. 706.
27. Ibid.
28. Ibid.
29. Ibid., p. 707.
30. Ibid., pp. 707–708.
31. Ibid., p. 709.
32. Ibid.

Chapter 3

1. Denis Brogan, *U.S.A.: An Outline of the Country, Its People and Institutions* (London: Oxford University Press, 1941), p. 65. Quoted in John Tracy Ellis, "American Catholics and the Intellectual Life," *Thought,* autumn, 1955, p. 353.
2. Ellis, "American Catholics," p. 386.
3. Thomas F. O'Dea, *American Catholic Dilemma* (New York: Sheed and Ward, 1958), p. 151. For a summary of the debate, see Frank L. Christ and Gerard E. Sherry, *American Catholicism and the Intellectual Ideal* (New York: Appleton-Century-Crofts, 1959).
4. Robert H. Knapp and H. B. Goodrich, *Origins of American Scientists* (Chicago: University of Chicago Press, 1952); and Robert H. Knapp and Joseph J. Greenbaum, *The Young American Scholar: His Collegiate Origins* (Chicago: University of Chicago Press, 1953).
5. Knapp and Greenbaum, *The Young American Scholar,* p. 48.
6. Gerhard Lenski, *The Religious Factor* (Garden City, N. Y.: Doubleday, 1961).
7. *Religion and Career,* p. 52.
8. "Entering the Mainstream," *Commonweal,* October 2, 1964, p. 33.
9. George Shuster, "New Statistics on an Old Problem," *Commonweal,* January 10, 1964, p. 436.
10. John Donovan, "Creating Anti-Intellectuals?" *Commonweal,* October 2, 1964, p. 39.
11. *The Changing Catholic College,* p. 50, and *From Backwater to Mainstream,* pp. 24 and 93.
12. Donovan, "Creating Anti-Intellectuals?" p. 39.
13. R. W. Mack, R. J. Murphy, and S. Yellin, "The Protestant Ethic, Level of Aspiration and Social Mobility," *American Sociological Review,* June 1956, p. 295.
14. "The Protestant Ethic: Time for a Moratorium," *Sociological Analysis,* spring 1964, pp. 20–33.
15. Joseph Veroff, Sheila Feld, and Gerald Gurin, "Achievement Motivation and Religious Background," *American Sociological Review,* April 1962, pp. 205–217.

16. "The Protestant Ethic: Time for a Moratorium," pp. 30–31, passim.
17. *Religion and Career*, p. 133.
18. "Sociology of Religion," *The Critic*, August–September 1962, p. 12.
19. "The Protestant Ethic: Time for a Moratorium," p. 33.
20. "Entering the Mainstream," p. 35.
21. *Religion and Career*, p. 18.
22. *Commonweal*, March 29, 1963, p. 17.
23. "The Catholic Message and the American Intellectual," *The Critic*, April–May 1964, pp. 34–40, passim.

Chapter 4

1. Mary Perkins Ryan, *Are Parochial Schools the Answer?* (New York: Holt, Rinehart, and Winston, 1964).
2. Ibid., pp. 161–173, passim.
3. John A. O'Connor, "The Modest Proposal of Mary Perkins Ryan," *The Catholic World*, July 1964, p. 220.
4. Andrew Greeley and Peter Rossi, "The Effects of Catholic Education, Part I," *The Critic*, December 1963–January 1964, pp. 34–38.
5. Andrew Greeley, Peter Rossi, and Leonard Pinto, "The Effects of Catholic Education, Part II," *The Critic*, October–November 1964, p. 49.
6. Andrew Greeley and Peter Rossi, *The Education of Catholic Americans* (Doubleday Anchor ed.), p. 91.
7. Ibid., pp. 91–92.
8. Ibid., pp. 76 and 117.
9. Ibid., p. 125.
10. Ibid., p. 185.
11. Ibid., p. 208.
12. Ibid., p. 239.
13. "Are Schools Worth It?" *America*, September 19, 1964, p. 286.
14. Quoted in "News and Views," *Commonweal*, August 19, 1966, p. 514.
15. Edward B. Fiske, "Study Evaluates Catholic Schools," *New York Times*, July 25, 1966.
16. "News and Views," *Commonweal*, August 19, 1966, p. 514.
17. "Degrees of Devotion," *Time*, July 29, 1966, p. 49.
18. "Parochial Benefits," *Newsweek*, August 1, 1966, p. 77.
19. Robert Cross, "The Greeley-Rossi Report," *Commonweal*, September 16, 1966, pp. 577–579.
20. Daniel Callahan, "Review of *The Education of Catholic Americans*," *Commentary*, January 1967, p. 83.
21. Mary Perkins Ryan, "Review of *The Education of Catholic Americans*," *The Critic*, December 1966–January 1967, pp. 77–78.
22. "The Catholic Campus," *The Critic*, October–November 1966, p. 84.
23. *The Changing Catholic College*, p. 59.
24. Ibid., p. 86.
25. "The Catholic Campus," p. 88.
26. *The Changing Catholic College*, pp. 176 and 185.

27. Ibid., p. 202.
28. Ibid.
29. Ibid., p. 203.
30. Ibid., p. 204.
31. *The Hesitant Pilgrim*, p. 10.
32. Doris Grumbach, "Review of *The Changing Catholic College*," *The National Catholic Reporter*, April 17, 1968, p. 13.
33. Daniel Callahan, "Academic Standards Are Secular," *The Saturday Review*, March 16, 1968, p. 77.
34. "Myths and Fads in Higher Education," *America*, November 11, 1967, p. 545.
35. *The Student in Higher Education*, p. 24.
36. Ibid., p. 9.
37. Ibid., p. 59.
38. *From Backwater to Mainstream*, pp. 147 and 149.
39. "Catholic Alumni: Seven Years After," *America*, January 25, 1969, pp. 96 and 100.
40. *Recent Alumni and Higher Education*, p. 172.
41. "The New Urban Studies—A Word of Caution," *Educational Record*, Summer 1970, pp. 232-236.
42. *Recent Alumni and Higher Education*, pp. 178-183, passim.
43. "Review of *Report on Higher Education*," *Journal of Higher Education*, October 1971, p. 613.
44. *Can Catholic Schools Survive?*, p. 26.

Chapter 5

1. "The Temptation of the New Breed," *America*, May 22, 1965, pp. 750-752.
2. Ibid., p. 750.
3. Ibid., p. 752.
4. "A Farewell to the New Breed," *America*, June 4, 1966, pp. 801-804, passim.
5. "The New Community," *The Critic*, June-July 1966, pp. 37 and 34.
6. Ibid., p. 36.
7. Ibid., p. 37.
8. *Come Blow Your Mind with Me*, pp. 93-94.
9. *The Hesitant Pilgrim*, p. 7.
10. Quoted by Peter Steinfels, "Andrew Greeley, Divine Sociologist," *Commonweal*, June 12, 1970, p. 286.
11. *The Hesitant Pilgrim*, p. 12.
12. Ibid., pp. 16-27, passim.
13. "Catholicism Midwest Style," *America*, February 12, 1966, p. 223.
14. *The Hesitant Pilgrim*, p. xvii.
15. *The Catholic Experience* (Image Books ed.), p. 49.
16. Ibid.
17. Ibid., pp. 46 and 62.
18. Ibid., p. 44.
19. Ibid., p. 63.

20. Ibid., pp. 74–76.
21. Ibid., p. 103.
22. Ibid., p. 104.
23. Ibid., p. 158.
24. Ibid., p. 163.
25. Ibid., p. 173.
26. Ibid., p. 180.
27. Ibid., p. 215.
28. Ibid., p. 280.
29. Ibid., p. 282.
30. "What Do the People Say?" *Commonweal,* October 11, 1968, p. 53.
31. "Roman Catholics: Clouded Future," *Time,* January 10, 1969, p. 63.
32. *Come Blow Your Mind with Me,* p. 122.
33. Ibid., p. 123.
34. Ibid., p. 129.
35. Ibid., pp. 132–133.
36. Ibid., pp. 134 and 133.
37. Ibid., p. 135.
38. Unpublished manuscript.
39. *Catholic Schools in a Declining Church,* p. 321.
40. Personal document.
41. Condensed from "The First Papal Press Conference—A Vision," *The Critic,* February–March 1969, pp. 14–19. Reprinted in *Come Blow Your Mind with Me,* pp. 222–233.

Chapter 6

1. Harvey Cox, *The Secular City* (New York: Macmillan, 1965), pp. 2 and 4.
2. Ibid., p. 4.
3. Daniel Callahan, ed., *The Secular City Debate* (New York: Macmillan, 1966) pp. 107 and 103.
4. Ibid., pp. 104 and 108.
5. Ibid., p. 115.
6. Ibid., pp. 124 and 126.
7. Thomas Altizer and William Hamilton, *Radical Theology and the Death of God* (Indianapolis: Bobbs-Merrill, 1966), p. 5.
8. Martin Marty, Stuart Rosenberg, and Andrew Greeley, *What Do We Believe?* pp. 117 and 123.
9. Ibid., p. 149.
10. Ibid., p. 153.
11. "There's a New-Time Religion on Campus," *New York Times Magazine,* June 1969. Reprinted in *Come Blow Your Mind with Me,* p. 26.
12. Ibid., p. 29.
13. Ibid., p. 30.
14. Ibid., pp. 31–32.
15. Ibid., pp. 33–35, passim.

16. Ibid., p. 35.

17. Guy A. Swanson, "Modern Secularity," in Donald Cutler (ed.), *The Religious Situation* (Boston: Beacon, 1968), pp. 811-813. Quoted in *Religion in the Year 2000*, pp. 32-34.

18. *Religion in the Year 2000*, p. 25.

19. David Martin, "Toward Eliminating the Concept of Secularization," in Julius Gould (Ed.), *Penguin Survey of the Social Sciences* (Baltimore, Md.: Penguin, 1965). Quoted in *Religion in the Year 2000*, p. 50.

20. *Religion in the Year 2000*, p. 51.

21. Ibid., pp. 68-69.

22. Ibid., p. 70.

23. Ibid., pp. 171 and 173.

24. "Superstition, Ecstasy, and Tribal Consciousness," *Social Research*, Summer 1970, p. 204.

25. "Religion Still Has Tenure," *The New York Times*, October 17, 1970.

26. *The Denominational Society*, p. iii, and *Unsecular Man*, p. 55.

27. *The Denominational Society*, p. 236.

28. Bronislaw Malinowski, "Magic, Science, and Religion, "in Joseph Needham (Ed.), *Science, Religion, and Reality* (New York: Macmillan, 1925), p. 82. Quoted in *The Denominational Society*, p. 36.

29. *Unsecular Man*, p. 1.

30. Ibid., p. 19.

31. Robert Nisbet, *The Social Bond* (New York: Knopf, 1970), pp. 303 and 308. Quoted in *Unsecular Man*, p. 23.

32. Clifford Geertz, "Religion as a Cultural System," in Donald Cutler (Ed.), *The Religious Situation*, (Boston: Beacon, 1968), p. 667. Quoted in *Unsecular man*, p. 58.

33. *Unsecular Man*, p. 93.

34. Henri Frankfort, *Before Philosophy* (Baltimore, Md.: Penguin, 1949), p. 15. Quoted in *Unsecular Man*, p. 89.

35. Ibid.

36. Piccard, quoted in *Unsecular Man*, pp. 74-75.

37. *Unsecular Man*, p. 75.

38. Ibid., p. 74.

39. *Unsecular Man*, pp. 248 and 247.

40. *Ecstasy*, pp. 1-2.

41. Ibid., pp. 121-122.

42. Ibid., p. 122.

43. Reprinted with permission of author.

44. *Ecstasy*, p. 4.

45. Ibid.

46. William C. McCready and Andrew M. Greeley, *The Ultimate Values of the American Population*, p. 156.

47. Ibid.

48. Jeffrey Hadden (Ed.), "Review Symposium: The Sociology of Religion of Andrew M. Greeley," *Journal for the Scientific Study of Religion*, March 1974, pp. 75-97, passim.

49. Ibid., p. 75.

50. "Andrew Greeley Replies to His Critics," *Journal for the Scientific Study of Religion*, June 1974, p. 230.
51. Ibid., p. 231.

Chapter 7

1. *Unsecular Man*, p. 1.
2. *Uncertain Trumpet*, pp. 25-55, passim.
3. *The Hesitant Pilgrim*, p. 241.
4. Ibid., p. 117.
5. *Uncertain Trumpet*, p. 36.
6. Ibid., p. 80.
7. Ibid., pp. 112-113.
8. Ibid., p. 114.
9. Ibid., p. 95.
10. Ibid., p. 101.
11. *The Hesitant Pilgrim*, p. 238.
12. *Uncertain Trumpet*, pp. 39 and 35.
13. Ibid., p. 23.
14. "Greeley on Greeley and Bishops," *National Catholic Reporter*, September 28, 1973, p. 15.
15. *Priests in the United States*, p. 90.
16. "Greeley on Greeley and Bishops," p. 15, and interview.
17. "The State of the Priesthood," *National Catholic Reporter*, February 18, 1972, p. 7.
18. Ibid., p. 15.
19. "After the Synod," *America*, November 20, 1971, p. 424.
20. "The State of the Priesthood," p. 10.
21. *Priests in the United States*, p. 107.
22. Ibid., pp. 196 and 198.
23. Ibid., p. 197.
24. Ibid., pp. 198-199.
25. Ibid., p. 204.
26. Ibid., p. 109.

Chapter 8

1. "The Rediscovery of Diversity," *The Antioch Review*, Fall 1971, p. 345.
2. Ibid., pp. 359-360.
3. Ibid., pp. 343-344.
4. Ibid., pp. 348-349.
5. Ibid., p. 350.
6. *Why Can't They Be Like Us?*, p. 19.
7. "Intellectuals as an Ethnic Group," *New York Times Magazine*, July 7, 1970.
8. Ibid.

9. "Civil Religion and Ethnic Americans," *Worldview*, February 1973, p. 24.
10. Ibid., p. 27.
11. Ibid., pp. 23–24.
12. "Malice in Wonderland: Misperceptions of the Academic Elite," *Change*, September–October 1970, pp. 32–39.
13. "Making It in America: Ethnic Groups and Social Status," *Social Policy*, September–October 1973, pp. 24 and 28.
14. "The New Ethnicity and Blue Collars," *Dissent*, Winter 1972, p. 276.
15. Richard Schermerhorn, *Comparative Ethnic Relations* (New York: Random House, 1969), p. 123. Quoted in *Ethnicity in the United States*, p. 291.
16. *Ethnicity in the United States*, pp. 315 and 297.
17. *Why Can't They Be Like Us?*, p. 33.
18. Ibid.
19. *Ethnicity in the United States*, p. 300.
20. Ibid., p. 296.
21. Ibid., p. 300–301.
22. Ibid., p. 300.
23. Ibid., p. 302.
24. "Report to the Ford Foundation, Second Year," *NORC Paper*, December 1972, pp. 4.
25. *That Most Distressful Nation*, p. xxvi.
26. Ibid., pp. vii and 29.
27. Ibid., pp. 34 and 36.
28. Ibid., p. 39.
29. Ibid., p. 48.
30. Ibid., p. 56.
31. Ibid., pp. 104–107, passim.
32. Ibid., p. 135.
33. Ibid., p. 249.
34. Reprinted with permission of the author.
35. In a communication to me Professors Shils and Janowitz confirmed that the Department of Sociology found Greeley's qualifications as a scholar "inadequate." They added that the *Voices* article was "hardly a responsible account."
36. Andrew Segal and Don Rose "Why No Protests over Andy Greeley?" *Hyde Park–Kenwood Voices*, July 1973.
37. Letter of July 18, 1973, addressed to the *Hyde Park–Kenwood Voices*.
38. "The 'Religious Factor' and Academic Careers: Another Communication," *American Journal of Sociology*, March 1973, p. 1253.
39. "Review of *Real Lace*," *The Critic*, March–April 1974, pp. 59–60.
40. *The Communal Catholic*, pp. 70 and 72.
41. "Confessions of a Loud-Mouthed Irish Priest," *Social Policy*, May–June 1974, p. 4.
42. Ibid., pp. 4 and 6.
43. Ibid., p. 7.
44. Ibid., p. 11.
45. Ibid.

Chapter 9

1. William Van Etten Casey, S.J., "Thank You, Dan and Phil," *Holy Cross Quarterly,* January 1971, p. 3.
2. *Commonweal,* quoted in David J. O'Brien, "The Berrigans and America," *Holy Cross Quarterly,* January 1971, p. 53.
3. Francine du Plessix Gray, "Acts of Witness," *The New Yorker,* March 14, 1970, pp. 44ff., and *Divine Disobedience* (New York: Knopf, 1970). Gary Wills, "A Revolution in the Church," *Playboy,* November 1971, pp. 159ff.
4. Noam Chomsky, "On the Limits of Civil Disobedience," *Holy Cross Quarterly,* January 1971, p. 27.
5. "The Berrigans: Phrenetic?," *Holy Cross Quarterly,* January 1971, p. 17.
6. "Turning Off the People," *The New Republic,* June 27, 1970, pp. 14-15.
7. American Political Science Association, September 10, 1971. See "Political Attitudes among American White Ethnics," *The Public Opinion Quarterly,* Summer 1972, pp. 213-220.
8. Noam Chomsky, "On the Limits of Civil Disobedience," *Holy Cross Quarterly,* January 1971, pp. 22-31.
9. "A Scrapyard for the Daley Organization?" *Bulletin of the Atomic Scientists,* February 1973, p. 12.
10. Ibid., p. 11.
11. "Take Heart from Heartland," *The New Republic,* December 12, 1970, p. 17.
12. "A Scrapyard for the Daley Organization?" p. 11.
13. "Take Heart from Heartland," p. 19.
14. "A Scrapyard for the Daley Organization?" p. 9.
15. Ibid.
16. *Building Coalitions,* pp. 24 and 25.
17. Ibid., pp. 88-90.
18. Ibid., p. 232.
19. Andrew S. McFarland, *Power and Leadership in Pluralist Systems* (Stanford, Calif.: Stanford University Press, 1969). Quoted in *Building Coalitions,* p. 229.
20. *Building Coalitions,* pp. 229-230.
21. Ibid., p. 235.
22. Ibid., pp. 247-248.
23. Andrew Greeley and Paul B. Sheatsley, "Attitudes Toward Racial Integration," *Scientific American,* December 1971, pp. 13-19; Andrew Greeley and Paul B. Sheatsley, "Changing Attitudes of Whites Toward Blacks," *The Public Opinion Quarterly,* fall 1972, pp. 432-433.
24. *Building Coalitions,* pp. 320-321.
25. Ibid., p. 32ln.
26. "For a Black Vice-President," *New York Times Magazine,* September 19, 1971.
27. Ibid., p. 35.
28. Universal Press Syndicate, August 6, 1974.
29. Ibid., July 30, 1974.
30. Ibid., 1974-1976.
31. Ibid., October 29, 1974.

32. Michael Novak, "The Communal Catholic," *Commonweal*, January 17, 1975, p. 321.
33. Mike Royko, "All a Matter of Experience," *Chicago Daily News*, March 11, 1975.
34. Universal Press Syndicate, December 21, 1974.
35. David Martin, "R.D. Laing: Psychiatry and Apocalypse," *Dissent*, June 1971, pp. 250-251.
36. "Nothing But a Loud-Mouthed Irish Priest," in Gregory Baum (Ed.), *Journeys* (New York: Paulist Press, 1975), p. 196.
37. "Moynihan and Drucker—Demythologizers," *Educational Record*, summer 1969, pp. 319 and 325.

Chapter 10

1. *Love and Play*, p. 21.
2. *The Life of the Spirit*, pp. 27-28.
3. *A Future to Hope In*, p. 107.
4. Ibid., pp. 125-126.
5. *The Life of the Spirit*, p. 22.
6. *The Friendship Game*, pp. 25 and 159.
7. Ibid., p. 18.
8. Ibid., pp. 27-28.
9. Ibid., p. 53.
10. Ibid., p. 69.
11. Ibid., p. 74.
12. Ibid., p. 60.
13. Ibid., p. 61.
14. Ibid., p. 115.
15. Ibid., pp. 109-110.
16. Ibid., pp. 18 and 96.
17. Ibid., p. 129.
18. *Ecstasy*, p. 52.
19. *The Friendship Game*, p. 125.
20. *Come Blow Your Mind with Me*, p. 134.
21. *The New Agenda* (Doubleday Image Ed.), pp. 148-149.
22. Ibid., p. 124.
23. Ibid., pp. 125 and 127.
24. Ibid., p. 127.
25. *Sexual Intimacy*, p. 85.
26. Ibid., pp. 86 and 100.
27. Ibid., pp. 99-100.
28. Ibid., p. 101.
29. Ibid., pp. 104-108, passim.
30. Ibid., pp. 119 and 121.
31. Ibid., p. 126.
32. *The New Agenda*, p. 141.
33. *Sexual Intimacy*, pp. 150 and 191-192.

34. Ibid., p. 198.
35. *Love and Play,* p. 64.
36. Ibid., p. 66.
37. Ibid., pp. 131 and 134.
38. Ibid., p. 161.
39. Ibid., p. 181.
40. Ibid., p. 7.
41. Ibid., p. 30.

Chapter 11

1. "Myths, Symbols and Rituals in the Modern World," *The Critic,* December 1961-January 1962, p. 18.
2. "Myths, Meaning and Vatican III," *America,* December 19, 1970, pp. 538-542; "Religious Symbolism, Liturgy, and Community," *Concilium,* February 1971, pp. 59-69.
3. *The Jesus Myth,* p. 25.
4. Ibid., pp. 32-33.
5. "Would He Be Crucified?" *Chicago Daily News,* April 6-7, 1974.
6. *The Jesus Myth,* p. 44.
7. Ibid., p. 69.
8. Ibid., p. 52.
9. Ibid., p. 72.
10. "The Holy Week Biography: Our Readers Respond," *Chicago Daily News,* April 13-14, 1974.
11. *The Sinai Myth,* p. 12.
12. Ibid., p. 43.
13. Ibid., pp. 54-55.
14. *What a Modern Catholic Believes about God,* p. 57.
15. Ibid., p. 61.
16. *The Sinai Myth,* p. 62.
17. Ibid., p. 216.
18. Universal Press Syndicate, January 21, 1975.
19. *The Touch of the Spirit,* p. 30.
20. Ibid., pp. 22-23.
21. *The Communal Catholic,* p. 155.
22. *The Devil, You Say!,* p. 35.
23. Ibid., p. 49.
24. Ibid., p. 53.
25. Ibid., p. 78.
26. *The Mary Myth,* p. 55.
27. Ibid., p. 121.
28. Ibid., pp. 157, 161, and 163-64.
29. *The New Agenda,* p. 90.
30. Ibid., pp. 32 and 39.
31. Ibid., p. 34.

32. Ibid., p. 267
33. Gregory Baum, introduction to *The New Agenda*, pp. 11 and 19.
34. *The Sinai Myth*, p. 117.
35. Ibid., pp. 118 and 126-127.

Epilogue

1. "The Next Ten Years," *National Catholic Reporter*, November 1, 1974, pp. 9-12.

Books by
Andrew M. Greeley

1959
The Church and the Suburbs. New York: Sheed and Ward.

1961
Strangers in the House. New York: Sheed and Ward.

1963
Religion and Career. New York: Sheed and Ward.

1964
And Young Men Shall See Visions. New York: Sheed and Ward.
Letters to Nancy. New York: Sheed and Ward.
Priests for Today and Tomorrow. Notre Dame, Ind.: Ave Maria Press.

1966
The Education of Catholic Americans (with Peter H. Rossi).
    Chicago: Aldine.
The Hesitant Pilgrim. New York: Sheed and Ward.

1967
The Catholic Experience. Garden City, N. Y.: Doubleday.
The Changing Catholic College. Chicago: Aldine.

1968
The Crucible of Change. New York: Sheed and Ward.
The Student in Higher Education. New Haven, Conn.:
    The Hazen Foundation.

Uncertain Trumpet. New York: Sheed and Ward.
What Do We Believe? (with Martin E. Marty and Stuart E. Rosenberg). New York: Meredith.

1969
From Backwater to Mainstream. New York: McGraw-Hill.
A Future to Hope In. Garden City, N. Y.: Doubleday.
Life for a Wanderer. Garden City, N. Y.: Doubleday.
Religion in the Year 2000. New York: Sheed and Ward.

1970
Can Catholic Schools Survive? (with William E. Brown). New York: Sheed and Ward.
The Friendship Game. Garden City, N. Y.: Doubleday.
The Life of the Spirit. Kansas City, Mo.: National Catholic Reporter.
New Horizons for the Priesthood. New York: Sheed and Ward.
Recent Alumni and Higher Education (with Joe L. Spaeth). New York: McGraw-Hill.
Youth Asks, Does God Still Speak? Camden, N. J.: T. Nelson.

1971
Come Blow Your Mind with Me. Garden City, N. Y.: Doubleday.
Complaints Against God. Chicago: Thomas More.
The Jesus Myth. Garden City, N. Y.: Doubleday.
The Touch of the Spirit. New York: Herder and Herder.
What a Modern Catholic Believes about God. Chicago: Thomas More.
Why Can't They Be Like Us? New York: E. P. Dutton.

1972
The Catholic Priest in the United States. Washington, D.C.: United States Catholic Conference.
The Denominational Society. Glenview, Ill.: Scott, Foresman.
Jesus Now. Chicago: Thomas More.
Priests in the United States. Garden City, N. Y.: Doubleday.
The Sinai Myth. Garden City, N. Y.: Doubleday.
That Most Distressful Nation. New York: Quadrangle.
Unsecular Man. New York: Schocken.
What a Modern Catholic Believes about the Church. Chicago: Thomas More.

1973
The New Agenda. Garden City, N. Y.: Doubleday.
Sexual Intimacy. Chicago: Thomas More.

1974
Building Coalitions. New York: New Viewpoints.
The Devil, You Say! Garden City, N. Y.: Doubleday.
Ecstasy. Englewood Cliffs, N. J.: Prentice-Hall.
Ethnicity in the United States. New York: Wiley-Interscience.

1975
Love and Play. Chicago: Thomas More.
May the Wind Be at Your Back. New York: Seabury.
Reconnaissance into the Sociology of the Paranormal (with William
    C. McCready). Beverly Hills, Calif.: Sage Publications.

1976
Catholic Schools in a Declining Church (with William C. McCready
    and Kathleen McCourt). Mission, Kans.: Sheed and Ward.
The Communal Catholic. New York: Seabury.
Death and Beyond. Chicago: Thomas More.
Ethnicity, Denomination, Inequality. Beverly Hills, Calif.:
    Sage Publications.
The Great Mysteries. New York: Seabury.
Nora Maeve and Sebi, New York: Paulist.
The Ultimate Values of the American Population (with William
    C. McCready). Beverly Hills, Calif.: Sage Publications.

1977
The American Catholic. New York: Basic.
Christ for All Seasons (with Nancy McCready). Chicago:
    Thomas More.
The Mary Myth. New York: Seabury.
Neighborhood. New York: Seabury.
No Bigger than Necessary. New York: New American Library.
An Ugly Little Secret. Mission, Kans.: Sheed, Andrews,
    and McMeel.

Index